Race Across Alaska

RACE ACROSS ALASKA

First woman to win
the Iditarod
tells her story

Libby Riddles and Tim Jones

Stackpole Books

Copyright © 1988 by Libby Riddles
and Tim Jones

Published by
STACKPOLE BOOKS
5067 Ritter Road
Mechanicsburg, PA 17055

All rights reserved, including the right to reproduce this book or portions thereof in any form or by any means, electronic or mechanical, including photocopying, recording, or by any information storage and retrieval system, without permission in writing from the publisher.
All inquiries should be addressed to Stackpole Books, 5067 Ritter Road, Mechanicsburg, Pennsylvania 17055.

Printed in the United States of America

20 19 18 17 16 15 14 13

Design by Ice House Graphics

Library of Congress Cataloging-in-Publication Data

Riddles, Libby.
    Race across Alaska: first woman to win the Iditarod tells her story/Libby Riddles and Tim Jones.
    p.   cm.
    ISBN 0-8117-2253-8
    1. Riddles, Libby. 2. Iditarod Trail Sled Dog Race, Alaska. 3. Sled dog racing—History. 4. Women mushers—Alaska—Biography.
I. Jones, Tim, 1942–   . II. Title.
SF440.15.R53   1988
798'.8—dc19   87-25273
                                            CIP

"Born to Run," lyrics and music by Paul Kennerley, © 1981 by Rondor Music (London) Ltd. (PRS). Rights administered in the U.S. and Canada by Irving Music, Inc. (BMI). Reprinted by permission.

"Let's Go Crazy," by Prince. © 1984 by Controversy Music. Reprinted by permission.

"The Iditarod Trail," by Hobo Jim. Reprinted by permission.

To my dogs
In the miles we've gone together,
you've trained me well.

ALASKA

Anchorage
1. Rabbit Lake
2. Skwentna
3. Finger Lake
4. Rainy Pass
5. Rohn River
6. Nikolai
7. McGrath
8. Takotna
9. Ophir
10. Iditarod
11. Shageluk
12. Anvik
13. Grayling
14. Eagle Island
15. Kaltag
16. Unalakleet
17. Shaktoolik
18. Koyuk
19. Elim
20. Golovin
21. White Mountain
22. Safety

Nome

ARCTIC OCEAN

BERING SEA

NORTON SOUND

Teller
Nome

YUKON RIVER
KUSKOKWIM RIVER

Nenana
Cantwell
Mt. McKinley

ALASKA RANGE

CHUGACH MOUNTAINS

Anchorage
KENAI PENINSULA
Seward
COOK INLET
GULF OF ALASKA

March 2, 1985

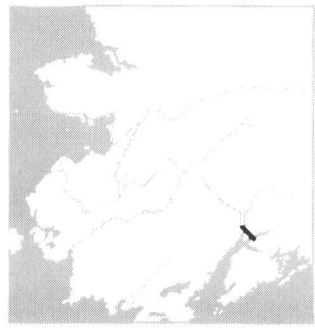

Anchorage to Rabbit Lake: 110 miles

Mostly sunny, high 25° and low 14°, with winds averaging 6 to 7 knots.

Libby Riddles has a trying first day: outside Anchorage the sled brake snaps in two, and the dogs are so eager to race that they run off without her. Nevertheless, she and the team reach Rabbit Lake without further mishap.

My brother Mike drove. In the darkness we saw other dog trucks on the highway—big plywood boxes in the beds, little doors cut in the boxes, and here and there a dog's nose testing the breezes. Our beat-up old Dodge was no match for some of the fancy rigs. New pickups with freshly painted dog boxes and signs naming the mushers and their sponsors kept disappearing ahead of us into traffic. I had to remind myself that it isn't trucks that win the Iditarod.

We stopped once to check on two dogs we'd had to double up in one compartment. They were already arguing.

We worked our way to a staging area, where race officials would assign parking spots on Fourth Avenue for the start of the race. Just a hint of morning lit the place where we sat waiting. A call came over the loudspeaker asking for anyone who carried an Emergency Medical Technician card. Joe had completed his EMT training the previous summer and headed toward the official's car—if you don't answer a call, you can even face charges. This would be his first emergency. But then the voice announced that the situation was under control, and Joe got back into the truck, relieved. On a day like this you have enough emergencies of your own.

Joe Garnie was my partner. At our home in Teller, seventy miles north of Nome, on the coast of the Bering Sea, we had bred and trained dogs to run the Iditarod, Alaska's most famous marathon for sled dog teams. If we had done our jobs, these fifteen dogs would take me the twelve hundred miles from Anchorage to Nome. If we had done our jobs well, and if I had the will and the stamina, I might finish in the top ten. But what I really wanted was to win.

We sat in the truck, Mike blowing his cigarette smoke out the window as the Dodge idled. We tried to figure out whose dog truck was whose. Our Dodge made its own statement. The faded dog boxes sported no sponsors' names or even our kennel name, and the sides were blank. Now and then we could feel the dogs shuffling in their boxes, and we'd hear an occasional growl from the grouchier ones. At last somebody called, "Number forty-six."

We drove a couple of blocks to our spot on Fourth Avenue, one of the main east-west streets of Anchorage. Starting here would be a new experience. In my first two races we had started from Mulcahy Park, not downtown. Trucks were arranged by number along each side of the avenue, lowest numbers closest to the starting line, so that as each team took off toward the start, the dogs wouldn't have to weave through other teams on the way. Snow had been trucked in and spread on the street for the race.

A banner stretched across the street proclaimed the start of the 1985 Iditarod Trail Sled Dog Race, big red letters outlined in yellow. Far beyond, the Chugach mountains seemed to block the end of the street; their outline never ceases to awe me, especially when they reflect a sunrise or sunset. The winter sun, still behind the ridge, was beginning to spread its light over the city.

Now the work could begin. We piled out of the truck and strung a tie-out chain, first around the truck and then back to a couple of parking meters to give us room for all the dogs. A snowfence lined the street from meter to meter, protecting the dogs and spectators from each other. Some of the racers toward the front were already putting dogs in harness. With sixty-four racers and fourteen to eighteen dogs per team, the area was noisy.

We started taking the dogs out of the boxes, in order. First out was Sister, a dog of Joe's who was so ornery we tied her to a parking meter as far away as possible. She was the oldest dog in the team and probably figured her seniority should bring her respect. She would mix it up with any other dog, male or female. She might have been so mean because she was so darned ugly—mostly white with a few washed-out gray spots, built square like a Mack truck, with scars all over her muzzle from her various encounters. The pigment in one eye was pink. But there wasn't a trace of quit in her, and I knew I could rely on her as a spare leader if things got tough.

In a few minutes she was ripping the snow-fence slats to shreds. In the dog barn at home she had a special stall made of corrugated tin. If we left her behind when we went on a training run, she would try to demolish anything within her reach, especially dog houses, and if she couldn't reach anything destructible, she'd start digging up the snow with her front paws, then tearing up the ground with her teeth. Other times she'd bark and squeal and jump straight in the air, "four off the floor." Did we want to buy the city a new snowfence? We put Sister back in the truck.

The next dog out was Minnow. She was a big dog, about fifty-five pounds. Her sister Tip was even bigger. The two dogs looked so much alike I occasionally mistook one for the other when they were tied in the dark dog barn and I could see only their faces and not the kink in Minnow's tail. The similarity could be a major nuisance because I could let Minnow run a little, knowing she would honor my "come" command. But Tip liked to explore the neighborhood, and she always took her time before submitting to being caught. If I mistook Tip for Minnow and let her go, I'd end up chasing her around the village. Today, Minnow was in heat, and we let her out for only a few minutes for her own comfort. Then she, too, had to go back into the truck, where she would be safe from amorous advances.

Two out, two back in; so far, about normal.

The only rookie in the team was Stripe. All the others had raced Iditarod at least once. Stripe was white and liver-colored with a pink nose on a face only a mother could love—and his mother was Sister. Stripe was also tough and liked to let the others know it. He wasn't as tough as his mother, but then, he wasn't as ugly, either. He had die-hard drive and a good attitude, a good head.

Whitey was his littermate, but in personality she was his opposite. Her favorite trick was to try to be invisible whenever there was any type of commotion. Like most huskies, she liked to work, to cover miles, but she also held rest in high esteem, and given any chance, she'd plop down in the snow. These were both Joe's dogs.

Joe's pride and joy was his leader, Dusty, a stout little red dog, his color suggesting more golden Lab than husky. Dusty was a giveaway pup from our neighbor Albert Oquillik. He would do figure-eights and back flips for Joe, and although he would lead for me in training, he was never as happy with me. I guess he was a one-person dog. He was fast, though, and even if I didn't trust him as much as my own leaders, he could be put out front to give them a rest. As for team dogs, there weren't many better than Dusty.

Four brothers were the core of my team: Dugan, Axle, Bugs, and Binga. Dugan would be the main leader for the race with Binga and maybe Axle to help out, along with Dusty and Sister.

Two more of Joe's dogs came out of the truck to the picket line, Brownie and Socks. Littermates, they were pups of Joe's retired leader, Ugly. Brownie had a flying trot and a tendency not to lope. He always seemed composed, self-contained, and didn't seem to care if I ever petted him. I'd pet him anyway. Joe had been trying to make him into a leader, and he was beginning to pick up the idea.

Socks was the smallest dog in the team, but built solid and strong. She could have been a bit faster, but somehow with her short legs she got the job done, and she was consistent. She was the only dog on the team who had a reputation as a chewer and I intended to keep a sharp eye on her. All I needed was for Socks to chew

The Lineup

*T*eams for the Iditarod comprise seven to eighteen dogs. The animals usually run in pairs, one on either side of the gangline, or towline, attached to the sled. Occasionally a single dog runs in the team, either because the dog works better alone or as a matter of logistics, with an odd number of dogs.

The leaders are the brains of the outfit and the steering wheel. They take the commands of "gee" and "haw" for right and left, respectively, and keep the team in the trail. They also must set the pace and get their teammates moving at their speed by keeping the gangline taut.

An all-around leader is a rarity. Some lead dogs dislike running into the wind or working their way through forest. Some take commands readily but cannot keep the lines tight. Others maintain a fast pace but cause tangles when called upon to turn. Many teams therefore include a command leader for tight steering and a pacesetter to keep the team moving on straight portions of trail.

All good leaders show an uncanny ability to find and stay on the trail. When a trail is covered by loose snow, the leaders must feel for the packed snow underneath; when the trail has been swept bare by the wind, they must use their sense of smell to find the way; when the trail cannot be seen or felt or smelled, some dogs find the way by an apparent sixth sense.

As the leaders turn, the rest of the dogs in the team may jump off the trail to follow them in a straight line, creating a tangle of lines and even over-

turning the sled. The two dogs behind the leaders, called swing dogs, *help steer by staying in the trail and forcing the rest of the team to turn in a wide arc that will bring the sled around the corner safely.*

The next several pairs of dogs are the team dogs. *They provide the muscle to pull the load and maintain speed.*

The last two dogs in line are wheel dogs. *They are trained to stay in the trail around curves, but the clue to their main function lies in their size. Usually the largest animals in the team, they bear the extra burden of being first to feel the load as the team starts out or pulls uphill. Sometimes, however, a small, agile dog is better able to keep out of the way of the sled runners. All wheel dogs must be steady animals, for the constant pounding of the runners close behind them can be unnerving.*

Drivers often move their dogs around, putting a swing or team dog in lead to give one of the usual leaders a break from the pressure or because it might do better under certain conditions. Sometimes two dogs develop a dislike for each other and have to be separated, or a female coming into heat may have to be moved away from males. A single lead dog might work better for a time, or a single wheel dog may offer more control of the sled on twisty trails.

Behind a team of sixteen dogs, the driver will be more than forty feet from the leaders.

through one of the lines and let all the dogs in front of her take off down the trail, leaving me and the sled behind.

Another dog of Joe's I was taking was Stewpot, a real one-of-a-kind dog. He looked like a collie crossed with a white arctic wolf, and he was almost as big as a wolf. Joe and I had feuded over which was the bigger dog, his Stewpot or my Bad Dog Bane, the father of Tip and Minnow. We never did weigh or measure them. That would have taken all the fun out of it. As a pup, Stewpot had had a fancy name, Sewlik, Eskimo for northern pike. When he was a couple of years old, we lent him to our friend Ray Lang, a dentist in Nome who used him in the All-Alaska Sweepstakes. Ray never could remember the dog's name, so he started calling him Stewpot. The dog was a big old pot-licker anyway. Stewpot was going to be my main wheel dog, right in front of the sled.

My favorite of the dogs from Joe's lot was Penny. She was the fastest and most consistent, and I also liked her pleasant manners. She did her work in the team and minded her own business. I hardly ever had to look at her when I was on the move—an invisible dog. Penny had perfect Siberian markings of gray and white. Her radar ears were always in constant motion as she high-stepped down the trail. If she heard any sound, her ears would swivel in its direction. If a dog in the team received a scolding, Penny's ears would lay back in submission.

The last dog out of the box was a coal-black female named Inca. She was a half-sister to Tip and Minnow. Inca had been born on my birthday three years earlier. She had a strong desire to please and would obey me better than most of the other dogs. Inca was loyal, a dog I could let loose. At home in training, I always cut her loose from her chain and let her follow me. She'd run ahead, then run back to me and jump up, sometimes throwing her whole body on me. I usually had to have an arm free to block her exuberant assaults. I used Inca for a herder when I took pups for walks, and if the pups got carried away with their temporary freedom, I'd just call Inca back, and the pups would follow along behind.

There was little to do once the dogs were out. I stood and regarded my team. For the next two weeks we would eat, sleep, and labor across more than a thousand miles of Alaska. I had high hopes for this pack of mutts. I wasn't one of the famous mushers, one of the people the press hung around and talked and wrote about, but I thought these dogs could even win the race if I could handle them right. I sure wanted to give them every opportunity, but there were a lot of miles and a lot of variables on the trail between Anchorage and Nome.

A few days before the race, Joe had been down at the Knik Bar with a group that included some racers.

"Don't you think you'd be right up there if you were driving that team instead?" they kept asking.

"You guys," said Joe, "are going to screw around and screw around and underestimate her and she's going to pass you up."

But what others were thinking didn't affect me too much. I had learned that in sled dog racing, as in most other things, respect must be earned. I'd run the Kuskokwim 300 twice since my last Iditarod and managed to beat some teams I'd never beaten before. Some of the racers had to know I was serious. And only two teams had been able to beat our dogs in the previous year's race.

Susan Ogle and Kelley Weaverling came by with egg burgers and coffee. They had helped me organize my airdrops of food and supplies for the checkpoints along the trail. To make my burlap bags distinctive, so that I could pick them out of a pile, Kelley had spray-painted them green and purple. We began hauling down sleds and gear from the top of the dog boxes and stretching out the gangline and preparing harnesses. Another friend stopped by and gave me an orange for the trail. Elwin Johnson and Katrine Zosel offered their services as dog handlers. Other people were stopping to wish me luck and look over my dogs. When neither of us was racing, I had been one of the walkers, wishing favorites well, strolling and looking at all the dogs. This year I had eyes for no dogs but my own.

A special friend arrived—Patty Friend. She had given me not only some of her dogs and a lead on a summer job, but also inspiration. In 1979, running the Cantwell 180 sled dog race, she had sprinted to the finish half a minute ahead of the competition and become the first woman—at least in modern times—to win a long-distance sled dog race.

Kelley and Mike went to work putting the new bindings on my fancy new Sherpa snowshoes. I had purchased them just a day before the race. I couldn't quite afford them, but they were lighter and smaller than the regular wood and rawhide snowshoes, and they packed a lot easier into the sled. I'd been sure I could jury-rig bindings, but as it turned out, these high-tech snowshoes would work only with the real thing, the expensive real thing.

I started sorting gear. When we had finished, a race official checked over the mandatory equipment for the sled and counted the dogs. Volunteers followed with cans of paint to mark each dog on top of its head, a way to make sure racers wouldn't add dogs to their teams. Mine got purple. I resented having the sticky paint on my animals' fine pelts, but I accepted it as a necessary evil.

Just after Minnow got her splash of purple, I stepped a little too close. She jumped and spread a nice blotch of purple all over my brand new L.L. Bean Thinsulate jacket.

All the time, the loudspeaker down the avenue was announcing one team after another as the racers left the starting line. Police were holding traffic. Part of the dogs' training was to get them used to crowds, but you don't find many crowds where we live. As it turned out, our dogs were so intent on chasing the teams ahead of them, they hardly seemed to notice the people.

On the first day of a race, dogs are usually pretty excited by the presence of the other teams and the overall commotion. They're also fresh, and fifteen dogs in the peak of condition can be mighty difficult to stop if they set their minds on going somewhere. And if you go down the wrong trail and have to turn around, you have to untangle a lively mess of dogs while other teams pass by. After a few days on the trail, the dogs would settle into a routine and be more inclined to behave themselves. I wondered whether the other racers dreaded the first days as much as I did.

The teams in front of us disappeared down Fourth Avenue one by one. I waited until the last minute to put my dogs in harness to keep them from going wild. Once they're in harness they reach an almost fever pitch in their excitement, yipping and yowling, lunging and jumping forward. They don't like being left behind. My old Bad Dog Bane used to grab the gangline in his teeth and pull back on it, pulling the other dogs with it. Then he'd let go, and the dogs taking up the slack and lunging forward would help him in his attempt to be on his way. Pretty slick.

Over the morning I'd collected quite a few handlers: Mike, Susan, Kelley, Patty, Dennis Lozano, Jack and Nancy Studer. Nancy was one of my strongest suppliers of moral support.

When the race officials told me we had fifteen minutes to go, we got busy. Sister and Minnow came back out of the truck, and I put all my handlers to work, showing them which dogs to put where. I had to resort to my list to make sure. For the first part of the race, officials wanted us to take a handler along to help with tangles and supply added weight to slow the dogs. Some handlers rode in the sled. We had decided Joe would ride a second sled, which we had borrowed from Jack Schultheis.

For the tight work of maneuvering through town I would use my two best leaders, Dugan and Bugs. Bugs especially was my "power steering" for this work. Behind them we put Inca and Binga. Behind them came Axle and Dusty, Sister and Penny, Tip and Minnow, Stripe and Socks, Whitey and Brownie. In wheel we put Stewpot by himself.

At last we received the signal. Each handler grabbed a tandem of dogs, Joe took the leaders,

Across Alaska

The forty-ninth state derives its name from the language of the Aleuts, who lived on what are now called the Aleutian Islands. Looking across the sea, they called the mainland alyeska, "where the waves begin, where the weather comes from." The weather is severe, and the Iditarod Trail across the state presents not only several kinds of weather—distinct climatological systems, really—but also an ever-changing terrain.

From Anchorage, in the southcentral portion of the state, the trail winds through spruce and birch forest, crossing frozen lakes and muskeg, or bogs, and following meandering rivers toward their sources in the Alaska Range. Weather south of the range is relatively temperate because winds blowing off the north Pacific Ocean keep the land warmer in winter and cooler in summer.

The trail rises into the mountains to Rainy Pass at almost 3,200 feet. Just to the north stands Mount McKinley, at 20,320 feet the tallest peak in North America.

Out of the mountains the trail drops into the great Interior and a second climate. This is Jack London's land of icy silence, where temperatures in the minus thirties are common and dips to minus fifty and even minus seventy are not unknown. The trail follows portions of the Kuskokwim River. Rolling hills and sparse spruce forests along the streambeds alternate with tundra until the trail reaches the Yukon, the Mississippi of Alaska. Here the teams encounter frigid temperatures and often face north winds of more than fifty miles an hour.

At Kaltag on the Yukon, the trail rises again to cross a low pass in the Nulato Hills, then drops to the Bering Sea coast and a third climate, where the effects of arctic weather are somewhat tempered by the ocean. Many miles of trail lie on sea ice, whose blanket of granular snow abrades dogs' feet. Shifting ice may move trail markers out of sight, and lost teams face the danger of going out on thin ice or being swept out to sea on an ice floe.

Nearing Nome, the trail approaches the northern tree line, above which only the scrub vegetation of the tundra can survive the long winter nights of cold and wind. Though temperatures are more moderate than in the Interior, mushers cannot escape the bite of the high winds howling out of valleys along the Seward Peninsula, winds powerful enough to knock dogs off their feet and overturn sleds.

and I rode the sled and the brake. The dogs surged ahead impatiently, dragging their handlers, but we managed to stop for the countdown.

All the preparations had come down to this. I was at the starting line, the dogs stretched out front facing the high white mountains at the end of the street. Race officials and photographers surrounded the sled. Some helped hold it so the dogs wouldn't pull us over the line in their screaming lunges to chase the other teams. The announcer made some cracks about Joe being in the second sled and noticed our single wheel dog. The countdown began. "Ten . . . nine . . ." Joe stood on the second sled behind me. At "two" I motioned the handlers away. I wanted a clear shot; I didn't want a tangle with the dogs running over somebody; I wanted the dogs to see where they were going. I glanced over my shoulder at Joe. He was ready. "One . . . GO!"

Big crowds leaned into the snowfences on both sides of the street as we sped down Fourth Avenue. We passed the spot where years before I'd watched my first race. I could hear the muffled roar made by the clapping of hundreds of gloved and mittened hands. I kept my eyes on the team.

We went about half a dozen blocks and then made a right turn. Earl Norris was right in front of us. He'd been running dogs around Anchorage since the 1940s but this was his first Iditarod. We passed him and then went over the hill and down Cordova Street. We took a curve around Mulcahy Park, where the race used to start, and went out of sight of the crowds.

The day warmed as we went along, the temperature rising to uncomfortable heat for the dogs. We let them stop frequently for a few minutes to cool off and bite a little snow. We crossed through a long meadow and reached a stand of trees on the far side, the lead dogs disappearing into the bushes around a sharp corner. As the sled came closer I could hear someone cussing up a storm. We stopped and Joe held the team while I went up to see what was happening.

One of the racers was crashing through the

underbrush, pulling lines and lifting dogs, untangling a team that had wrapped itself around half a dozen trees. Worse, I hadn't stopped in time, and the front end of my own team was tangled in the same trees. I unwound them and they came free just as the team ahead pulled away. I went back to the sled, gritted my teeth and prepared to negotiate what remained of the turn and keep the rest of my team on the the trail.

But instead of following the trail around, the dogs went flying through the alders, bouncing our sleds off trees until at last we hit the trail again and returned to business. I made myself a note to come back one day and personally chainsaw that patch of alders.

From there the trail was good, alternating wide stretches and narrow portages.

Then Dugan and Bugs started down some sort of narrow trail, following a couple of sets of tracks. By the time I saw this new adventure, it was already too late. Two by two the dogs jumped over an old wringer washing machine iced into the trail. The sled hit it and I flew over the top. I heard Joe shout just as he was knocked off the second sled and then my sled went over. I hung on to the drive bow while the dogs dragged me until I righted the sled and regained the runners and stopped. I set the hook into the snow and waited for Joe to catch up. He'd slammed into a tree and banged his knuckle badly. I shook my head and shrugged. A washing machine in the trail, of all things.

Less than an hour into the race and already my expectations and fears for the first day were starting to fulfill themselves. For a while we continued along a fairly normal trail, some sort of road, but then I spied half a dozen boulders dead ahead. I figured the boulders kept cars off the road. Someone had removed one boulder, leaving a space between the side of a bank and the second boulder for us to pass. The space was only about four feet wide—not a lot of maneuvering room for a sled skidding on a slippery surface. We had fast trail, and with the dogs so fresh and excited we were doing about twenty miles an hour.

Joe shouted, "Get off your brake and steer."

I always figure that if I'm going to crash, I'd rather crash going slowly, so I laid into the brake. That takes away some maneuvering ability, however, so I compromised, letting off the brake just as we came to the opening. My heart rate accelerated a little and my breath stopped but we slipped nicely between the boulder and the bank. Later I heard that some other racers hadn't fared so well. Armen Khatchikian broke his collarbone there and had to drop out of the race at Eagle River. Joe Redington, Sr., also crashed there and hurt his arm badly. I don't imagine anybody had fun going through there.

Beyond the rocks, the trail smoothed out, and we had an easy time into Eagle River. We passed quite a few teams, and a few passed us while we rested the dogs in the heat. I was in no hurry. I wanted to go easy on the dogs during the warm part of the day. It was a long, long way to Nome, and the way the day was going, I didn't even want to think about how far it was. Soon the last few miles of energy in those egg burgers wore out. I was starting to get that shaky feeling that comes from hunger. I remembered the candy bar Dennis Lozano had slipped me back on Fourth Avenue and dug it out of my pocket. I made my second note of the day. Maybe even before I chainsawed the alders I'd thank Dennis.

We pulled up a long hill into the chute at Eagle River and I could see my pit crew already there waiting to haul us by truck across open water and a tangle of roads to the restart at Settler's Bay. We made our way through crowds past the VFW post that was being used as the checkpoint. The old Dodge was parked just around a corner.

The dogs looked hot and dry when we rolled in, and though my own hunger and thirst were wearing at me, from now on the dogs had to come first. We gave them water out of a cooler in the truck, and most of them drank quite a bit. An old friend, Penny Moore, popped out of the crowd. I hadn't seen her since the last Iditarod, and we talked, catching up, but I was distracted. Now the race was going and I had to keep track of my time. The crew agreed to watch over the dogs while they rested so that I could grab a bite to eat.

The VFW volunteers had cooked a big batch of stew and made corn bread, along with coffee and other snacks for the racers. I took advantage and wolfed down as much as I could. When I'd thoroughly stuffed myself, I thanked the women there and headed back to the truck. We loaded up the dogs and started out to drive the forty miles to Settler's Bay, the restart and at last, the release from the city to the comfort of the open trail away from crowds and traffic.

We didn't stop anywhere, counting on fierce traffic all the way. The previous year we'd stopped at Palmer to change the runners on Joe's sled, and he had barely made it on time. By race rules, drivers can leave exactly three hours after arriving in Eagle River, and I didn't want to stay a minute extra. We were on race time now.

It looked like all of Anchorage had emptied out to go watch the restart and we settled into the flow. Settler's Bay is a development of recreational and residential homes on the west side of Cook Inlet just across the bay and a little north of Anchorage. Its golf course provides good open country for the race, with plenty of room for spectators. We followed signs and arrows pointing the way for racers to find the staging area, where officials directed us to a parking lot. Stakes in the snow held paper plates with the mushers' numbers on them. All manner of vehicles were scattered through the area: dog trucks, motor homes, pickups, a few cars. A forest bordered one side of the parking lot, and there we found Number 46.

We backed in toward the woods and strung our picket cables in the trees. This put the dogs where they wouldn't be bothered so much by the knots of spectators wandering through. Once we had the dogs out of the truck, we hauled down the racing toboggan sled and started packing for real. I had thought of picking up some of my gear at the next checkpoint, which was Knik, about seven miles or so away and the last stop on the road system. But I de-

In the Sled

Iditarod race rules require mushers to carry equipment essential for driver and dogs to survive under severe winter conditions: arctic sleeping bag, axe, snowshoes, eight booties for each dog, at least two pounds of dog food per dog, a day's food ration for the musher. Before leaving each checkpoint, the driver is required to show these items to an official.

But these requirements are the minimum. A driver needs considerably more to traverse the nearly twelve hundred miles of trail in relative comfort and safety. Most drivers carry a dog food cooker, a cooler to keep the dogs' food warm, feeding pans, a dipper for ladling dog food, tools for sled repairs, electrical tape for fastening dog booties, spare lines and harnesses, chains for tying dropped dogs, headlamps and batteries, compass, topographical maps, and personal items, like camera, needle and thread, notebook, cooking pot and utensils, tape player, comb, and toothbrush. Many drivers carry firearms—heavy-caliber handguns are favored—to protect their dogs if a moose attacks the team.

Several drivers also pack what is called in Alaska a "red sled," a four-foot-long plastic child's toboggan favored by Bush residents for hauling firewood and water around their cabins. Lightweight and easy to pull, it eases the musher's chores of hauling dog food and water at checkpoints.

cided I didn't want to waste any time there—once we were gone, I wanted to stay going. Besides, the trail committee might consider that planned help, a disqualifying offense.

I put the heavy cooler full of dog food in first, toward the back of the basket. The sled steers better with the weight in back. The food in it was cooked and all ready for our first real stop down the trail. Then I put in the new snowshoes, tied together. The sleeping bag and the cooker went in next. Dog pans went up in the front. I tied the axe in its leather sheath to the outside of the sled bag, where I could grab it easily. I had a smaller bag tied between the back supports of the sled, below the drive bow, for personal items: dry gloves, snacks, headlight, goggles, sunglasses. While I was packing, friends came by, talking when we could. Dan and Karen Owens visited. I usually see them for an hour or so each year at Settler's Bay for the restart and that's about all, even though they've been friends of mine probably longer than just about anybody I know in the state.

Several other friends came by, talked for a moment or two and left. Susan and Kelley brought more burgers. I wasn't hungry but I figured it might be several hours before I could eat again, so I tried to stuff one down.

A checker from the race committee looked over my gear, checking the mandatory equipment. At least we didn't have to sign in at this checkpoint this year. The previous year one driver had neglected to sign the sheet at Settler's Bay. Faced with returning seventy miles to the checkpoint to sign or being disqualified, he withdrew.

Three old friends from my days at the Bureau of Land Management stopped to talk. LaDonna Westfall, Charlene Montague, and Nancy Reagan had all helped the last time I raced, preparing some of my personal food. They took some pictures and wished me luck again, saying they wanted me to know they were still behind me.

LaDonna pulled me to one side. The night before, she said, she'd been inspired to write something for me. She handed me an envelope

19

marked "Libby." I tucked it into a pocket, its message unread. This was something to save. Somewhere down the trail, I was going to need a little boost and the time would be right to take out that envelope. Then the three of them faded back into the crowd.

Time passed quickly in the bustle of packing and organizing and visiting, and when I finally checked my watch, I had only fifteen minutes left. For some time Joe had wanted me to hook up, but again I didn't want the dogs to wait long in harness, expending energy in their excitement. With fifteen minutes to go, though, we were getting down to the wire and I gave the go-ahead.

With all the help experienced by this time, the dogs were harnessed and hooked into the gangline in no time and we were just about to go to the starting line when a woman with two children in tow came up. I recognized her face right away even though it had probably had been twenty years since I'd seen her. She was my cousin Phoebe, who'd just moved to Anchorage from Wisconsin.

The team was more than ready to go, and with close to a dozen handlers, we edged through the trees to the restart line. I stood under a banner again, this time looking up a long hill, the trail lined by snowfence, the snowfence lined by people. The run to Eagle River had tamed the dogs some, but they were still lively, and I was nervous.

While waiting for the countdown, I asked about the trail ahead. Somebody warned me about a corner at the bottom of a big hill, but that only added to the nervousness. My first goal was to get to Knik, six or eight miles, and then take it step by step from there.

We took off through a snowfence chute and climbed the long hill. People cheered, and I couldn't help waving as I passed along the fence. For a mile or two we cruised the golf course, past spectators taking pictures and calling out their good luck wishes. At last I was alone with the dogs. We approached a split in the trail with no markings for which way to go. Two photographers were standing there and when with unfailing accuracy I picked the trail that turned out not to have sled tracks, I had to call them for assistance. Once the team was stopped, the dogs had to be turned 180 degrees in a narrow trail—one of the best ways to tie forty feet of ropes and fifteen frisky dogs into a knot. Luckily for me, the two photographers were willing to help. I asked one to stand on the snow hook and hold the sled; the other helped me turn the dogs. I was ordering both of them around, perfect strangers, but I had to get out of that mess.

Every one of the dogs was tangled somehow. The lines were so tight I couldn't even get them loose. If people hadn't been around to help, I might have lost a dog. Minnow was caught in a nasty knot and almost choked. Her expression was pitiful. All the other dogs were straining forward, making her situation worse. The photographer pulled back on the other dogs so that I could free Minnow from the stranglehold. The rest of the team grew increasingly impatient to be on the way, jumping, barking, lunging, and doing anything else difficult they could think of. It was all the two men could do to hang on to the sled while I worked with the rats' nest of dogs. After a couple of quarts of sweat, I finally managed to free them and line out for the proper trail. When I was finally ready, I thanked my rescuers profusely and then geared my mind toward whatever disaster might be in store for me next. The day was fulfilling my worst expectations.

We were approaching the steep hill I'd been warned about. An old boat lay rotting in the snow at the bottom of the hill, and beyond it, the trail swung sharply to the right. I stood on my brake with both feet trying to keep my speed at a minimum in anticipation of the corner. A roostertail of snow kicked up behind me. We swept around the corner beautifully, and through the curve we came out onto the tidal flats of Knik Arm. Now and then I touched or rode my brake to keep control over rougher parts.

I began to feel some looseness in the brake

when I pressed down. At first I tried to ignore it: "It can't be what I think it is." When I finally did look down, I saw that the bar, a half-inch-thick bar of steel, had snapped at one of the rounded corners. It was broken clean through. I looked at it several more times in disbelief.

Panic turned to anxiety. I had to get it fixed. I was within a couple of miles of Knik, but I wasn't sure how I was going to repair it. For the time, I had to concentrate on those next few miles and then somehow stop the dogs and park them without the use of a brake. I had no idea whether my pit crew had been able to fight the traffic and reach Knik. I might be alone there, with no brake and no way to get a new one or fix the old one. And going on without it was out of the question.

Near Knik the trail wound through thicker woods, then rose sharply to the road, where volunteers were stopping traffic. Across the road we dropped into the parking lot at the Knik Bar and into a sort of picnic area next to Knik Lake. As soon as I came up over the road, I hollered for help, since I had no brake to help me stop. Several people, including some of my pit crew—they had made it after all—managed to grab the team and guide us over to some trees where I could tie the dogs. Joe and Mike figured there was a good chance someone in the crowd might have the same type of sled, and maybe we could borrow or buy a brake for my sled.

Dean Osmar, who had won the race the year before and was helping his son, Tim, this year, offered a brake, but it was too short. Raymie Redington's handler, Gary Longley, an old friend of ours from Nome, said he had one we could use. There was some confusion as to whether it was Raymie's or Gary's brake, but I wasn't being too particular at the moment. I got it bolted into place and we were ready to go. In all, we'd lost only about twenty minutes.

If that brake had snapped any farther down the trail, I'd have had to backtrack to Knik, and by the time I returned to Knik, no one would have been there. I might have spent hours tracking someone down to find another brake. No way would I have headed up into the mountains without a brake. My luck had been good bad luck.

I gave Joe a last hug. It would be the last I'd see him until Nome.

"Wish me luck," I said. "If this keeps up, I'm going to need it."

We tore off down the lake and then climbed the bank onto the trail I'd been using for training over the past couple of weeks to keep the dogs in shape. Debbie Altermatt's house, where we had stayed, was just three miles away, and I started to worry that my leaders might try to head back to her house. Dugan, good as he was, had a stubborn streak, and if he had it in mind we were going back to Debbie's dog yard to eat a a big dinner and sleep on fresh straw, he'd try it.

Fortunately, Debbie and a friend had chosen that intersection to watch the race, and they were in position when Dugan made his dive. His attempt was only half-hearted, however. I think the dog really knew that we were Nomeward bound, he was just making sure I didn't want to change my mind.

I finally felt like I was really on the way to Nome. A great weight had lifted and I recalled the same feelings of relief the other two times I had raced. All the busywork and preparation for the race were over. The hassle of the city and the start were behind us. Before us the quiet trail opened up to Rabbit Lake, and beyond, so far ahead I didn't even want to think about it, Nome.

Somehow this year was different. All of my energy was focused on the team and the trail. I was deadly serious about racing this year, and in my concentration I was looking ahead to each mile of trail, mile by mile, instead of the grand experience of the whole. Nothing I'd heard about the upcoming trail did anything to make me feel relaxed or complacent.

This first, familiar, stretch of trail wound through a forest of birch and spruce. At one turn I recognized Jack Schultheis taking pictures along the trail, and I hollered my thanks for the borrowed sled. Except at checkpoints, we wouldn't see too many more people standing along the trail from here on, and we settled into an easy pace, eating up the miles.

I'd raced twice before and had a good idea of the time schedule I'd need. But it was critical to be flexible, to fit the schedule according to the dogs and the weather. I wasn't going to burn up the trail—and burn out the dogs—in the first part of the race, just to keep within sight of the front runners. Still, I didn't want to be any more than six hours behind in those first few days; less would be better. Closer to Nome, I wouldn't be able to let anyone get more than an hour in front.

With all the teams in front of us, the trail was pretty chewed up. Brakes left deep furrows on the downhill stretches. The dogs and sleds and mushers left behind a trail of loose snow, making it tough going for the dogs while we twisted through the forest. We easily passed the obstacles I knew about, a big birch on an inside corner, and then, beyond two lakes, a rock on a forty-five-degree turn that could catch a sled runner. At the rock, thick alders on each side of the trail complicated matters. I hopped off the sled and ran around that corner, taking away any chance of tipping over.

I pulled a can of Squirt from the sled bag and swigged it down between trail bumps in about three swallows. Not even twenty-four hours into the race and already I felt dehydrated.

The trail curved around a few big hills through thick woods, then across a big open area of frozen marsh and small ponds and onto another road. That was as far as I'd gone on my training runs. From then on, the trail would be new to us, and the time had come to pay even more attention. The dogs took the winding trail smoothly without mishap and we passed the miles with no problems finding the proper trail. About twenty-five miles out of Knik I thought it was time to give the dogs a little breather and let them snack on some of the treats in the sled. I began looking for a good place to stop, where I could anchor the team to something sturdy and wouldn't interfere with teams coming up from behind.

I stopped by a fairly sturdy scrub spruce and tied the sled to it with a heavy-duty rope about fifteen feet long. I pounded the snow hook down, too, even though in four feet of powder it couldn't gain much purchase.

I had to unload most of the sled to reach the cooler. I gave each dog a scoop of food and repacked. I wanted to let them rest a little bit, twenty minutes or so, but they were restless. When they're tired, they dig a little nest or circle around until their ground is just right and then curl up. If they're not tired, they just sit or lick their paws or stand and look at me. Today the dogs were too restless even for that. But if I let them run too much, they'd be sore and tired the next day.

A couple of teams passed while we were resting: Bob Bright, Terry Adkins, and Victor Katongan. They were all good teams, but I tried especially to get a look at Victor's. It was a tough outfit he had, and he was a determined driver.

My dogs watched those teams go by, too. They were jealous, barking and whining, trying to give chase. They didn't care to watch others go down the trail, leaving them behind. They began barking and jumping up and down, even doing a couple of four-off-the-floors. They lurched forward once, and again, and all of a sudden they snapped the little tree I had them tied to. The couple of feet they gained fired their efforts. They started yapping and throwing themselves forward in their harnesses, gaining on the tree little by little. The tree held, but my faithful, easy-to-untie, hitch-the-dogs-up knot was now underneath, and the knot cinched so tight I couldn't budge it.

Hindsight tells me if I had had a brain in my head, I would have waited to get help from another driver. But one of the ideas of the race is to take care of yourself, and that's what I proceeded to do.

The dogs kept their pressure forward, so there was little chance of untying the knot. I would need that rope every time I camped, so I wasn't keen on cutting it. I decided instead to take a few chops at the tree with my axe and then make a grab for my sled. Trouble was, by this time the sled was about seven feet from the tree, farther than I could reach if I chopped through the tree and it let go. I chopped at the tree a couple of times and then stepped onto the runners and encouraged the dogs forward, thinking they might break it. No luck. So I went back and tried to pull the knot again. After my encouragement the dogs were almost frothing at their mouths with excitement, jumping and leaping forward. I decided to take a couple more chops at the tree. On the third swing, the dogs jumped and broke free. I grabbed for the only thing I could see, and that was the hunk of tree flying by, still tied to my snub line. I held on to the axe with my other hand, gripping both for dear life. The axe was mandatory equipment, and so were the dogs and sled.

Axe in hand, I was sledding along the trail on my face at twenty miles an hour, pulled by fifteen wired-up dogs, hollering while I tried to dig my boots into the snow to bring the team under control.

"Whoa, dammit!" I yelled.

But nothing dampened the dogs' enthusiasm to go catch those other teams. I hung on for all I was worth while they dragged me through the deep snow on the trail. My grip on the rope was weakening all the time, then I lost it. I stopped, face in the snow, my fifteen mighty huskies loping off into the night without me.

It was too cruel. My dogs could get tangled in an alder path, maybe choked to death. My race was down the drain. All the months, the years of preparation, the money, all the people who had helped . . . In anger and frustration and fear I picked up and chased after them, glad no one was close enough to hear me as I ran after them, cursing and hollering, wavering, slowing to walk, close to tears.

"Come back here, you miserable dogs! Oh please, *please* stop."

For fifteen or twenty minutes I slogged through deep snow, running and walking, hollering and unzipping layers of clothing as I heated up. I'd lost my whole outfit, but I still had that

26

Dog Power

Sled dogs love to run. In their eagerness to hit the trail, they have uprooted small trees and snapped heavy ropes. One team of ten dogs is known to have pulled at their harnesses with such vigor that they dragged the pickup truck to which they were tied; the truck was in gear with the parking brake engaged.

Including the driver, a sled loaded for the Iditarod weighs between three hundred and five hundred pounds. With a team of sixteen dogs, that means twenty-two to thirty-one pounds per dog, much less than the drivers' rule of thumb: that a dog should not pull more than its own weight.

The dogs are trained to trot at a pace of eleven to twelve miles an hour pulling that load. Loping, they can attain a speed of twenty miles an hour, and with an unloaded sled, they are limited only by their own top speed. When rest stops are figured in, a top team averages between seven and eight miles an hour, a pace that the dogs must maintain over the course of the race if they are to remain in contention.

crazy axe, for all the good it would do me now. A headlight came through the trees behind me and I flagged the driver. I was out of breath but tried in quick bursts to explain. The stranger got the point quickly and told me to hop onto the sled; we'd go look for my team.

He introduced himself as Chuck Schaeffer. I'd never met him before and I couldn't even see his face in the dark, but I knew he was from up north in Kotzebue. He had less trouble figuring out who I was—there were just a handful of women in the race. I felt guilty for imposing my extra weight on this racer's dogs, but he said it was no problem giving me a lift. That's one of the great things about the Iditarod. Even if drivers are expected to keep their own acts together, even though they're all competing, if you ever need help, someone's always glad to oblige.

Chuck's dogs kept up a steady pace as I sat on his sled, clutching my axe and mumbling about my doggone dogs. After half an hour we saw something ahead reflecting our lights. I had two strips of reflective tape on my sled, but I didn't really believe it was my team until we got closer and I could see the dogs' eyes reflecting the light. There they were, all lying down resting. The gangline was tied off in three places and the sled turned upside down, so even if they had gotten loose, the sled would have slowed them down. Somebody had done a fine job of rescuing my team for me. I didn't know who, but I vowed to find out and buy him a couple drinks at the end of the trail.

I tried hard to be mad at my dogs, let them know what bad dogs they were for ditching me, but I couldn't quite pull it off. I moved along the team, checking them for injury. They all looked at me so innocently, their expressions seeming to say, "Aw, we were just funnin' ya." And truly, what they'd done was instinctive. Although I was drenched with perspiration from running and shaken by the whole experience, my thoughts were positive. I had my team back, and my chance at the race came back with them.

I begged Chuck to stay until I got the dogs ready. He helped me untie them from the trees and get their tuglines hitched, which took a while because whoever had tied the dogs had done it well. I righted the sled, never once letting go of it, and sent them off.

I lose my team maybe once every season, and although I'd had several nightmares about that, even during the summer, before training started, I'd never lost them in a race. Still, I felt a little relieved. Everything bad that could happen had already happened to me. I wasn't even worried about moose: I'd already received more than my share of bad luck. I don't tangle with moose, I don't get lost, I just lose my team.

About ten miles along I came upon a campfire and stopped to find out how far it was to the Rabbit Lake checkpoint. A man and a woman were sitting by the fire and I poured out my story about losing the team. They turned out to be friends of Dennis Lozano's whom I'd met before. I couldn't stay long. I'd left my team in the trail and I didn't want to block it for anyone coming from behind. When Chuck pulled in, I moved on through the darkness and eventually found my way to Rabbit Lake a bit after one in the morning.

March 3, 1985

After attending to chores at the checkpoint, Riddles heads off into deep snow and moose country. She is ill and discouraged.

Rabbit Lake to Finger Lake: 79 miles

Clearing skies, high 18° and low 14°, with winds averaging 6 to 7 knots.

Teams were parked everywhere. About twenty mushers had reached Rabbit Lake ahead of us, and all the dogs were resting alongside the trail and down through the trees. A friendly, familiar face emerged from the darkness—Jack Niggemyer, one of the Rabbit Lake checkers. He'd been doing volunteer work for the Iditarod over the past few years, trailbreaking and handling checkpoints. He'd also let me borrow his big pickup truck to make my airdrops for shipping. He helped me find a place to park the team while he passed on the news. Susan Butcher's team had been attacked by a moose. Susan was there, nursing the injured dogs, one of them even in Jack's sleeping bag. I wondered again about the .41 Ruger I'd decided to leave at home.

Jack had had a pretty tough time of it himself, just setting up the checkpoint. Most of the checkpoints along the trail are villages, with buildings or lodges. But at Rabbit Lake, they use tents. By the time the checkers arrived, the tents that had been dropped earlier were covered with snow. Jack and the others had to find them and then dig them out. And because the trailbreaking snowmachines hadn't arrived yet, they'd spent the rest of the day trying to pack a trail on snowshoes.

I was parked close to a water hole out on the lake ice. Rick Mackey was parked to my right. I picked up the two gunny sacks of food I'd sent to Rabbit Lake and then set off again to fetch water. Every time I left the team, the fear they'd run off gnawed at me. I had chopped a good groove into the lake ice to anchor my hook and then dropped sacks of dog food on top for secur-

29

ity. In time the dogs know when they're supposed to rest, and they seemed content that this was a checkpoint. Maybe they'd found out that making off without the driver wasn't so much fun as they'd expected.

The race committee supplies Blazo fuel for cook stoves. I picked up a can and then searched for my charcoal. I'd used a pressurized fuel camp stove on the first two races. Now I had two round galvanized pails. The bottom one, the stove, has airholes and two bars welded across the top. I put the charcoal in and poured on half a gallon of Blazo, then carefully touched it off with a match. The cooking pail, full of dog food, sits on the bars. The charcoal makes a hot fire and keeps going a long time—no stopping to refill the fuel or pump up the pressure again. I needed only the little bundles of kindling that Elwin and Kelley had made to increase the heat for cooking my second batch of dog food. I could throw burnable trash in there, too, and I could always soak one of the gunny sacks with Blazo and put that on the coals as well.

Some of the racers didn't like the charcoal cookers. They said it hogged too much Blazo. My feeling was we're paying money, our entry fee, for Blazo, and if necessary, I could even burn wood in my cooker—something they couldn't do with a camp stove.

I took the food bucket and a dog dish to use as a scoop and went over to the water hole punched through the lake ice. Every step away from the team bothered me, but the dogs weren't moving.

With the water on and flames shooting several feet into the air, I began chopping my frozen meat into pieces small enough to cook quickly. All the sacks had been sitting outside, so everything was frozen, some of it in big blocks. I used my axe to chop at the frozen beef, chicken, fish, liver, and lamb. Back in Anchorage, I had pressed the beef flat in the bags so that it would be thinner and easier to break. Still, it was in fairly large frozen pieces, and I used one chunk for a chopping block to cut the rest of the meats. Chopping in deep snow was a real pain. My beef

At the Checkpoints

*A*t the two dozen or so checkpoints along the Iditarod Trail—the number may vary each year—drivers sign in and show the equipment required by race rules. In the villages, a local person is usually appointed checker, but at the remote stations the Iditarod race committee sends volunteers to man checkpoints that sometimes are little more than tent camps. The checker often has three or four helpers, since mushers can arrive at all times of the day or night.

Also at each checkpoint are a ham radio operator and a veterinarian. The network of radios enables race officials to relay requests for supplies, discuss problems, and, through reports of arrivals and departures, know whether a musher is overdue and perhaps in trouble on the trail. Since the radio line is essential for official business, phone patches for the drivers are discouraged.

Since race rules prohibit drivers from carrying most drugs, the veterinarian is the main supplier when medicines are needed. The vet also has the authority to force a driver to drop a dog he or she believes should not continue, though most often a word of advice is all that the driver needs to hear. A dropped dog must be left at the checkpoint with a chain and two days' worth of food. If the dog cannot be shipped out within that time, food bags belonging to mushers who have scratched from the race can be used. The dropped dog is flown to Anchorage or Nome, where it is cared for by volunteers until the musher or his friends can retrieve it.

Once drivers have checked in, they are directed to their food drops, the bags of dog food and supplies sent out to the trail before the race, and their work begins. However tired and hungry they may be, their dogs must come first. Water must be hauled and heated, frozen blocks of meat must be chopped. Each dog must be carefully checked for signs of illness; booties must be removed and feet inspected for injury. To help the dogs rest, drivers often ship straw as bedding and seek quiet campsites where the animals can sleep undisturbed, even going back out onto the trail to get away from the village and its commotion.

Checkpoints have their advantages, however: water is available in its liquid form, and villagers may offer hot meals. Help at checkpoints is allowed as long as it is available to all drivers, but most racers are careful lest too much help be deemed a breach of the rules. By design the Iditarod tests the ability of men and women to rely on their dogs and their own resources.

chopping block sank farther and farther into the depths while I chopped. Once I ran out of chopping block, I bashed it around in the soft snow, chasing the little pieces as they split and sifting through the snow to find them.

I dumped all the chopped meat into the water just before it boiled. Then I went to get more water. While the dog food was cooking, I had a few minutes to turn off my headlamp and lie down on my sled. I actually felt a little dizzy. I was too tired to think much or feel anything beyond dizzy. It was a long, long way to Nome, and I hoped the next thousand miles wouldn't be as tough as the first hundred. Nome seemed impossibly far. I just wanted to concentrate on Skwentna, the next checkpoint and only thirty-four miles ahead. I was suffering first-day symptoms.

I crawled out of the sled, took the boiling dog food off the fire and mixed in some commercial dry dog food "friskies." I let them soak up some moisture, then poured in some cold water to cool the soup enough so the dogs could eat it.

"Lead dogs first, guys," I announced. I worked my way back through the team dishing up their food. They all ate enthusiastically, a good sign.

As the second batch of dog food cooked, I went through the team, examining the dogs' feet. All looked good—no cuts, no sore pads—and I let them sleep while I finished my work. I added some cold water to the hot dog food and put it in the cooler. Then I hauled my trash to a refuse pile, returned the rest of the Blazo, and loaded my gear into the sled. Time to be moving again.

We pulled out of the Rabbit Lake checkpoint around four in the morning. There was a lot of traffic on the trail. I hated to stop to check the dogs for fear somebody would come up behind me too fast. But because of that deep snow, the dogs' feet demanded a lot of checking to make sure snow wasn't balling up between their toes. I just had to look them over as quickly as I could, then run back to the sled before the teams behind me got too upset waiting. The trail was so narrow and the snow so deep that passing another team became a major event. If a slower team passed us while we were stopped, we'd have to pass them again a few minutes down the trail.

I was traveling with Rick Mackey off and on and also Roger Nordlum. We passed Bob Bright in the dark. He had managed to squeeze off to the side of the trail and it looked like he was examining his dogs' feet.

The sky began to brighten about six o'clock. Though I had run the dogs longer than I should have, they still looked good, leaning into the harnesses and trotting along steadily. But they could hold up only so long. The three of us who were running together decided on a truce and stopped together on the trail to give our dogs a quick snack.

Rick Mackey parked right behind me and shared some of his coffee while we visited a little. Rick was one of the better racers and had won the Iditarod in 1983. He had a gun with him. I told him I didn't, but as long as I was in front, I'd sure let him know if there were any moose for him to shoot. We tried to figure the distance remaining to Skwentna. I felt like I'd traveled several hundred miles that night. Surely it couldn't be much farther.

By the time we packed up again and hit the trail, we could see where we were going without headlamps. Roger Nordlum was half a mile ahead when I gained the top of a small rise and saw an ominous brown shape in front of his team. It was a moose. Rick stopped behind me, and I told him he might as well get his pistol out. He was just far enough back down the slope that he couldn't see at first, but I think he got his gun. I watched Roger's team pull sharply off to the right, then make its way in a wide circle around the moose.

Figuring if one team could make it past, so could another, I set out nervously. It was a small moose, but its head was down, and it was giving me a very dirty look. I envisioned smoke coming out its ears. The team was quick to pick up on the seriousness of the situation. When a moose flees into the brush, the dogs know

Lords of the Trail

*L*ike all travelers in winter, moose prefer hard-packed trail to deep snow. And these large ruminants are reluctant to yield ground. A moose on the railroad right-of-way may even challenge an oncoming train. If the moose does yield, the dogs instinctively give chase, and the driver must hang on to his sled while his uncontrollable team tears through the brush.

Confronted by dogs, the moose may see not domesticated animals but a pack of wolves and attack. Should they engage, the dogs are at a disadvantage. The moose, which may weigh sixteen hundred pounds, kicks and stomps, while the dogs become tangled in their own lines.

Alaska state law allows the killing of a wild animal in defense of life and property. Iditarod rules state that if an animal deemed edible, such as moose, is killed in defense of a team, the driver must stop and clean the carcass and report the incident at the next checkpoint.

Many moose inhabit the lowlands between Knik and the Alaska Range, and few teams pass through that area without seeing at least one. In 1985 several teams had close encounters.

The moose that was blocking Libby Riddles's trail had stood its ground for some time. Tim Osmar drove his team right past: "Showed him who's boss," he said. Lavon Barve, behind him, was more conservative, stopping at a distance and waiting for the moose to move. When it didn't, he put on his snowshoes and packed a detour around it, leaving

32

the race trail to the animal. Riddles followed Barve's snowshoe trail.

Later the moose knocked Monique Bene off her sled and stood over her for twenty minutes while she lay motionless in the snow. Eventually the moose shuffled off, leaving a frightened musher and cowering dog team.

Susan Butcher was less fortunate. On the first day a moose attacked her team, killing one dog and injuring several others. Duane Halverson came up from behind and found the moose still kicking its way through her team. He shot it with his pistol four times before it fell. A second dog died of its injuries the next day, and Butcher dropped out of the race.

they're safe and are more likely to give chase. But they seemed to sense that this moose, standing there challenging them with its head down, wasn't going to be any fun at all.

I kept a close eye on Joe's leader Dusty, who was behind the swing dogs, three from the front. He had a reputation for chasing game, and our friend Ray Lang in Nome had entertained us with several good stories of Dusty chasing moose during the Nome Sweepstakes Race. All the dogs' ears bent forward and heads popped up as the moose gave us the evil eye. But at the crucial moment they took the "gee" turn on the side trail and we scooted past.

The rest of the trail into Skwentna was up and down short hills, mostly through spruce forest or down on the Yentna River. The temperature turned cold toward dawn, dropping well below zero before the sun started to rise. Skwentna is a small settlement where the Skwentna and Yentna rivers converge, and there were several turnoffs to cabins and side trails. As we went along, I began looking for the turnoff to our friend Duke Bertke's cabin. He'd tried to describe it to me back in town. I missed it and ended up going too far down the river. Duke and his wife, Becky, found me at the checkpoint. They were with one of my sponsors, Steve Jones and his wife, Mary, who had snowmachined in from Big Lake to watch the race pass through Skwentna.

Joe Delia checked me into Skwentna. He's certainly got to be one of the nicest guys in the world. He has lived out there for more than twenty years as a trapper. He's also the postmaster, and a lot of people call him mayor even though there's no government around, at least not of the municipal kind. Donna Gentry, my old racing buddy and this year's race marshal, lived there, too.

We had pulled in at nine-thirty, and the day looked like it was going to be sunny, maybe too hot for the dogs. I figured on giving them a fairly long rest to compensate for the long, hard night. Also, I had to be pretty careful not to overdo it in this warm weather and get them overheated.

33

Duke pointed out a quiet place to keep the dogs. Unfortunately, it was across the river and far from my food drops and water. I tried talking with him while stumbling through my cooking routine, but I don't guess I was carrying much of a conversation. Duke finally gave up, inviting me to come over to their cabin and get some shut-eye when I was done tending to my dogs.

I wrestled my gunnysacks full of dog food across the river, but it was too far to pack water, so I melted snow instead even though it was slower. It seems for every ton of snow, you get about two drops of water. I had trouble getting the stove hot enough to cook the second batch of food. The bundles of kindling that Kelley and Elwin had painstakingly chopped and packaged speeded it up for a while, but the thin wood strips burned out fast. I didn't dare pour more Blazo on it; the whole thing might explode. Finally I soaked a gunnysack and used that.

Every once in a while one of the youngsters staying at the Bertkes' whizzed by on a machine to see if I was ready to come up to the cabin. I had to tell them "twenty more minutes" three times before I finally was done.

It felt indescribably wonderful to set my body down on that snowmachine seat. It was something I hadn't thought about, but except for the brief naps at Rabbit Lake and maybe a minute or two here and there on the trail, I'd been standing up for more than twenty-four hours, a lot of that time pushing the sled or pumping, or lugging heavy bags. Just bending my knees in another direction felt good. But luxury doesn't last long on the Iditarod Trail. The snowmachine wouldn't make it up the river bank with two of us, so I had to walk up.

The guys had taken off for a few hours to try some ice fishing and just the ladies were at the cabin. Although it didn't seem right so early in the race, I already felt tired and rummy and filthy. I was certain that I looked and acted as if I came from Mars or somewhere worse. Reality was becoming a little distorted, and you just feel it in your bones that you're not like normal people.

As I walked into the cabin, I started getting out of my gear. It felt like such a luxury to get my feet out of those damp shoepacs. My face felt hot and flushed as the warm air hit me. My sinuses started to swell, and soon it was almost impossible to breathe through my nose.

I was extremely thirsty and downed several glasses of water. I was getting punchy and beginning to experience a relapse of the cold I'd had the week before the race. Walking indoors seemed to trigger it. My appetite was gone, but I forced myself through the plate of food Becky gave me—I needed to eat.

Upstairs I found Raymie Redington already sleeping on the floor, half out of a sleeping bag. He sat up, muttered some complete nonsense and then was down for the count again, soon snoring away happily and dead to the world. I looked at him for a minute. He had a respectable dog team. I was just as tired and worn out as he was, and I was sniffling from my cold besides. I realized that if he could sleep this soundly on the trail, and if he slept like this again somewhere down the trail, I could probably get the jump on him.

I flopped down on that amazingly comfortable bed and tried to sleep. But my face, already wind-burned, began to burn in the heated cabin, and I couldn't breathe through my nose at all. Despite the bed, I never did fall asleep, just spent an hour tossing and turning. I was also worrying about my team, alone across the river with just a snow hook holding them. They were tired, too—probably sleeping better than I was—and the kids were posted on guard duty, but that chase on the trail still haunted me.

Sleep was impossible. I had some coffee, and Becky found me a couple of pills for my head cold. I was feeling pretty sick, but it was time to get going to Finger Lake. I changed my socks and the felt liners for my boots and sorted through my gear. Duke had returned and offered to lend me a gun. Two moose had been standing on the river just outside of town all day, he said. I declined. I figured we were past some of the worst places for moose. Besides, I thought,

35

surely by now my bad luck had run its course.

In late afternoon the temperature was still pretty warm but I expected it would drop as night fell. I hitched the dogs' tuglines and turned them toward the trail. Just outside of town several trails crossed and I managed to turn off onto one of the wrong ones. A man came by heading for town on a snowmachine and I asked if he'd be kind enough to help me. He turned and guided me to the trail I wanted. By this time Becky had seen me having difficulty and had driven out to help, too. To be in trouble again so soon—it was not a good omen.

The trail followed the Skwentna River to the west and a little north and then into the mountains ahead. At first the trail was laid over the river ice, then later wound through spruce forest and alder into the lower hills that eventually would grow into the Alaska Range, which in turn builds to the highest peak in North America, Mount McKinley, 20,300 feet high.

I didn't know how many teams had left Skwentna ahead of us. Even this early in the race I didn't want to get too far behind and I kept pushing. The dogs had rested well in Skwentna and moved along nicely as we traveled up the river, even though the surface wasn't the best. We had no trouble locating the trail; it was the only one around and the rest of the landscape was covered by five or six feet of snow. That was the problem.

It was fresh trail, just broken through the deep powder, and there hadn't been time for it to set up, time for other teams to run over it and freezing temperatures to pack it hard. It was bottomless trail, just loose snow going down forever.

The teams that had gone ahead of us had churned the snow, making the trail even worse. The dogs' legs and the sled runners sank into that loose snow. In some places it must have felt to the dogs like they were running in loose sand, and when I stepped off the sled to check them, I sank at least up to my waist in the looser, even deeper snow off the trail.

These conditions were just about perfect for ruining dogs' feet. Ice balls were forming be-

Footwear for Dogs

Fabric booties protect the dogs' feet from ice, which abrades the pads, and from snow, which can ball up between the pads, causing discomfort and injury. Mushers use the booties to avoid problems, but if a dog suffers a cut, a bootie can protect the injury and keep the animal in the race. Mushers often dab foot ointment on each boot to keep the dogs' pads supple.

Booties may be made from canvas or the nylon cloth used for lightweight backpacks, but many mushers prefer polypropylene or Polarfleece bunting. Two pocket-shaped pieces sewn together make a pouch that slips over the dog's paw. The bootie is fastened around the leg with a strip of electrical tape or with sewn-in Velcro; some mushers even make elasticized Velcro cuffs. A bootie must be fastened carefully: too tight and the dog loses circulation to his paw, too loose and the dog can flip it off easily.

Bootie manufacture is a chore for a musher's best friend. Since a team may trot through a thousand of them in the course of a race, many a musher's friend has spent long hours cutting and sewing dog boots.

tween the pads, frozen to the guard hairs. I removed them gently, either by crushing them or melting them out with my fingers so as not to pull out the protective hairs and leave the dogs in worse shape than before. I put boots on the dogs that were picking up ice balls. Booting them took a lot of time, but so does picking ice from their feet.

Although I enjoy sewing, stitching up hundreds of dog boots took so much time that my friend Nancy Studer had had to take over for me. I used a lot of her dog boots for protection through that stretch of trail. Those feet had many miles to cover, so I did my best to keep them in good shape.

As the late afternoon light faded into darkness, I stopped and rummaged through the sled to find my headlamp. I checked a few dogs' feet and prepared for the night shift. I tried to get radio stations on my Walkman, but I was already out of range of the Anchorage stations. I put a tape on instead: Bob Marley and the Wailers, a little reggae, soothing music to keep me happy. Here we were just a little more than a day into the race and coming off a long rest stop at Skwentna, and already I was feeling fatigue. If I was this tired now, what kind of shape would I be in when we got to Unalakleet?

The dogs were doing pretty good without my help; they never seemed to notice that I was drifting off. I kept fading in and out as the team moved down the trail in their own steady rhythm. It was hypnotic.

I remembered seeing Joe Redington, Sr., on my first race in 1981 with a fat lip and a scarred face. He explained he'd been sleeping on the back of the sled and had whammed into a tree branch. Until I'd been down the trail myself, I couldn't see how you'd ever get that sleepy. Patty Friend had told me that when she dozed off at the back of the sled, her knees usually buckled, and if she didn't wake up in time, she'd fall off the sled. Eventually she started using a safety line, tying herself to the sled so that the dogs wouldn't run off without her.

I didn't have that problem. It was easy enough

to catch two- or three-minute naps on the back of the sled. The Walkman helped, too. With the Wailers blasting away in my ears I couldn't fall asleep for too long. It wasn't much fun, being so tired I couldn't keep from fading out. I swear sometimes I was sleeping with my eyes open. What I saw sort of faded away into sleep. I tried to get more comfortable at one point and leaned over the drive bar to rest on top of my sled, but the trail was too bumpy to find any comfort that way.

A lot of things went by that night in the dark mist of my sleep. I vaguely remember passing people in a clearing illuminated by a big campfire. I tried to remember what this section of the trail had been like on previous races, but all I could recall was that it always seemed farther from Skwentna to Finger Lake than the forty-five miles the race people said it was. The terrain was more interesting than some, with river travel and spruce forest and hills to climb, but in the dark it seemed endless.

Still fighting to stay awake, I saw a big hill up ahead. The checkpoint had to be somewhere this side of that hill. Maybe it was on the hill. But the hill looked closer than it was, and we still took almost forever to get there. At last I heard a dog bark from off in the distance. We dropped onto a frozen lake and then up on the side of a hill, and I could see the warm lights of a cabin at the hilltop. It was a little after two in the morning. One of the checkers had seen my light coming and rushed down the hill to check me in and show me a place to park my dogs.

Already eighteen teams were resting around the little cabin. With a little extra effort from behind the sled, we reached the summit of the steep lake bank and found a good place for the dogs next to a big old spruce tree sturdy enough to anchor the sled and team.

The dogs went into their nesting routines, digging little holes or circling and packing down little places in the snow to sleep. While they made themselves comfortable, I went to drag the sacks of food over to the sled, one at a time. Fortunately, by this time the other drivers and teams had packed paths through the deep snow.

I fell into my own routine and soon had dog food cooking. After the mutts had eaten and I had cooked the second batch for the cooler, I trudged over to the cabin.

The checkpoint at Finger Lake was in the home of June and Gene Leonard. They had checked racers through since the first race in 1973, and Gene had run the race a couple of times, leaving June to manage the checkpoint herself. The race people had told us at the drivers' meeting before the race that this year we were not to expect to use the Leonards' cabin while we were at Finger Lake. This, according to Gene, was a mistake. We were welcome, he said. Even if it hadn't been a mistake, I wouldn't have blamed them. Imagine having your house invaded for three or four days, night and day, by dozens of weary, smelly dog mushers. But this is Alaska, and the people are special. The Leonards' home was one of several that somehow survived the Iditarod year after year.

Gene was sitting at a table, talking dogs and racing. This was my third time through the checkpoint but I had never met June. Every time I raced, I got to Finger Lake in the middle of the night, and she had showed enough sense to sneak away to get some sleep.

With many of the eighteen drivers inside, the small cabin was crowded. A few drivers were out cold, snoring on the couch, on the floor, on any horizontal surface and even a few almost vertical ones. The rest were cradling bowls of soup or cups of coffee.

Once I had my wet clothes hung up, I found a bowl and had some wonderfully hot soup. The bustle of the cabin was too much for me, though, so I went back to my sled, warmed by the food. I set the alarm on my watch for an hour of sleep and then pulled my sleeping bag over me, boots and all. I only napped, dropping into light sleep and waking again, somewhat uncomfortable in the narrow confines of the sled bag. Cold and stiffness woke me for good before my alarm went off.

As the world came into focus I realized why I

39

was so uncomfortable. I was so chilled I shivered uncontrollably as I tried to stuff my sleeping bag back into its sack. The chill was my own fault for not having the sense to take my boots off and climb all the way into the bag. It wasn't the first time I'd done this and I knew better. At least I hadn't found so much comfort that I'd overslept.

    The chilling hadn't done my cold any good at all. I was certainly glad for the nearby cabin and the hot coffee waiting inside. I slogged over there and once inside I stayed close to the warm stove for a good while, feeling even more tired after my nap. I chugged down an Alka-Seltzer Plus cocktail, then tried a cup of coffee. Not that the coffee would do much good, but at least it was warm.

    Enthusiasm was sorely lacking.

March 4, 1985

Finger Lake to Rainy Pass: 30 miles

High 18° and low −16°, with slight winds.

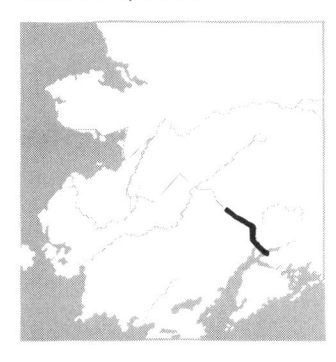

From Finger Lake the trail cuts across a deep canyon, where Riddles takes a bad spill, and then rises into the Alaska Range. A severe storm threatens the race, and two of Riddles's dogs take sick.

Now we had to go down the other side of that tricky hill we'd come up six hours earlier. Victor Katongan helped me get started around the first part of the hill. He grabbed the leaders' lines and swung the front end over for me, and we took off down the hill. We passed teams parked all over the hill as we worked our way out of the checkpoint. It took a bit of fancy steering and a lot of muscling to maneuver the sled around the first couple of corners. I was straining and leaning and shoving the sled around the tight corners until on a particularly sharp one, I felt something give. All that work when my muscles weren't properly warmed and limbered finally caught me. I had pulled some of the muscles around the right side of my hip. Not a sharp pain, but an ache. For the rest of the race, every time I had to run or pump behind the sled, those pulled muscles reminded me of that turn.

We were on the trail a little after eight in the morning. I was glad it was daylight because the coming stretch was particularly tough going. At first the trail wound tightly through the trees, still over soft snow, and on some of those corners I wondered if the trailbreakers weren't trying to pull a joke on us.

In one place at the bottom of a short hill a small tree growing at a forty-five-degree angle almost blocked the trail, and it looked like the snowmachines breaking the trail had gone right under it. The dogs tried a different route, hopping over the tree. By the time I could react, all I could do was brace myself, expecting to slam into the tree and wedge the sled underneath. Somehow that didn't happen. The sled followed the dogs over the tree and miraculously re-

41

mained upright. I wondered how the rest of the teams would fare at that spot, but I didn't get too much time to think about it. The trail was demanding my undivided attention. My dogs had seldom trained in tree country; the forest was more exciting to them than to dogs that were more used to it. They hummed around those corners, probably expecting to see a hare or something else fun to chase around the very next turn.

The scenery was really beautiful, but I was too busy concentrating on our maneuvers to enjoy it. I started thinking I'd been living up on the treeless coast for too long. I used to miss the forest, but now I could hardly wait to get out of those sled-busting trees. I felt claustrophobic. We whipped through the woods like a snake. Every once in a while the leaders would turn completely out of sight around a curve. The sensation of being pulled along by an invisible force was almost funny, if you had a warped sense of humor. The farther we went, though, the more nervous I got, anticipating the Happy River descent.

After Finger Lake the trail rises at a steeper grade until it reaches thirty-four hundred feet at Rainy Pass in the Alaska Range. En route it crosses a canyon cut by the Happy River. This canyon presents one of the greatest obstacles on the race, and getting across is always an adventure. The trail makes a steep descent and then climbs back up the other side before climbing higher into the mountains. The drop creates all the problems.

When I raced in 1981, the descent had been divided into three steep, straight chutes, each with a platform at the base, like landings on a staircase. That had worked out pretty well. The last turn at the bottom of the hill had been so sharp to the left that the trailbreaker cut a wide loop to the right, swung all the way around like a cloverleaf on a superhighway, and then crossed the trail to get us going back in the right direction. I was hoping they had done something along the same lines this year.

I was a ways behind the leaders, but in at least

Over the Edge

For the perilous descent into the Happy River canyon, drivers have wrapped chains around their sled runners to slow their speed, dragged logs to brake the dogs, and unhooked tuglines to reduce the dogs' pulling power. But none of these measures would have helped Burt Bomhoff in 1985.

The dogs of the race leader, Lavon Barve, had missed a hard left turn and overshot the trail, but because he saw no tracks, he stopped and swung his team around. Burt Bomhoff's dogs just kept going, following the leading team's scent and tracks twelve feet beyond the turn. Then they ran out of trail.

"I was looking at the Happy River, a thousand or fifteen hundred feet below," recalled Bomhoff. "Suddenly my lead dogs disappeared. Then the swing dogs went out of sight. I stood on the brake, leaped, grabbed my hook and dug it in, but by then three or four pairs of dogs were over the cliff. I worked my way up the gangline hand over hand and saw my dogs dangling over the canyon. Hanging by their harnesses with their feet out, they looked up at me as if to say, 'What now?' I whistled them up, and with me pulling, they scrambled back up."

Bomhoff took a few minutes to chop the branches off a spruce tree and build a fence to block the false trail. "I thought somebody would get killed," he said.

one place that turned out to be fortunate for me, since I could see ahead where other people had crashed. We were traveling along the edge of a hill, and every time I looked down I got the shivers. It was a long, steep way to the bottom.

We traveled along the edge of that cliff, looking way, way down. God, I was getting nervous. It was a long way down. It looked impossible, even though I'd made it before, twice. We rounded the corner and the trail dropped out from under us.

I thought, "Oh, boy, here we go."

We were heading downhill fast. I laid into the brake for all I was worth and tried to keep the heavy sled straight. We were side-hilling down the slope with trees on both sides, the dogs heading straight down, the sled shushing down sideways. We were two thirds of the way down the hill. As I went down, I looked at the tracks of sleds that had gone ahead of me to see what happened to them while trying to keep my team and my sled under control. Each one of those tracks that marked somebody's adventure went by in a heartbeat—not much time to figure out exactly what had happened, or what I should do.

We careened wildly. Then I saw where somebody had wiped out. The unlucky musher was gone but had left a huge crater in the snow. I panicked. "The last guy crashed here, now I'm going to." Our speed didn't give me enough time to go through all the options, let alone try one. I wasn't using good sense. The sled slewed sideways, the right runner caught in the deeper snow off to the side, and the whole sled somersaulted with me still hanging on. It turned upside down. The snow hook flew loose and ripped my jacket and slammed into my hand. Then all motion stopped.

I was in snow up to my armpits. I looked at the dogs. "Oooh, dogs. Don't you dare. Don't you *dare* take off and drag me on my belly the rest of the way down this hill."

I told the team "Stay!" in my most serious tone of voice. They stood waiting for me while I foundered in the snow—snow so deep I had a

43

hard time just getting back to the trail to gain some purchase so that I could reach back and drag the sled back. I didn't bother to survey the damage. I didn't have time. I just wanted to get off that hill, get the rest of it over with. I managed to horse the sled upright and got on the runners on my knees. Then I told the dogs, "Go ahead, easy, easy." Just as we began moving, a corner of the sled snagged on a tree. I had to pull back and away from the tree and quickly hop on as the team took off down the last stretch. I found out later that some of the racers had renamed the Happy River descent: "Kamikaze Hill."

About half a mile past the bottom of that hill, a few of the mushers had stopped to snack their teams. If they were feeling anything like me, they stopped, too, to regain their composure after that hill. I was shaky.

Rick Mackey was there ahead of me, Roger Nordlum and Sonny Lindner, too. Rick offered me a swig of his coffee, as he usually did when I ran into him. He said he'd crashed on the hill, too, only two of his dogs had gotten tangled. He'd had to cut their lines quickly to keep them from choking.

Two more drivers joined us, Fred Agree and then John Barron. Fred, Sonny, and John had made the hill without crashing. Impressive. I tried to regain some measure of calm. I was feeding the dogs out of the cooler when I began to notice a throbbing in my right hand. I took off my glove and what I saw looked scary. I'd been stupid enough to wear a ring, and my snowhook had bumped the knuckle when I crashed. The finger was now swelling up like mad, and the ring was close to cutting off the circulation.

Rick produced one of those handy seven-in-one tools with a file on it so that I could cut the ring off. But I wanted to wait. I didn't want to cut the ring off unless it was absolutely necessary. It was a plain silver ring with a black Australian opal. I'd worn it on my other two Iditarods, and as much as I hate to admit to being little superstitious, I considered it my lucky opal—just to be contrary, of course, because it's bad luck if you buy it for yourself. It *was* bad luck, come to think of it—for the one finger anyway. I put some snow on the finger to try to keep the swelling down and managed to talk Rick into letting me borrow his gadget until we reached Rainy Pass Lodge. He was taking a big chance, lending it to me. If anything went wrong with his sled in the next twenty-five miles, he'd have no tool to work with.

We had more tough trail ahead and the sky was beginning to darken as snowstorm clouds moved in from the north. Rick and Roger started packing to leave and I followed as quickly as I could.

After the ridge and the wild rides through those chutes, the trail resumed a steady rise into the Alaska Range. I was still in territory familiar from previous races and recognized the trail. We crossed a frozen lake, then passed two cabins on its far side. On a previous race I had made a quick investigation of the cabins, and now I recalled that the trail had gone off the lake and up into the woods right next to the cabins. This year our route was different—the trail led across the lake.

Sonny Lindner was parked toward the end of the lake, feeding his dogs and emptying his cooler to lighten the load in anticipation of a lot of side-hilling on the trail ahead. I didn't remember it as being that tricky, but I paid attention. A lot of these guys raced nearly every year, and they knew the trail better than I did.

We drove back into the trees and the closeness brought back the claustrophobic feelings. The going wasn't bad, though, just close. It might have been that after the last stretch along the Happy River, anything would have seemed better.

I was looking forward to the last miles of trail into the Rainy Pass checkpoint. The forest thinned as we began to climb toward tree line in the mountains. I carried an image of clean, unbroken hills, dotted with fat little spruce trees, with blue-white mountain peaks rising from a broad valley. Conditions were warm as we passed noon and I was stopping the dogs often to give them snacks and let them cool off. I stopped on one big open area, probably another frozen lake, and gave each dog what I call a popsicle, my homemade, frozen whitefish snacks. John Barron rolled up and decided to snack his dogs, too. As warm as it was, there was no sense being in any hurry. We'd just wear the dogs out.

A helicopter landed on the far side of the lake. We couldn't tell who they were or what they were doing. Another team came across the lake. John and I tried to figure out who it was. Finally the team trotted close enough for us to holler, "Who the heck is that?" The bearded driver passed by, shouting, "Paulsen. I'm one of those darn Minnesota drivers. That's why you don't know me." Barron and I packed up and moved on. I pulled a little bit ahead of him and traveled alone the rest of the way to the Rainy Pass Lodge.

The scenery was slightly less awesome than what I'd seen in 1980 and 1981, but the trail gave the dogs smooth sailing. In other years the mountain peaks were ahead and to the north and south. This year they were obscured by trees and close hills. The dogs were traveling at an average speed, around ten miles an hour— good considering the higher temperature, almost thirty, I guessed.

I watched my team carefully as they moved along. I knew them well and I was looking for little telltale changes. Sometimes a dog holds his ears back a little, telling you something's wrong.

Two of Joe's dogs, the big old wheeler Stewpot and little Socks, the smallest in the team, were showing signs of sickness. I could tell they were both a little off their usual health. If they were getting dehydrated, they would lose weight fairly fast, and the physical effort of the race would take them down even faster. Maybe they had picked a bug off the trail or were getting stressed out. I guessed it was viral.

"Hey there, Stewpot," I called, trying to happy him up. "How's old Stewbones? How's my big wheelie? And you there, Socks. How's my girl? You think a lot of yourself, don't you, Socks?

You're not going to let a bug get you down, hey Socks?"

Dropping them at the next checkpoint had to be one of my options as I looked at these two still struggling in harness. But before I made that decision, I planned to wait and see how they looked after they had rested.

In my fatigue the last part of the trail to Rainy Pass Lodge merged into a white blur. What revived me was passing some bright blue, five-gallon Blazo cans and then a couple of fifty-five-gallon drums of aviation fuel, sure signs we were approaching civilization. Two checkers waited on the steep banks rising from frozen Puntilla Lake to the big frame lodge. Again eighteen racers had arrived ahead of me. The checkers said airplanes hadn't been able to fly on the other side of the mountains and there might not be dog food at the next two checkpoints. Even at three in the afternoon the sky on the far side of those mountain peaks looked black, and it sure didn't look like anyone could fly those clouds. With the possibility of not having food at the next checkpoint and maybe the one after that, most people planned to wait it out at Rainy Pass.

My problem was, I had planned to take my mandatory twenty-four-hour layover to rest the dogs at the next checkpoint, Rohn River, and that's where I had sent the extra food for a long stay. I hadn't planned to stay so long at Rainy Pass, and I might not have enough to feed the dogs for the next twenty-four hours and still have food for the run over the mountains. Nevertheless, I declared my twenty-four, too. No sense sitting there for twelve hours before starting the official twenty-four clock.

While the officials checked my gear, I surveyed the area, trying to scope out the best place to put my dogs. If we were going to stay a while, I wanted to make the dogs as comfortable as possible. I went out ahead of the leaders to break trail down a little hill. I pulled them along to a good sturdy tree where I could tie them and not have to worry. The snow was pretty deep in places and I sank into it with almost every step.

We were close to where the airplanes were landing and taking off. Other than that, it was a good spot.

I floundered and sank through deep snow to tie the sled and unsnap all the tuglines. I tied the front end of the gangline to a bush to stretch it out as far as I could so that the dogs wouldn't bunch together.

A few of the dogs merited special attention. Minnow was still in heat and still capable of getting herself in trouble. No need to agitate the males in the team. I tied her to a tree away from the other dogs.

Little Socks wasn't feeling at all well, but she might still have energy to gnaw on the rope. I wasn't about to let her chew the whole team to freedom, so she got her own tree, too. Besides, if she was sick, she'd probably prefer to be by herself.

Stripe had a fondness for barking and insulting whichever dogs were tied next to him, especially after he'd rested for a while. One of those insulted dogs might just get its feelings hurt badly enough to try to take him on. "You old scrapper, you," I chided as I led him to a tree off by himself. I slogged along the team and took off their boots, checked their feet, and petted them a little. Penny took a bit of teasing: "How's Penner? How's the sweet girl with the shabby fur?" She scrunched up her face in modesty.

By accident I had parked close to the dog food drops. I picked out my sacks easily enough; the green and purple stripes stood out in the mound of bags. Then everything came out of the sled. If we were going to be here a while, it would be a good place to go through all the gear and reorganize.

As I fetched a can of Blazo and hauled some water from a hole chopped in the lake ice, I was getting jealous of Swenson and Lindner, who were carrying "red sleds" to use for their hauling. These children's toboggans of molded plastic were just the right size for hauling water and small loads of firewood. I used one all the time to haul dog food buckets at home, and I sure missed it on the trail.

Champion Dog Food

When the teams left Anchorage for the first race along the Iditarod Trail in 1973, drivers were prepared to feed their dogs according to their experience with sprint sled-dog racing. But the food formulas that had worked well for short distances did not sustain dogs running long distance.

Because it supplies high energy in cold weather, fat has become a large part of the dogs' trail diet, but that fat must be highly soluble. Beaver meat, which combines a high protein content with soluble fat, was a popular choice for a time, but more sophisticated, more easily obtained formulas have been developed since. Seal blubber is another source of fat, but it, too, is rarely used. Only Alaska Natives can hunt most marine mammals, and a nonnative can obtain seal products only if they have undergone processing.

Food formulas have become as complicated as chemical formulas—and as closely guarded. Beef, beef liver, ground chicken, lamb, and commercial dry dog food form the basis of the cooked meals that most dogs eat at Iditarod checkpoints. Approximately one ton of these ingredients must be cut, measured, and packaged for shipment to the villages along the trail.

Dehydration is a serious problem, particularly in colder temperatures. Because the dogs may not drink plain water, the meats and dry food must be mixed with considerable amounts of liquid. Melting snow, however, is a tedious job—each armful of snow *yields only a small amount of water—so mushers take advantage of the readily available water in villages and prepare two batches of dog food at a time, one for immediate feeding and another, carried in a five- or six-gallon cooler, for feeding along the trail. The cooler insulates the warm food against freezing.*

To maintain their energy level, sled dogs need snacks at intervals along the trail. Riddles snacked her dogs on fish, mostly whitefish caught in the Imuruk Basin near Teller, and on chunks of lamb; both were eaten raw.

Racing dogs do not generally leave untouched much of their food—a minimum four pounds per dog at checkpoints plus two pounds in the sled.

In winter training and during the summer, mushers use many of the same ingredients but cut costs by increasing the proportions of fish and commercial dry dog food. The dogs need the same nutritional values year-round, just not in such prodigious quantities as during the race. Maintaining a dog team costs whatever the driver can afford. Riddles's thirty animals consume nearly $20,000 worth of food and veterinary care each year.

While I waited for the food to cook, I went to look for the veterinarian, Ginny Johnson. With all the teams already in the checkpoint and more arriving every few minutes, she was busy. Actually, the drivers needed more doctoring than the dogs. It seemed everybody had trouble with the Happy River hill.

"I knew the trail was bad," she said, "when the quiet people, the people who don't normally complain, came in and said 'Oh, God. The trail was awful.'"

Jerry Austin had broken bones in his hand. Terry Hinsely had a cut over his eye that would have required stitches if it hadn't already started to heal.

While Ginny was working her way over to the team, one of the race officials told me he'd heard I'd broken my hip and was going to scratch from the race. I wondered how that one had started. I couldn't remember telling anyone about wrenching my hip going out of Finger Lake. Rumors really fly around the checkpoints along the trail, but a banged knuckle is a long way from a broken hip—and not even worth mentioning compared with some of the accidents. It did remind me to return Rick Mackey's multitool, though. The finger wouldn't get any worse. I'd tied it with the black tape I used for dog boots to keep down the swelling, and it seemed okay. The knuckle was damaged, however, and a year passed before I could take the ring off.

The dog food was still cooking when Ginny came over. She examined the sick dogs and gave me some diarrhea medicine. She also gave me some extra foot ointment. I liked to grease down all the dogs' feet whenever I had time. It was a big help on those feet that might be developing small sores.

The dark clouds over the far peaks weren't looking any better, and it was becoming obvious we'd be there a while. I'd have to stretch the dog food. I mixed the cooked feed with more water and friskies and started relaying dog food to the front of the team. It was more work to feed the front end of the team first—the full bucket's heavy—but I always fed my dogs like that, even

49

when it was just snacks. The leaders shoulder an extra burden and I like to let them know they're special. Socks just nibbled, then lost her interest. Stewpot, whose name only suggests what quantities of food he ate, sat there looking glum, turning away from the good meal I'd placed before him. If they kept this up, they would get dehydrated and weak, lose weight, and have to be dropped from the race. I told Ginny I wanted a little time to work with them first.

I can't stand to see dogs suffer. In the fall, when Inca's and Minnow's puppies were three months old, the whole group contracted parvovirus, even though they had been vaccinated. The nearest veterinarian was seventy air miles away, and once the pups got sick, they couldn't travel anyway, so I had to treat them as best I could in a corner of the house. Two of Inca's pups I kept alive with intravenous fluids, antibiotics, and Kaopectate; the other three died, along with Minnow's seven. One of the lucky ones showed such spirit I had to smile. She was almost too sick to move, but whenever I came near, she'd thump the tip of her tail against the floor; I named her Wags.

Socks and Stewpot didn't have anything so deadly as parvo, but they felt miserable, I could tell. I was depressed. I wanted to hold my team together. I sat with the two sick dogs and offered seductive snacks, trying to tempt them: lamb, liver, little pieces of blubber. I kneeled in the snow with them and tried to get them at least to nibble at the morsels, but neither Stewpot nor Socks would even so much as sniff at my offerings.

Spending all this time with the team, I was beginning to take on their moods, and the way the two sick dogs looked was getting to me. To keep my humor up while I did the rest of the chores, I dug out my Walkman and played a new UB 40 tape. It seemed I could do things twice as easily with some tunes playing. I chopped up another round of dog food, keeping time by humming along with "Geoffery Morgan." I hoped I wasn't within anyone's earshot.

Rumors had been racing through the pack of

drivers about who was leaving or staying, and I wondered what was real. Then Donna Gentry, the race marshal, told me we were all going to be there for a while because there was no dog food at the next two checkpoints. The airplanes couldn't fly.

I didn't have enough dog food, and I supposed many of the others were in the same shape. I put just a small amount of chopped meat in the second batch; it would be skinny soup. Gears started going around in my mind, trying to figure the best plans for the situation. A few drivers had planned well enough, or were financed well enough, that they had plenty of dog food, but I wasn't one of them. I kept to my vague plan: Play it by ear.

Several drivers were attempting to use whatever connections they had to get meat flown in to them. It would be so expensive, if I could even locate an airplane that would fly to Rainy Pass in this nasty weather. Roger Nordlum said one of his buddies was going to be bringing him a planeload of horsemeat and that he could probably spare me a fifty-pound block of it . . . if his pilot could make it up to Puntilla Lake. And it sure didn't look like flying weather.

There were rumors that the officials would put the race on hold. I wanted to talk with Joe. Among the several cabins around the main lodge, one of the smaller ones had been allotted to the ham radio operators, who could patch through a phone call. By the time I trudged up the hill to the radio cabin, night had fallen. I shook the heavy snow off my boots and then ducked inside. Burt Bomhoff was on the radio arranging for some dog food to be flown up for his team. I sat down on a bench, flushed from the sudden heat, and waited my turn. More than a dozen people were waiting, and I listened to their banter. Dogs and trail, Happy River and dog food, freezes and food at Rohn, Ptarmigan Pass, Rainy Pass. I was too tired to participate and felt more than a bit out of place in human rather than canine company. Most other mushers were in zombie states like me.

Finally it was my turn. The radio operator told

me to write Joe's phone number on a slip of paper. I'd never used this type of radio phone before. The operator waited for traffic to clear as he tried to put the call through.

I sure hoped Joe was home. Only two days earlier we had said good-bye at Knik, but it seemed so much longer. Joe answered. The operator handed up the microphone and I wondered if I had to say "roger" and "over" and all the other radio talk, as he had done. I told Joe what was going on, that I was planning on keeping the dogs full of skinny soup and getting lots of water into them. There really wasn't anything he could tell me that I didn't already know, but it was good just to talk with him a bit and get a little support. As I walked out of the cabin, I heard one of the operators say to the other, "That's the sort of thing that makes this job worth it." The call had cheered someone else besides me, then.

I tucked my team in, gave each one a little scratch and a word. Now that I knew we were going to be there for a while, I peeled off the harnesses so that I could get them dry. I gathered all my other damp gear, which was most everything, and my sleeping bag and sludged over to get my first look at the lodge so kindly contributed for our use.

Inside, I felt a flush of sudden heat. Gear was hanging from every available nail, from the rafters, even from a pair of snowshoes hung on the wall, anywhere there was room, but especially around the two stoves. I found a place for my boots and wore just the damp felt liners around the lodge, even though the floor was wet from all the tracked-in snow. They had a huge coffee maker in the lodge, but the brew was going fast. It sure tasted great. Some of the rooms in the back of the lodge had beds but they all seemed occupied. I kept looking around till I spotted an empty bunk; my luck was good. This time I got all the way into the bag, at the last minute setting my watch alarm for six.

The noise of conversations in the next room faded slowly, and my last thought was how grand it was to be sleeping on a mattress.

March 5, 1985

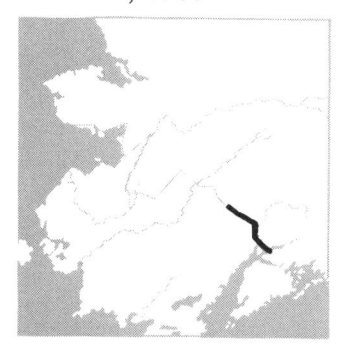

Rainy Pass

Occasional snow, high 24° and low 1° with slight winds.

Racers hole up in Rainy Pass, waiting for the weather to break. Riddles nurses her sick animals and rations her dog food.

I woke before the alarm went off. When the world came back into focus, I walked barefoot on the wet carpet to get my liners and boots. Outside it was cool enough, but with the promise of temperatures in the twenties, and snow. The sky still looked black over toward the other side of the range where the airplanes would have to fly food into the next two checkpoints.

The mutts were happy to see me, standing up to shake and stretch, wagging their tails. Socks and Stew got up with the rest, but they weren't smiling. Nasty little pools of diarrhea were frozen in the snow beside them. I gave them medication and tried to happy them up a little.

"How's the pot-licker today?" I asked, rubbing Stewpot behind the ear. "How's Socks? Yes, you, the Socks-dog with the sharp ears."

The rest had done them some good. It even looked like they'd been behaving themselves. I had to make skinny soup again with a few extra friskies thrown in for some bulk. I sure wanted to be feeding my dogs better than I was. While they were eating, I began to wonder if there wasn't something I could do besides sit and wait for airplanes that might or might not make it through the weather. I walked back to my cooker and was quite pleased to find that although the whole unit had melted quite a way down into the snow, I had a pot full of warm water ready for a second batch. That's one of the joys of charcoal. I didn't have much of it, though, and making it last would be tricky.

I searched the immediate area for some dead wood and located a few pieces here and there. Then I swiped the burlap sack that I'd given Axle to lie on the night before, soaked a little Blazo into it and set it alight.

53

I hated to bother the couple who lived there, but I desperately wanted to get some more food for my dogs and I finally got brave enough to ask them if they had a fish or two, or anything else I could buy for dog food. I wasn't the first to ask; others had been there, too, and they were diplomatic enough to make a policy of not selling anything to anyone. One last resort. Joe and I had caught the whitefish for the dog popsicles with a net through holes in the ice at Teller. I wondered out loud if it were possible to catch fish through the ice of Puntilla Lake. No, they said, there were precious few fish in the lake.

I was making a nuisance of myself, but I just had to give it a try, for my dogs. There wasn't much else to do, so I busied myself by first gathering some more dead wood, small stuff mostly, making a little pile to use the next time I cooked. I filled the cook pot with water. This time using my head, I walked to the lake, not even fifteen feet away, then out another ten feet and started to scrape away the snow with the dog food dipper I'd brought along for a scoop. Under the snow, overflow water started to seep into the little hole I'd scooped out. Joe had told me about that little trick. It was slow, but I was quite pleased not to have to tote water from way over at the water hole. I tried to explain the process to Kazuo Kajima, a driver from Japan, because he was packing water all the way over to his little yellow tent, which was still farther away from the water hole than I was.

To make the hounds more comfortable, I nicked off a few spruce boughs and made a bed for each dog. They were all for it and stood anxiously by until I was done. Then they made themselves at home, poking and scraping, rearranging, circling and finally dropping down to rest on their new beds.

The coffee was still brewing when I entered the lodge, and several dozen racers were milling around. A whole tribe of coffee drinkers were waiting for the morning brew. Now and then someone would check the color of the coffee in the viewing tube, and when it finally turned dark enough, we lined up around the pot.

Donna came into the room as I sipped my coffee and summoned us to a big meeting down on the ice. There she laid out the situation.

"It's bad," she said. There was no dog food at the next two checkpoints. We had two options: we could stay in Rainy Pass until dog food could be delivered by plane, or we could hope for the best and go for it. She gave us five minutes to talk it over before we would vote. Swenson asked if our decision had to be unanimous. It had to be unanimous to hold the race, Donna said; otherwise everybody was on his own. Rick smiled a wise sort of smile. Dog drivers are never unanimous about anything. People split into smaller groups of conversation. The front guys didn't want the hold, especially those who stay way out front and had raced hard to get there first.

Bomhoff had been the second team to arrive at Rainy and thought the hold would really hurt his chances. He voted against it. Swenson did, too. He had enough food there at Rainy to take him and his dogs the two hundred miles to McGrath if need be. Not many of us had that, including me. I voted to stay. I was almost out of dog food and it wasn't worth it to make it to Rohn only to find out the dog food hadn't gotten there yet.

The weather was still too scary to attempt the pass, and it looked as if everyone would be staying until the weather looked a little better. The trail wasn't marked well, if at all, and with all the snow anybody who left would have a massive trailbreaking job.

The group broke up, everyone talking as they made their way back to their sleds or the lodge. A few who were coming off their twenty-fours packed up. I decided to check over the dogs and find something constructive to do. I went back to the warm water on the cooker and made a new batch of feed, even though the dogs wouldn't need to eat for a while. All were resting happily on their spruce beds.

The dogs might get stiff from sitting still for so long. One at a time I took several of them for walks out on the lake to limber them up. Then,

55

having run out of things to do, I went back up to the lodge. It was fun to have all the drivers together. I got to meet some racers for the first time and had a chance to shoot the breeze with some of those I already knew. The atmosphere was fairly relaxed, considering this was a race. Everyone was still working at drying gear and making something to eat, sipping coffee and telling stories and jokes.

A few reporters wandered around in the mayhem. They filmed once in a while, the television lights sharpening everything. They interviewed Swenson and some others about what they thought of the race so far. I even got my picture taken, but probably just because I was sitting between Herbie Nayokpuk and Roger Nordlum. It was pretty crazy in there, but it sure felt good to sit around relaxing and drinking coffee. I heard several horror stories about the descent to Happy River. That afternoon, those drivers who had tried to leave came back, saying they couldn't find any trail. Donna went out on a snowmachine looking for markers, too.

During the afternoon some airplanes managed to duck under the clouds and land on Puntilla Lake. One of them was Roger Nordlum's pal, and true to his word, Roger saved me a box of meat. Several other planes brought in dog food and people food from Anchorage.

When I returned to my team, I found the box of meat. I couldn't believe my eyes. I was sure it must have been a mistake. Then Chuck Schaeffer wandered over. He and Nathan Underwood had parked their teams next to mine. Chuck said they had made sure to snatch a box for me and bring it over. It was pretty nice of those guys to help me like that, a real lifesaver. We were watching out for each other. I knew now I'd make it through our stay at Rainy Pass without having to try ice fishing or other desperate measures and still have enough to get across the pass to Rohn. I'm sure the owners of the lodge relaxed a little, too. I don't think they appreciated the jokes we'd all been making about their horses.

Donna reported severe trail problems. There

Frozen in Rainy Pass

Mushers' bags of food and equipment are usually shipped to checkpoints well before the race, but because the Rohn River stop is just a campsite, not a village, food has to be flown in at the last minute, lest wolves devour the cache. But by the time the mushers had reached Rainy Pass Lodge in 1985, severe weather to the north of the Alaska Range had prevented airplanes from making their drops.

The first afternoon and night, drivers were taking their mandatory twenty-four-hour layovers. Race marshal Donna Gentry was hopeful that the planes would soon reach Rohn, but the weather reports gave no cause for optimism. When drivers started coming off their twenty-fours, it became apparent that at daybreak some would move anyway.

Herbert Nayokpuk had a reputation for going out into storms, and he was getting ready to go. Gentry watched his preparations. "Herbie had the food to make it; so did Swenson and Lindner," she recalled. "They had the food and the experience to travel the two hundred miles to McGrath with just what they could carry in their sleds. Once those three started to move, they were all going to go, and not all would be happy dog teams at the other end."

In thirteen years of Iditarod competition, the race had never been frozen officially, and Gentry did not want to set the precedent. "What the Iditarod is all about doesn't include that type of interfer-

ence," she said. "But there was no dog food until McGrath, two hundred miles and at least two days away. And the trail wasn't marked all the way. I hated to take decisions away from the mushers, but I had to consider what was best for the race as a whole. I got five ulcers trying to make up my mind."

For a second opinion Gentry consulted veterinarian Ginny Johnson. "That's a long way to go without veterinary supervision," she said. "Some can do it, and some can't."

Her stomach in a knot, Gentry announced her decision. All the racers would stay put until there was food at the next checkpoints.

The freeze brought its own complications. By now most of the teams had reached Rainy Pass. Since few had planned for a long stop, and planes had been unable to deliver fresh supplies, food and medicine for both dogs and people ran short.

"I had to make judgment calls about who needed what the most and save medicine for the sickest," said Johnson. "But after four days, treating the animals was easy. I didn't have anything to give them."

In Anchorage the radio stations reported that the teams were stranded in Rainy Pass. People donated food from their freezers, and when the planes finally could land on Puntilla Lake, Johnson helped unload the sacks of fat, fish, meat, and commercial dog food. Each driver received about twelve pounds.

"People were very generous," Johnson reported. "A few packages of dog food looked good enough . . . well, the race judges had steak dinners that night."

were no markers. Toward evening everyone was coming off their twenty-fours. Drivers were starting to get restless and when daylight came, they were going to be moving, if not before. Herbie was getting ready; he had been through Ptarmigan Pass before without much of a trail.

Then Donna stopped the race; we would be frozen in Rainy Pass until the planes could make their drops. I went back up and fed the dogs around eight o'clock, this time with a little thicker soup, now that I had more meat. I talked to them and rubbed them down. Brownie acted like he was putting up with something slightly beneath his dignity. Such a serious dog. Socks didn't let on that she enjoyed it, either, but she had a little more fun in her.

Back at the lodge, drivers were still busy swapping lies. I managed to find an empty bed again; it was early. One of the other beds contained an exhausted rookie, Ron Robbins. It's really too bad we didn't have a snoring competition. My money would have been firmly on Mr. Robbins, seeing as how Marc Boiley, another musher, and Stinky Hardy, the famous Nome pilot, weren't there. The snoring produced in that bed was shaking the floor and rattling the rafters. That guy could have competed with my chainsaw.

Vern Halter and I exchanged glances. "What are we going to do about this guy?" I was scared to wake him up. I didn't even know him. We had to do something, though. I shook the guy enough to wake him and then Vern hollered at him to turn over. He quit snoring long enough for me to fall asleep.

I woke up an hour later with the chainsaw buzz in my ears. It was just too much. I reached down in the dark to grab a pillow—there was a pile of them on the floor—to wing at the snoring rookie. What I grabbed was the middle of Bomhoff's face. I don't know which of us was more surprised. I yelled; Burt grabbed my arm in a deadly grip. Then he woke up.

"What the hell are you doing, Libby? God, it felt like an owl landed on my face."

I told him sorry, I'd mistaken his face for a pillow.

57

March 6, 1985

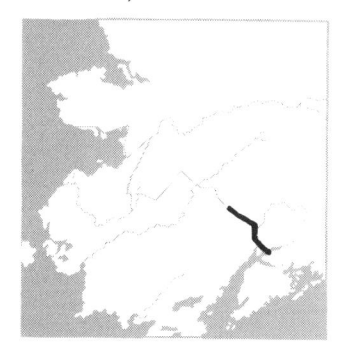

Rainy Pass

Snow, high 29° and low 21°, with slight northwest wind.

The race is now officially frozen. Riddles spends the day resting and worrying.

After two days of rest, the dogs were getting frisky. Stripe, even tied to his own tree away from the others, had started bad-mouthing his neighbors and tugging at his hitching post. I moved him even farther away to a somewhat sturdier tree.

Stewpot and Socks stood up and stretched. They were looking a little better. I could tell they were beginning to mend, just the way they moved. I gave them some pills from the vet and tried to tempt them with different treats again, but they still weren't eating normally.

It was getting harder to find sticks of firewood. Still, I sure was glad to have the charcoal cooker that could use wood in a pinch. The race people were rationing Blazo and I wondered how the guys with only Coleman stoves were doing. While breakfast cooked, I worked on the dogs a little. A couple of them got rubdowns, and all of them got a little petting and their necks scratched. While I worked along the team, my mind began to wander. When would we be leaving? Would the food last? What all lay ahead of us? Musing, I pulled up Brownie's collar and scratched the fur that was matted down underneath.

Everyone was talking about going through Ptarmigan Pass instead of the usual Rainy Pass route. Rainy Pass would be a short but screaming, twisty downhill run around boulders and across ice bridges over open water that dropped a thousand feet in about four miles. Tough trail, and with the heavy snows, the avalanche danger was high. Ptarmigan would have a gentler incline and decline with less avalanche danger but would add almost thirty miles to the route. That meant more dog food to carry.

Donna Gentry had considered the trail options

and held to the Ptarmigan route because of the avalanche danger.

The checkpoint bustled with activity that afternoon. Some relief people and dog food had made it in. We stood in lines waiting for the race officials to divide up the deliveries.

I received a surprise jug of honey from my friend Charlene in Anchorage. I was amazed that she had been able to get something to me personally at Rainy Pass. I was glad to get some people food, too, because I was trying to save what little I had for the long haul across the pass to the Rohn River checkpoint. I bummed some extra dried fish from Fred Jackson, also an up-north guy, and got a taste of stew up at the lodge. The hot meal was a welcome change. I was regretting not having brought along some jars of seal oil. It was something I had learned to appreciate, living in Teller on the northern coast.

In Teller the favorite social events—besides checking the mail at the post office, going to church, and playing bingo—were the traditional feasts. People would spread food on a table or a board on the floor and fill up their plates or eat off cardboard. The men had long knives, the women, ulus, to cut the dried fish and seal meat. We dipped the pieces in small dishes of seal oil, then sprinkled on salt. I especially loved the black meat, but I wasn't keen on the pieces of blubber unless it was forty below outside. After that, greens in oil, carrots, and turnips. Each guest would then head for the basin to wash hands and face, knives and plates. For dessert, we ate berries with sugar or *kamamik,* Eskimo ice cream, which is made with seal oil.

I had some *kamamik* with me, but I craved the straight stuff. Chuck Schaeffer had given me a taste of his seal oil the first day, and I had dipped some dry meat in it, but I didn't want to be too much of a bum. I was getting hungry just thinking of all the food that was supposed to be waiting for me at Rohn.

Later I sat on the sled, watching the dogs and looking toward the weather. Darkness was coming and it was snowing—thick, wet stuff. The

Alligators at the Lodge

To veterinarian Ginny Johnson fell the responsibility for doctoring sick dogs during the long freeze at Rainy Pass. Moving from team to team through deep snow was exhausting work: "By the end of a day of postholing around the field," she recalled, "I was tired."

Libby Riddles's team was close to the lodge, and Johnson passed them frequently. "Every time I walked by," she said, "she was with the dogs. It wasn't me and my medicines that cured her sick animals. It was Libby."

The race marshal, too, was glad that Riddles stayed with her team. "That was one dog team you didn't walk up to in the dark," said Donna Gentry. "They were alligators. They were unbelievably protective. Once I came up beside them. That whole team came at me. I couldn't move in the deep snow. Fortunately, Libby was there and called them off. I should have explained to her that she could have been disqualified if her lead dog had eaten the race marshal."

wind was picking up a little, too. It didn't look very promising. I went up to the lodge to sack out and found out they had gotten some dog food into Rohn, but not all of it. Still, it was progress. The trailbreakers on snowmachines had gone all the way to Farewell Lake, past Rohn. They had said there were eighty trail markers in the eighty miles between Rainy Pass and Rohn, but when Donna Gentry went out, she couldn't find any. All the markers were on the river, where the soft snow was. There was nothing going through the pass. Donna called the trailbreakers back.

By the time they returned up the South Fork, most of their trail had fallen into the river. The ice on the river was breaking up.

At about eight Donna called a meeting. We all stood on the lake in the evening darkness and heard that the race would be unfrozen at ten o'clock that night. The trailbreakers would be coming back by daybreak tomorrow. The weather was still marginal, and it would be foolish to attempt the pass at night.

People sat around the lodge talking. One guy was complaining about not being able to get up in the morning. Lavon Barve, the first guy into Rainy Pass Lodge, looked up and said, "It ain't very important to you if you can't even wake up for it."

Word was, in spite of the weather and trail, a certain group was planning on sneaking out of the checkpoint at three in the morning. I figured the weather was too bad to leave, but I set my watch alarm for three anyway, just to check. I made sure my main gear was hanging where I could find it easily and then tried to get some sleep. With the dogs all rested, they were pretty lively, and Donna had warned people about the danger of dog fights. Two dogs did get killed in a fight over some food that was left out, and I remembered how Rick Mackey lost his chance to win the race three years earlier when during a long rest in Shaktoolik his dogs had jumped into a fight. I hoped mine would behave one more night.

I woke up at three to take a look-see. I tiptoed

61

on bare feet over the wet, cold carpet to the main room. Not a soul was awake, unless they were faking it. Mummy bags were scattered in every direction and a symphony of snores filled the room.

In the midst of all those mounds of color was Barve, boots on, coat on, headlight on over his hat, sleeping soundly on his back with his knees up. That sure tickled me.

I went past him and eased the door open, then stepped out onto the porch. My toes cringed at the ice underfoot. There was no action in the dog area. For a moment I savored the quiet, watching the sky, the wind whipping clouds past the full moon. Then before my toes froze, I picked my way across the sleeping drivers, heading back to the comfort of the bed. I climbed into my still-warm sleeping bag and tried to rest. The remainder of the way to Nome there'd be little time for such grand relaxation.

March 7, 1985

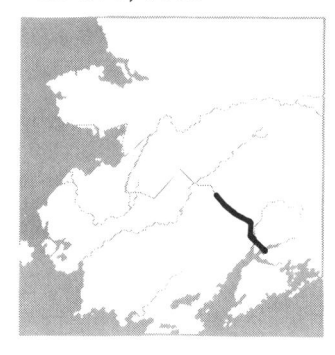

Rainy Pass to Rohn River: 75 miles

Clear, high 21° and low 2°, with slight winds.

Soft snow and creek overflow make the trail difficult, but the dogs have recovered. Riddles experiments with different leaders, looking for the combinations that will get the team through the many miles yet to go. As darkness falls, wolves begin their rounds.

Morning came soon enough and with it the mass scramble for gear and coffee. Nobody wasted much time on conversation. All the racers scurried around feeding dogs, packing, gathering trash, doing chores. I think I lost a few things under the snow and I hoped the whole place wouldn't be too much of a mess after the snow melted in the spring.

The first teams started to leave just before ten in the morning. The trailbreakers, who had been out all night on their snowmachines, didn't get even half an hour's rest before they went back out in front of those first teams. Not knowing who left first made me even more anxious to get going.

The night before, I had Stewpot eating again and even Socks had tried a few pieces of meat, though unenthusiastically. In the morning they ate more. They both still had diarrhea, but their appetites told me they were on the mend. If it hadn't been for the race freeze, I would probably have ended up dropping the two dogs.

I tried to figure out what I was going to eat. Even the dogs' horsemeat was starting to look good. I had a package of instant oatmeal I'd bummed from Betsy McGuire—it would help to get something hot into me before I hit the trail. To make the oatmeal a little more high-powered, I added cheese. Major mistake. The mix had more calories, but it tasted *awful*. I forced myself to eat some. Then I had to wash that sticky, gummy stuff from my cook pan. I should have had the horsemeat.

When everything was ready, I looked around for a dog handler. With all that rest, my dogs would be wild. I shanghaied Ginny Johnson and

63

Homer Hoogendorn, the pilot from Nome who was following Bob Bright in our buddy Ray Lang's airplane. They kept an eye on my takeoff in case my dogs decided to go chase horses or drive through the middle of another team. Homer hung on to the back of the sled until he was sure the dogs were headed in the right direction.

But the dogs weren't of a mind to do any goofing off. They seemed to want to get to Nome as much as I did. And after a three-day rest, they felt really strong. One of the photographers was standing at the top of a hill, shooting as we climbed into the pass, finally away from Puntilla Lake and Rainy Pass Lodge.

After six days of overcast, snowy weather, the sky opened crystal clear and blue, exposing the high, jagged peaks of the Alaska range as we made the gradual climb through a broad alpine valley toward the summit of Ptarmigan Pass. Wind was blowing, but it was grand to be on the trail again and moving. We'd left a little after eleven in the morning behind several other teams. Several more followed us into the pass. As long as we were only an hour or two behind the front runners, I was happy with our position. Stewpot and Socks had recovered fully. They leaned into their harnesses like they'd never been sick. "Looking good, guys," I called out. "Keep it up."

I stopped after a couple of miles to check feet and put on a few dog boots. The trail wasn't too tough right there, but a couple of dogs were getting ice balls between their toes. Despite the wind, the temperature was fairly warm for the dogs, in the twenties, so frequent stops for boots also gave them chances to cool off and catch their breath. I wanted to let them work back into the routine slowly after three days of rest.

Not too far along we climbed past tree line and the country opened, quite a bit like our training trails back home, a lot less claustrophobic and a lot more comfortable. A broad expanse of white flowed from the high ridge line to our right, down across the valley and up to the high ridge on our left, broken only here and there by

Eating on the Run

For the strenuous work of driving a team in below-zero temperatures, one driver estimated his daily needs at sixty-five hundred calories, compared with the twenty-five hundred recommended for the average person engaged in normal activities. Counting the calories in his food drops before the Iditarod race, the driver came up short and supplemented his rations with quarter-pound sticks of butter.

Although mushers have refined their dog food formulas with the precision of chemists, they often shortchange themselves on the trail. And after working with the dogs and completing other chores at a checkpoint, an exhausted driver may choose sleep over food, or drink coffee, which may keep him alert but cause dehydration.

Popular foods for the racers combine high energy value with ease of preparation. Many wrap steaks in foil with large pats of butter and reheat the meat atop the dog food cooker. Prepared pizza, sliced and frozen for the trail, and fried chicken have also proved favorites.

Besides steak, fried chicken, and pizza, Libby Riddles packed French toast and peanut butter sandwiches, fruit juices, dried moose meat, frozen berries, carrot cake, bacon, corn muffins, ready-made popcorn, frozen yogurt, cheese, commercial trail mix, powdered milk, English muffins, pecan pies and rolls, frozen melon balls, and kamakmi, or Eskimo ice cream. She drew publicity for the high proportion of "junk food" in her drops.

"We don't have as strict a diet as many professional athletes do," she acknowledged. "We concentrate on what the dogs eat. We do know we have to eat well to cope in the cold, but when I'm tired, I won't eat." And it is for precisely that reason that she packed pizza instead of health food in her shipments. "I like to look forward to what's in the bag at the next checkpoint," she said.

stunted little spruce trees, the advance troops in the forest's endless campaign to regain territory lost to elevation and latitude. Foot soldiers, they were.

I was keeping an eye out for the first landmark I recalled from a rough map of the route through Ptarmigan Pass, a white tent. But everything was white. Conditions became a little tense when the wind started blowing snow across the trail and I had difficulty figuring out where the drivers ahead of me had gone. By the time I passed, their tracks already were erased by drifting snow. We couldn't find much in the line of trail markers, either, but I was able to check the trail by finding faint sets of tracks every once in a while. Then the snow obliterated even those, and all sign of the trail was gone.

Dugan, my lead dog, would have to find the trail for me, catching the scent of the dogs that had passed before him or feeling the firm snow underneath. He started veering off to the right and I "hawed" him back to the left to keep him going in the direction we'd been following. He went that way for a while, then he turned the team sharply to the right again.

Raymie Redington and another team were following behind me and I was sure they were wondering what was going on with me and my leader. I was just about to give Dugan a piece of my mind for turning without my permission when, through the blowing snow, I made out the white tent, straight ahead. Boy, did I ever feel like a fool. I had to learn to trust this little dog more.

I stopped the team and slogged through the deep snow to the front of the team. I knelt down in the snow and apologized to Dugan. I told him what a fine fellow he was and scratched him behind the ears. He hadn't been trying to get away with something, after all. His instinct had proved correct, and I let him know he'd done the right thing. I gave him another quick scratch before returning to the sled, but he was too humble to accept the praise. He shook himself, then stood leaning forward into the harness, all blue eyes and muscular legs.

It was a long way through the pass in the heat of the day. The incline wasn't so bad: the trail rose from eighteen hundred feet at Rainy Pass Lodge to something a little less than twenty-seven hundred at the summit, over a span of about eighteen miles. But the trail was soft and punchy, through deep snow. Worse, as melting begins in late winter and ice still lies thick in stream beds, the water has to have somewhere to go, and that's sometimes over the top of the ice. We began running across some areas of overflow along the creeks and lakes. I tried to command the team off the trail to a drier path, but the snow was so deep it made that option just as difficult. The dog boots got wet and had to be changed.

I'd sent plenty of dog boots in my drops, but the conditions were so tough on feet that my supply was already running short. I had to save the icy ones and hope to find a way to dry them somewhere farther along. In the meantime, I was having fun snatching up boots that the dogs ahead of us had thrown off their feet. If the boots aren't fastened tightly enough, the dogs flip them off. Every time I saw the dark shape of a bootie in the trail ahead of me, I leaned down and tried to scoop it up as we passed. I was a regular bootie pirate.

Despite frequent stops in the heat, we covered ground steadily. Past the tent we had an easier time finding the trail. At times it seemed endless in that broad expanse of mountain pass. Looking ahead to the mountain peaks along the trail made it seem a long way to go.

We came upon Rick Mackey and Tim Moerlein stopped in a small creek bed. They were taking a break, and my dogs were jealous. They voted themselves a rest by pulling off to the side of the trail when I asked them to pass the stopped teams.

For a moment we wrestled. I wanted to go on; they didn't. I was a little tired and crabby and started to get mad, but maybe the dogs were a little tired and crabby, too, and needed a blow. In a good-natured way, Rick told me I looked like I could use a break. I gave each of the dogs a frozen snack, then dug around until I found something for myself. I sat on my sled to shoot the breeze with the guys. Rick seemed in good spirits, and made me feel a little embarrassed for almost losing my temper with my dogs. It turned out my main problem had been a lack of fuel; a little trail mix improved my mood considerably.

I didn't know Tim Moerlein well, but I knew he was running some of my old friend Rod Perry's young dogs, so I looked his team over. I recognized some of Rod's dogs, especially the cocoa-red ones, which anyone would know were Rod Perry huskies, most out of a little red dog named Torch. Rod was one of my first teachers—he and his wife Patty had taught me the importance of being organized when racing sled dogs—and one of my first sources of dogs. He had a real knack for pinning appropriate names on his dogs: Fat Albert, Lugnut, Crazy Legs. It was Rod who had named my Bad Dog Bane, a bully of a pup and truly the bane of the litter.

Bob Bright came along and stopped, but just for a minute. We all decided to get moving. It wouldn't be long until dark and we needed to make the best use of the daylight. I was hoping Bob would go ahead of me for a while. He had the best dog booties in the race, I had found. They had elastic on the Velcro fasteners to hold them on better. Behind him I might be able to scoop up a couple.

There was a cabin up ahead before Hell's Gate. We were traveling on a river by this time, high in the mountains near the source of the South Fork. The trail was fresh snow over ice and rocks of the shallow river's bottom. I could feel the rocks whenever I had to touch my brake down. The heavy snow was a blessing on this part of the trail. The traveling would have been miserable without it, pounding over rocks, gravel, and ice.

We had crossed the Ptarmigan Pass Divide. The rivers and creeks we'd followed and crossed until now all drained to the east and south, toward Cook Inlet behind us. The South Fork drained the other way, to the west and north into the interior of Alaska. We started down, gradually at first, but heading for Hell's Gate, which must have had that name for some reason. We even passed a Styx Lake. We were moving quickly on a slight downhill grade, always conscious of the river bottom under the fresh snow.

We came to the tracks of an airplane on skis and a marker the pilot must have used to guide his landing. A man and a youngster were sitting on a snowmachine there. They said it was just a couple of miles to the cabin. The site was picture-book Alaska: regal spruce lining the river, mountains all around, fresh snow. Then add what has to be the freshest air in the world, crisp and fragrant and invigorating.

I could see several teams tied along the river bank as we rolled up and looked for a place to park my team. I pulled as close as I could to the trail leading to the cabin, within reach of a two-by-four where I could anchor the sled. I dipped some water out of an open crack in the river ice and watered down the dog food in my cooler. The dogs were all thirsty, even Stewpot and Socks, and everybody drank.

Someone told me there was coffee on at the cabin. I hustled over there to check it out. I was as thirsty as the dogs, and when I found out some Tang was available, I bummed a couple of glasses of that instead of coffee. The open cabin and the coffee for the drivers were welcome surprises. No one had expected anyone to be staying on the trail there.

The couple who owned the cabin asked me to sign my name under my picture on a page of mushers' mug shots from one of the Anchorage papers. It was the first time I'd seen the photo, taken at the banquet back in Anchorage. I looked about half dead. Eventually, this picture was circulated worldwide by the Associated Press. Figures.

The hosts were packing to leave in the next half hour, ahead of another incoming weather front and the darkness. I thanked them and then hustled back out to the dogs. I was still nervous about leaving them unattended. Despite the climb that day, they were pretty frisky after their

The Iditarod Dog

The pedigrees of most Iditarod dogs would give an American Kennel Club registrar fits. Even though few carry papers, their lines are studied as closely as those of any Scottish terrier that promenades at Westminster.

Sled dogs can be traced to three basic ancestors. The Alaskan malamute is a registered breed named for the Malmuit Eskimos of Alaska's northwest coast, where white men first encountered them. Malamutes are large dogs, weighing fifty to one hundred pounds, with heavy coats. Their size and fur make them cumbersome racers, but many modern sled dogs show traces of the breed.

The second progenitor is the Siberian husky, also a registered breed. Smaller than the malamute, a Siberian may have brown eyes and red, black, white, or pinto fur, but the breed has tendencies toward blue eyes and a two-toned gray coat. First used by Russian traders in Alaska during the nineteenth century, Siberians were reintroduced in 1909, when a Russian entered a Siberian team in the All-Alaska Sweepstakes at Nome. His dogs finished third. That summer a Nome miner and sportsman, one Fox Maule Ramsey, journeyed to the Anadyr River country in Siberia and selected sixty dogs to bring back to Nome. In the 1910 sweepstakes, Ramsey entered three teams of Siberians, and despite the scoffs of onlookers, his little dogs finished first and second. Driving the winning team, John "Iron Man" Johnson set a record for the sweepstakes that has survived to this day. The

Siberians had arrived. Other mushers began training and running Siberians. One of them, Leonhard Seppala, won the sweepstakes three years in a row: 1915, 1916, and 1917. Later, when the 1925 relay to carry diphtheria serum to Nome caught the attention of the world's newspapers, Seppala's Siberians became the model for the Alaska sled dog. When he left Alaska for New England, the Siberians he took with him became the basis for many racing teams in the Northeast.

The third ancestor of the Iditarod athlete has no registered name, and his history is obscure. This is the generic husky, the sled dog, the Indian dog of the Interior villages, a tough, fast animal that has interbred over the years with hounds, bird dogs, and strays.

With all three strains in their veins, modern team dogs may look like mutts. Certainly, few match the pictures of the purebred Siberians and malamutes. Yet mushers can trace the lineage of their dogs, for since the Iditarod began in 1973, they have bred their dogs carefully in the search for the ideal long-distance racer.

In the 1970s large dogs were favored, animals in the fifty-pound range and even up to one hundred pounds. In the 1980s preference shifted to smaller dogs, forty to fifty pounds. And other characteristics are carefully watched. Feet must be tough; the coat must be neither so heavy that the dog overheats when working hard nor so light that it cannot stay warm; attitude should be good, since a happy dog works better and is easier to work with; constitution should be strong and immune to stress-caused illnesses; speed and

Rainy Pass vacation. I wanted to keep moving, too, to take advantage of the short amount of daylight left and maybe get a jump on the next storm.

I was trying different dogs in lead with Dugan, with varying success. Bugs, my other main leader, wasn't performing well at all in front. At home, whenever I put Bugs in lead, I had to tie off the front end while I harnessed the other dogs because he loved leading so much that he would go whacko, winging left and right, rolling around on his back, spinning around to badmouth the swing dogs behind him, even to the point of shaking up his more timid teammates. But now he had a crush on Minnow, who was still in heat. He was distracted, and he kept forgetting about the job to go sniffing.

"Bugs," I scolded, "you bad dog, you. Get up there, you airbrain, you turkey." But it was no use. "All you boys are in love with Minnow, is that it? She's a foxy dog, she's a looker."

Minnow herself was a supercharger in lead, but I didn't want to distract Dugan by placing the Sweet Young Thing next to him. I tried Binga, but I could tell he didn't quite have his heart in it.

"Poor Binga," I said after a few hopeless miles. "What are they doing, making that poor brown-eyed dog run lead when we all know he doesn't like it up there? Okay, buddy. Okay, Binga. I'll move you back. Dusty? Your turn, you red dog, you fat little varmint. Let's try you next."

Dusty had been a fat little rascal of a puppy, but he had surprising speed. "Shakin' bacon," we called it when he stretched out at the head of the puppy pack. One week before the Iditarod, I had had him in the lead when we saw a moose along the trail. Dusty relished a chase after game, but he stayed in the trail when the moose headed off to the right. Whew, I thought. A mile or so down the trail, we came to an intersection, and without my permission, Dusty turned right. I gave him a "haw" command to turn left; he refused. I didn't want him to get into the habit of disobeying me, so I put my snow hook in and led him over to the right trail. He knew he was in trouble and tried to one-eighty us back to camp.

69

I couldn't let him do that, either, so I pulled him back the right way again. We went through the whole dance a second time, but when I finally got him straightened out, he showed some resentment and wouldn't keep his line taut; he wouldn't pull at all. He just wasn't happy leading for me anymore. It was frustrating, especially now, knowing he would do it for Joe but not for me.

Sister I was saving for emergencies.

"Let's put your brother Axle up here, Dugan," I said when I moved Dusty back into team. "Axle, you're my good dog. You're going to pick up tricks from your brother, ain't ya, boy? Going to be a lead dog when you grow up, ain't ya, Axle?"

I'd never had much luck with him in lead during training, but I used him constantly in swing, right behind the leaders. He did his job well there, staying in the trail on turns and following the front guys. However, he began performing wonderfully in double lead. He was my choice for the descent. He was still a turkey leader, though, and he proved it immediately by trying to take me up to each of the teams parked all the way down the river bank.

"Axle, doggone it, you bone-headed idiot! Get your tail out of there!" When he heard me yelling, Herbert Nayokpuk pulled my front end over away from the other teams. Finally we sped off in the right direction.

"Go get 'em, Libby," Herbert shouted.

Despite the warning signs in the sky, the weather still was fairly mild, and we journeyed into some of the most beautiful country on the Iditarod Trail. I had lived in mountains near Anchorage once, and this area was similar. It almost made me a little homesick. The air smells different in the mountains, and weather can move in and out with alarming speed. The sun was dipping toward the mountains as we dropped down into Hell's Gate.

Hell's Gate had a nasty reputation, but I didn't know what the big deal was. I thought it was a lot easier and safer than Rainy Pass. I could see it would be real trouble if there wasn't snow,

endurance must be adequate to enable the dog to trot long distances at eleven to fifteen miles an hour; and conformation should be that of a thoroughbred racehorse—heavy in the chest and shoulders, thin at the waist, muscular in the haunches.

Because few drivers were ready with long-distance runners when the Iditarod began, many of today's dogs can trace their ancestry to the few dog lots of the 1960s. Almost every dog team in the state has the blood of the senior Joe Redington's dogs, in Knik. Many dogs can be traced to Jerry Riley's animals, who come from a line of dogs developed by his father at Nenana in the early part of the century, when he hauled freight in the Interior. Herbert Nayokpuk maintained dogs at his home in Shishmaref after other villagers had switched to snowmachines, Joe Garnie's Teller breed dates back many years, and Emmitt Peters's dogs are descended from the Yukon River village dogs of the past; their three lines have formed the bases of several other teams.

though. They get some outrageous winds through that valley. The floor of the canyon is two thousand feet in elevation and only about a quarter of a mile wide. Mountains on both sides of the trail rise steeply to more than six thousand feet, like walls to the sky.

Half a foot of new snow lay on the river through there, and if it hadn't been for that, the trail would have been pure misery. As it was, my brake was catching on fair-sized rocks. On the river itself, we had to cross glare ice.

Darkness began falling as we made our way down the river. The mountains loomed above us on either side, giant blue shadows against the deeper-blue sky. It was getting harder to find the trail, but with both Dugan and me working together on it, we were managing. He had an excellent nose for the trail, and I kept scanning the river for tracks with my headlight.

The sun sank behind the mountains while we ran down Hell's Gate, and we passed through dusk into darkness. Suddenly the dogs began to act a little strange. Penny's radar ears came up. Then Inca and Bugs started lifting their noses for something I couldn't see. All along the team other ears rose and swiveled and the dogs started looking off to one side. Over the quiet shush of the sled runners and the pants of the dogs, off in the distance I heard a howl. It sounded like a dog, but we couldn't be close enough to Rohn for that to be a dog. It was a wolf.

Our dogs were never exposed to wolves at home. The only wolves in the Seward Peninsula are way up in the mountains where very few people see them and even fewer are caught in traps. Even so, the dogs seemed to have a healthy respect for what they were hearing. Despite the wolf in their ancestry, they showed little interest in recognizing any kinship. The wolf's howls brought the whole team to complete silence and total attention. We stopped. I pulled off my hat so that I could hear better. All the dogs listened, very quietly, standing at attention in the dark. A few hackles went up.

Two wolves seemed to be conversing, one

howling and one almost barking. It was a thrill to hear them and a thrill to be traveling through their country. I wondered whether they were gray or black. Very few people have ever seen a wolf in the wild. I wished I could catch a glimpse of them. We listened for almost ten minutes and then jumped to it again. The dogs leaned into their harnesses and seemed a bit nervous for a while, turning and looking in the direction of the wolves as they trotted, the wild animals still on their minds. They were anxious to be putting miles between themselves and their cousins.

As we moved on down the South Fork, the new silence and darkness combined to make me sleepy. I dug out the Walkman and plunked in the Pointer Sisters. "Breakout" helped me keep my attention sharply on the trail. I sang along for the dogs. They were used to it.

This section of trail you had to be on the ball, eyes glued ahead the whole way, light on all the time. This part was tricky and very wearing. We had little track to follow, hardly any trail markers, and it was night. Sloughs cut off the river in every direction, opening false trails to follow. Most of the track had been obliterated. Patches of snow alternated with glare ice. The sled would swing wildly on the ice then suddenly catch on a patch of snow. This was the stage for one of the best performances I'd ever seen out of my Dugan dog. Down on this river, with all its sloughs and creeks, he was following scent with barely a track to follow.

But Dugan made one mistake. He turned left into a slough, mistaking it for the trail, and even though I saw the right way to go, it happened so quickly we were already part way up the slough before I could turn the team. I "geed" Dugan to the right bank, and as the rest of the team moved over, Axle managed to get his legs tangled in the ropes. He was an expert at that. As a pup he had been spindly and sickly, and my friend Susan Ogle had called him bug-eyed and ugly; I always thought he was a handsome devil, if a bit clumsy. I set my hook, and as I walked up to untangle him, I noticed how strange it felt to be off the runners for a minute. It almost made me dizzy—something like how odd it feels not to be rocking and reeling with the waves after you've been at sea.

At one turn of the river we came upon a bunch of survey tape strung out along the edge of a creek. Dugan wanted to turn but I stopped him. Another driver was bringing his team back up that part toward us, looking like he'd just checked out a creek. It was Rick Armstrong. That marking was confusing. I guessed the trailbreaker had been accustomed to marking trail for snowmachine races, where lots of tape means a dangerous area. For a dog driver, all that flagging signals an important turn. I thought I saw a trail and directed Dugan toward it. We searched a bit before finding it.

The rest of the way was more of the same, trying to find trail. Hour passed upon hour as Dugan picked his way downriver. It seemed such a long way. They'd told us at Rainy it was only thirty miles farther than the old route. That made it about seventy. I felt like we'd already gone ninety miles, and there was still no end in sight. Jeez, Louise, that was a long way.

At last some reflectors showed up in my headlight, but we were going so fast the front of the team had passed the turnoff before I saw the sign. I put my hook in and turned the leaders up the trail into the woods to the checkpoint. It was tough to set the hook on the river ice. Once the leaders were headed in the right direction, I let the dogs pass me and grabbed the sled as it went by. It felt strange to be on a tight, winding trail through thick woods after the more open river travel. I heard voices and saw lights through the trees and we rolled up to the cabin, the Rohn River checkpoint.

We'd been on the trail for fifteen hours. It was a little after two in the morning when I met the two checkers. One helped fetch my dog food, all four sacks that I'd planned to use on my twenty-four-hour layover, and volunteered to help me find a place to park the dogs. I wanted to have a clear shot through all those trees when I left the checkpoint, so I asked the checker to take me as far down the trail as he could.

73

Before I knew it, we were farther from the checkpoint than I'd planned. The guy had misunderstood me. I walked back in the direction of the cabin and found a spot.

The next step was to turn the dogs around on the narrow trail, not an easy task with all the spruce trees to weave around. The extra weight of the food bags made the sled top-heavy. In the process of turning the dogs around, we managed to tie the forty feet of ropes and fifteen dogs into a series of all but impenetrable knots, which tightened as the dogs struggled to step out of tangles and pulled against each other. Result: one giant ball of mayhem. I led this mess over to a place between two trees where I could tie it off. Untangling a massive dog knot was not my idea of a good time.

Chuck Schaeffer, who had been second into the checkpoint behind Joe Redington, Sr., told me that one of Joe's dogs had choked when his seventeen-dog team had gotten tangled in the same trees. I felt bad for Joe. I could only imagine how tough it'd be to lose one of your good dogs in a freak accident like that.

It had been a long, hard day for the team, and they deserved a good, hot meal. They went for my cooking, plus frozen lamb for dessert. I put more wood on the fire in an attempt to dry the dog boots. Some dried a little more than others and all definitely were smoke flavored. I hoped none of the dogs had developed a taste for barbeque.

I never did hike over to the checkers' cabin for the stew they had offered. It would have taken too much precious energy to walk there and back, so I stuck to my frozen snacks, pizza and popcorn, frozen blackberries, Kentucky Fried Chicken, and frozen peaches to quench my thirst while I waited for the cranberry juice to thaw.

My Norwegian friend Britt Thorstensen had mailed a huge bar of Norwegian chocolate to me at Rohn. But the checkpoint is just a cabin, and nobody lives in it except at race time. Rohn is not a normal place to receive mail. It isn't even on most maps. The chocolate had gone instead to McGrath. In McGrath the post office had given it to Ray Howell, who was going to be the checker at Rohn. He had given it to me when I had checked in. What a treat!

After the massive restart at Rainy Pass Lodge, we drivers had to sort ourselves out again and figure out who was racing and how. One thing was sure: no team would sneak out without my seeing them. As I collapsed into my sleeping bag, another team pulled up and parked across from me. I silently cursed the invasion of my peace and quiet.

I was feeling a little low. The time had come for a lift. I rummaged around in a pocket for the envelope LaDonna Westfall had given me back at Settler's Bay. Like everything else, the envelope had gotten damp, and the ink spelling "Libby" was runny and smeared. I opened it and read.

The day has come to make the run
from Anchorage to Nome.
Some leave the nest, some never rest,
and some are headed home.
The trail is wide, the snow is deep
through mountain and "the burn."
There's endless nights and northern lights;
it's something that you earn.
With Safety here the end is near,
gone Nikolai and Ophir.
It's many days since Grayling haze
and soon it will be over.
The finish line is just in time
to run through or to crawl.
The dogs were good, you knew they would
be out there giving all.
So give them steak and take a break
'til winter comes again.
Take them out and give a shout
and see those huskies grin.
The life you lead is run and feed.
Some people think it odd.
But you can say with pride that day,
"I ran Iditarod."

March 8, 1985

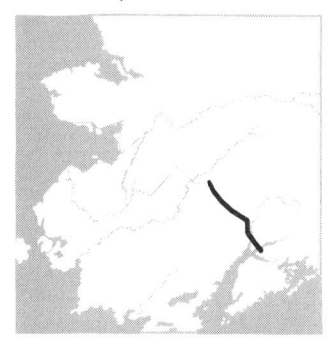

Rohn River to Nikolai: 70 miles

Snow, heavy cloud cover, and some fog, high 34° and low 13°, with winds from the south up to 25 knots.

The team heads into the Interior of Alaska. The trail is easy, but now three dogs show signs of illness. After nightfall, heavy snow cuts visibility, and Riddles's sled falls through the thin ice of a creek.

A driver talking to his team on the way out of the checkpoint broke into my sleep. Reluctantly I shed my bag. More and more teams passed me on their way out. In daylight I recognized Ted English as the driver who had parked across from me and intruded into my peace. He was fixing his sled and I gave him a good, heavy piece of wire from my airdrop to reinforce a broken piece of wood.

Once the second batch of food was secured in the cooler, I burned my trash while I waited for some juice to thaw for my Thermos. With all the food I'd sent to Rohn for my twenty-four hour layover, I could barely close the sled bag, but it was going to take a lot of snacks to get the dogs across the Farewell Burn to Nikolai, at least seventy miles. I left a few pieces behind in the woods and hoped that after all the race people and dogs had left, the wolves would find them. The sled looked and felt a lot heavier than it should have been.

The sled wasn't quite as heavy as the one I'd used the first time I'd run a distance race. I had gone up to Cantwell with the fullest sled anybody ever saw. It was a big old freight sled, and I guess I thought I had to fill it. It was piled high with a big bucket of tallow for the dogs and a couple of gallons of stove fuel and chocolate mints and all sorts of gear—everything except a load of firewood, actually—with only nine dogs to pull it. You'd have thought I was going to run the Yukon Quest, but it was just the Cantwell 180. There were a lot of hills at the start, and the sled was so heavy it kept pulling off to one side, driving me crazy. I was the last team to reach

77

the Maclaren River turnaround, and I didn't want to be last forever. After a glass of milk—which is another story, because I was so tired I knocked two glasses off the table before I managed to drink a drop—I took off for the finish. When I saw the lights and buildings of Cantwell, I started to feel real proud of myself. I drove the dogs up the street looking for the finish line—it had to be there someplace—and then back down the street, still looking, but I never did find it. I was so late they'd taken it down.

About one in the afternoon we were off again. The trail led a short way through the trees, then came out on river ice. The dogs slid around with the heavy sled swinging back and forth behind them. Each time it slid sideways, I had to maneuver it like a pair of skis, going with the slide. Whenever a runner caught on a rough spot, I had to catch myself or go flying off the sled. The action wrenched my cold muscles unmercifully. Raymie's team was ahead of us about half a mile. He was having the same sort of fun on the ice, trying to keep his sled upright and tracking straight. Brake marks from the sleds ahead of us had torn white scratches in the green ice everywhere. The ice demanded intense concentration and didn't leave much chance to enjoy the outstanding scenery.

After muscling the wildly swinging sled across the ice, I felt relief when we finally went back up into woods. We climbed up a narrow ravine to gain the top of a ridge. Although there were record depths of snow along most of the trail, this part had only a dusting—the wind had just blown it away. The snow didn't stick to the ice any better than we did.

The heavy sled was difficult to steer and I had trouble negotiating the narrow trail. I kept scraping the right side against trees. Most of the time I had to ride with both feet on the left runner, leaning to the left and pulling the drive bow to keep the sled from slewing to the right and hitting the trees. Bouncing off trees is not fun.

I came up behind Terry Adkins's team but had to wait until we found a clearing to pass. Gradually the trees began thinning. We were slowly

Sleds

*T*he basket sleds of light hardwoods, such as hickory, ash, or birch, resemble those used by drivers in the early days, when dogs hauled freight and mail. No nuts, bolts, screws, or nails are used in a traditional sled; all the wood is tied together with rawhide or heavy twine, which allows the sled to twist and bounce on uneven trails without shattering.

Vertical stanchions rising from the runners form a basket. A curved brush bow protects the front of the sled from collisions with trees; the higher drive bow at the back enables the musher to hold on and steer by shifting his weight. The runners extend about four feet behind the sled to provide the driver a place to stand. For purchase, the tops of today's runners are covered with strips of motorcycle tire. Plastic, bolted to the bottoms, permits easy sliding over the snow and protects the wood runners from abrasion. The plastic wears, however, and needs to be changed two or three times in the course of the race. Most sleds now have curved metal sleeves; the plastic runners, whose grooves match tongues on the metal, slide in and out quickly, saving time at checkpoints.

A new sled design, called a toboggan, has been developed since the Iditarod began. A sheet of heavy plastic running the length and width of the sled is bolted to the runners, and a triangular framework forms the basket and the handlebar.

To slow and stop a sled, the musher steps on the brake. On a basket sled this is a two- or three-pronged piece of *metal attached to a wooden brake board that runs under the basket; on the toboggan sled it is a U-shaped bar of metal with two prongs. A spring or elastic bungee cord holds the brake up and off the snow until the driver applies foot pressure.*

Once stopped, the driver sets the snowhook, which resembles a gigantic double fishhook with large, flattened curves. The sharpened tines are pounded into the snow, and the flat areas anchor the team.

A bag sewn of heavy canvas or nylon tenting fits the contours of the sled basket. Food and equipment are packed inside, and the bag is secured with zippers or toggles.

An empty sled weighs from forty to a hundred pounds; loaded for the trail, it weighs three hundred to five hundred pounds, including the driver. Sleds are commercially available, but many mushers make their own.

moving out of mountain country. In one clearing I stopped and looked back. My heart rose into my throat as I felt the awe inspired by the beautiful land around me, by those cool blue mountains—and by our having traversed it. I thought again of the good job my Dugan-dog had done for me on the river the night before. What a pro. I closed my eyes and took myself back to the sensation of gliding through the darkness with the wind at my back, the dog uncannily finding his way.

The first year I'd raced, I had reached the Post River over bare tundra and found it wide, with overflow water and no trail markers. Few teams had gone ahead of me because most of the drivers had taken their twenty-four-hour layovers at Rohn, and I was waiting to take mine at McGrath. The only tracks I had seen were brake marks heading downstream. But I missed the turnoff, and we began running into small trees that got thicker and thicker. I had to pull the dogs out backwards two by two. An hour had passed before I backtracked to where I'd first turned onto the river. When I had finally found a trail marker, across the creek and slightly downstream, I had made a big arrow on the ice out of electrical tape to mark the turnoff for the teams behind me.

This year we crossed the spot with relative ease. The next fun obstacle was the Waterfall, a steep, overflow-covered hill. I'd heard of drivers climbing up it on their hands and knees, trying to coax the dogs along with them.

In anticipation, I was carrying a single ice creeper, a spiked contraption to strap onto a boot and give some traction on ice. The dogs must have recognized the Waterfall from the previous year with Joe, because they headed up it without much trouble. I pushed with my cleated boot.

The weather had turned fairly warm. While the dogs were snacking and resting, I took out my camera and snapped a couple of quick pictures of them and the Waterfall. Now that we were past the ice, I put boots on the dogs that needed them. I heard a team coming from somewhere back down the trail and quickly got the dogs moving again.

The trail alternated between meadows and forest. The trees here were older and larger the farther we descended into the Interior. We passed many more large birch trees than we'd seen so far.

Rounding one corner, I came upon the caved-in Pioneer Roadhouse. In 1981 I had stopped to cook dog food there and taken time to look the place over. A dog barn was crumbling on one side of the trail. The roof was caved in, but the stall dividers made of saplings were still there. The roof of the main cabin also had collapsed. A seed at one time had fallen onto the sod roof and taken root, and eventually the tree grew heavy enough to collapse the rafters. Inside the cabin I had found old cans and jars and weather-stripping of moose hide around the door. While my dog food cooked, I had wondered about the gold seekers, mail drivers, and freight haulers who had followed this trail, who had inhabited this cabin. The creek out back was one of the prettiest places I'd seen. It must have been a welcome haven for travelers. Could they have imagined a thousand-mile dog race going past the roadhouse some fifty to sixty years in the future? I recalled feeling a bond with those people of the past, whoever they were, as I lay on the floor looking up at the sky through the caved-in roof. But this year I couldn't afford to stop for more than a minute. Two-thirds of the way to Nikolai lay ahead of us.

As I was jostling the sled around a corner, I happened to notice something red on the outside of the sled bag. It was the red blade of my camp axe, sticking out through a rip in the material. The bag had torn, no doubt, from all the bumping and scraping against trees on the narrow trails. For a flash I felt a little giddy thinking how easily I could have lost the axe . . . the same axe I had clutched so desperately while chasing my runaway dogs on the first day.

I found a needle and dental floss in my yellow gear bag and knelt alongside the sled. I had gotten handy at repairs since I had moved to

Teller. Stores that sell replacement parts for all the things that break were always farther away than we wanted to travel, and money—or the lack of it—was another consideration. This sled bag repair was going to have to be another improvisation, just something to baste the rip before it could tear more. It took about ten minutes. All the time, in the cold, I was wishing for my thimble to help push the needle through the heavy fabric. I had to hurry because I had stopped in the trail and couldn't hold up another team. And sure enough, a team did come up the trail. I had to throw the needle and floss into my pocket and move on. I began looking for a place to pull over. The dogs needed a longer rest soon, anyway. It was hard to find a good place, and when I came upon Raymie and saw a place behind him, I jumped at it. A loud "gee" from me and the dogs pulled off the trail and stopped. They were ready.

Some people would rather stop to rest alone—less distraction for the dogs. I prefer that, too, but this was the first decent opportunity to get off the trail, and I figured Raymie wouldn't mind. He was pretty easy-going, never seemed to lose his temper, and always said hello whenever one of us passed the other, which seemed to be frequently. We were running at about the same speeds. He had a voice just like his dad, Joe Senior, soft and gravelly.

I snacked my dogs again and then did a more respectable job of patching my sled bag, going back and forth over the tear with mint-flavored dental floss. It made a huge lump in the bag, but it was the best I could do without having a scrap of material to make a patch. When I was satisfied that it would last until Nome if necessary, I repacked my repair kit and pulled out my goodie bag. I ate some chicken and frozen fruit. Raymie tried a bagel and a couple of other snacks and we talked for a few mintues. About fifteen minutes after he moved out I packed up and hit the trail behind him.

We left the mountains in the distance as we rolled out into the broad, level interior of Alaska, bordering on the Farewell Burn. The peaks continued to recede into the horizon. The first time I had traveled through the burn, there had been little snow, just tundra and brown grass and precious few pieces of flagging to mark the trail. I had been astounded at having to cross so much bare gravel and tundra. I had stopped my team while I took a couple of pictures for proof and looked for the trail. As I was walking around, I encountered some fresh piles of scat. Huge piles of scat. A gigantic bear, I thought, a bear that was sure to be lurking behind the next bush. When I finally found some runner tracks on a patch of snow, I lost no time getting out. I felt like a real dummy when they told me at Farewell that the scat had been buffalo.

I didn't see any signs of buffalo this year, but in time we came across some people signs, so I knew we must be close the Farewell Station. The station is an outpost of the Federal Aviation Administration's weather reporting and navigation systems and had been a checkpoint the last time I raced. This year we passed by Farewell and went straight across to Nikolai. The seventy miles seemed even farther without Farewell as a checkpoint.

We traveled for a while on some sort of road or trail made by Caterpillar bulldozers and used to haul equipment and supplies to the mines. It seemed ironic to be driving dogs down a Cat trail.

Ahead I saw some action on a big cleared roadstrip leading down a hill. Tim Osmar and Burt Bomhoff had stopped at the top of the hill to talk with a stranger, probably from Farewell Station. He had a loose pup. Now all sled dogs like to chase loose pups. And when your fifteen dogs have their minds bent on a wild chase, you find yourself behind quite a lot of dog power. I maneuvered a sharp corner around Osmar, then passed Bomhoff. The dogs were straining after that pup. I braked and stopped but couldn't find enough snow to set the hook. When the team pulled my hook out, we zoomed down the hill toward a lake, chasing this fat, boisterous pup.

Halfway down the hill, I saw trail markers cutting across the road and off into the woods, a turn we needed to make. But the team was half out of control and at the speed we were going, I had no hope of stopping. If my leaders sensed that I was out of control, they might pursue their own ends—in this case, the fat pup. And if they followed the pup on down the hill, we'd end up across the lake—if we didn't wipe out on the way.

I hollered "gee" for all I was worth. Dugan instantly swung across the road and up the trail, making the turn without missing a step. We turned so fast I had to hold on tight. I was amazed. The turn surprised the pup, too. He'd gone on down the hill, and by the time he recovered to return to the game, we were gone.

Ahead was the Farewell Lake. Crossing all the lakes in that country was tricky: they were blown free of snow, so the going would be slippery, and the only flagging was where the trail came up off the lake on the far side and went back into the trees. Some of those lakes were pretty good-sized, and spotting the flagging all the way across wouldn't be easy. Fortunately, there was plenty of light left for us.

I stopped several times to check feet, and during one of those stops, Bomhoff passed me. I ended up traveling about a mile or more behind him and tried to compare our speeds. He had a hot team, one of the better ones on the trail, but after a while I figured my speed was very close to his. That was reassuring. What always slowed me down was stopping so often to check feet. Instead of booting my whole team before leaving the checkpoint, I had booted just the few dogs I knew were susceptible, so that they wouldn't all have to suffer the indignity of wearing that floppy footwear.

Time passed slowly on the lakes. I put a tape in the Walkman for entertainment. I sure enjoyed being out in the open and away from the trees, which I considered more and more of a nuisance as the miles wore on. Just riding the runners and coasting—instead of running up hills and muscling the sled around corners—didn't hurt my mood, either. I could see all of the sky again.

83

One by one the lakes fell behind and the mountains continued to sink into the horizon. I felt a thrill of triumph, having safely negotiated the pass. The worst of the trail was behind us, at least the toughest we'd expected. I gained such satisfaction from knowing the team and I had survived a few more tough times. And each horror that I'd lived through had given me a portion of confidence to carry on to the next task. Patience was so important yet so hard to maintain when I was hungry and tired and all beat up from the trail. I was trying to cultivate it.

I turned my concentration back to the trail ahead as we entered the Farewell Burn area. In 1977 a wildfire had burned for most of two months and left little but charcoal on 362,000 acres. While I was working for the Bureau of Land Management in Anchorage, I had watched the firefighters come and go and listened to their reports. That had been a dry year and the firefighters were kept pretty busy all summer around the state, but the Farewell fire was the largest ever recorded in Alaska.

Eight years later there was little regrowth and little protection from the wind. But it seemed it would be fairly good traveling through the burn because most of it was covered by snow. The other two years I'd run there had been more bare ground than snow. That made it harder to find the trail, harder for the dogs to pull, tougher on the sled, and miserable for the driver, who had to run behind on the bare ground.

At least in 1981 I'd had a toboggan sled that didn't break as easily. In 1980, driving a freight-style stick sled, I had broken the top rail and a crosspiece toward the front of the sled. Every time my sled would slam into another charred stump as we careened our way across the burn, I'd clench my teeth and hope it was the stump that broke and not another piece of my sled. I ground a quarter inch off my teeth that day. In 1981, when Donna Gentry and I went through there, it was more than marginally demoralizing to be hoofing it behind the sled over bare ground and see hunks of runner plastic and pieces of sleds that had shattered before us.

Long Johns and Loose Lips

Crossing the Farewell Burn in 1981, racer Donna Gentry had pulled off the trail to rest her dogs and enjoy a nap in the sun.

"I knew it was unlikely that anyone was going to come up behind me," Gentry said, "and it was two or three hours since Libby had passed me. I went rolling along, and as it got hotter and hotter, I kept peeling off more and more clothes. By the time I came over a little knob and saw Libby down in a gully, where some snow had collected—she had her dogs lying in the snow to cool off—I was down to my union suit. Before I realized what she was up to, she had whipped out her little Instamatic and snapped a picture.

"I thought about stopping to take my long johns off and put my regular clothes on, but there wasn't even a bush to get behind. Then I came over the top of a rise and lo and behold, there was Jerry Riley . . . and here I was in my long johns. I had to scramble to cover up.

"When I got to McGrath, everyone came out chuckling. It seemed Libby had talked to Frank Gerjevic from the Anchorage Daily News, and I was the headline on the front page of the sports section.

"She'd already taken to calling me Long John Gentry. After that I called her Loose Lips Libby."

On top of that, the temperatures had been higher than normal. Donna had gotten a little down and was muttering something about a helicopter, but we persevered and made it across. Later she told me, "When I die I'm going to heaven, because I've already been through the Farewell Burn."

This year, with lots of snow, we breezed through the burn. It was hard to believe it had been such a rough trail in 1980 and 1981.

The ups and downs of the trail still kept me busy. I helped the dogs up a series of small hills as the sky gradually became obscured by clouds. The gray remained bright and I ran with my goggles on to keep the glare down and the wind off my face. The mountains receded to a two-dimensional image on the edge of the horizon behind us while ahead I began to make out the hills that would take us through Ophir and Takotna. What a feeling, even when the going is tough, to have trail in front of you and trail behind. Life is so uncomplicated for a time. I had only to keep moving forward.

On the far side of the burn I followed some tracks off the main trail and stopped to snack the dogs. Three of the dogs had not been looking good, and I was starting to worry about them. Two of the brothers, Bugs and Binga, were a little down, but Inca had lost her appetite completely. While the other dogs ate, I unsnapped her from the gangline and took her back to the sled.

My Incadog, my favorite dog. I let her rest on top of the sled bag, quite a treat compared with sleeping in a snowbank. I tried to happy her up and said nice things to her while I scratched behind her ears, but she wasn't responding, obviously not feeling up to par. This was not the Inca I knew, the queen of the dog barn, the imperious Inca that threatened any loose dog that dared to walk past her stall. No matter that she sometimes got huffy with her teammates; she was my most loyal dog. Once I was using a puppy team to haul ice, with Inca in lead. When I walked away from the sled, the pups pulled out the hook and made a break for it. I called Inca,

85

and she managed to turn the whole team around and bring them back. It wasn't as slick a turn as one I'd seen in a movie about the famous dog driver George Attla, but it was darn good. Another time I lost a team of adult dogs out on the bay ice and stood watching them head for home, calling them even though I knew I'd have to walk. As they loped away, Inca kept looking back at me. She was in swing, her usual position, and didn't have the strength to turn this team, but I knew that if she could have, she would have.

I tried to tempt her with my own food and finally got her interested in a few pieces of dried moose meat. She chewed the little pieces as though the idea of food was repulsive, testing them in her mouth just out of curiosity. She also had a bite of Kentucky Fried. She kept looking up at me, asking me a question. Finally she relaxed and laid her salt-and-pepper muzzle on my leg.

I didn't really want to rest for so long when there was just an hour or so of daylight left, but I knew the dogs needed it, so I let the sun slip away as they slept and Inca and I rested on top of the sled. The sky had turned deep gray and a wind was gathering.

All of a sudden, the sky opened up and it began to snow with incredible thickness. I decided we'd better move on quickly because if we stayed where we were, everything, including us, would be under three feet of snow and I'd have to snowshoe to Nikolai. And that was not my idea of a good time. I stood and motioned for Inca to follow me. She shook the snow before stepping slowly off the sled bag. I walked her to midteam instead of swing, where she usually ran, and snapped her into line. She could coast there until she felt a little better—the middle of the team would be less stressful.

By the time I pulled the hook and headed for the main trail, I was wired for light and sound, stereo and headlamp, had sustenance easily available and two cassette tapes in my pocket. Darkness was coming quickly. I tried to use my goggles to keep the snow from bombarding my eyes, but it was getting too dark to see through them. I had to keep lifting them off to locate the trail markers or just find the direction the trail took.

Soon it was pitch black except for the beam of my headlight. We were traveling through a universe of flying snow, somewhere out in the middle of nowhere.

The snow fell even thicker than before, now with a good breeze driving it horizontally. All signs of the trail were rapidly disappearing ahead of Dugan and Axle. I'd never seen it snow so heavily. In the darkness I knew I was treading dangerously near that fine line often encountered in the Iditarod, the line separating being in contention from being knocked out of contention, being okay from being in danger.

The trail started to get to me. Here I had dogs turning sick again; a wall of snow was hitting us; darkness had fallen over the end of a long day on the trail. I had to lighten the situation somehow, so I plugged into Prince and the Revolution, full blast. It seemed insanely appropriate to be listening to wild music blasting in my ears while I searched for trail markers in a silent snowstorm.

Let's go crazy . . .

The snowflakes blew ceaselessly before us, making a hypnotic pattern in the beam of my headlamp. It was hard enough just to see the ground; nothing at all showed beyond the borders of the light. I couldn't tell if there were trees or hills. It was a void.

. . . in this life things are much harder . . .

I turned the Walkman off for a minute and found the silence oppressive. I traveled the rest of the night accompanied by music.

. . . and in this life you're on your own . . .

The country was so big and the weather so fierce that I could count only on myself, and my dogs. I couldn't rely on someone rescuing me.

. . . are we gonna let the elevator bring us down? . . .

Dugan found the hard-packed trail under the new snow and kept us going in the right direction that night. He plugged along, following the trail beneath that snow without missing a beat. Axle was beside him. I kept wishing to see a tree off the side of the trail, but there was nothing.

. . . *Oh no, let's go crazy* . . .

Every time I saw a reflector I had a short measure of relief until we passed it and I started scanning with my headlight for the next one.

. . . *everything be all right, ain't a thing go worse* . . .

It wasn't cold. The big danger was getting lost, but I might as well have relaxed. Dugan drove unhesitantly through the snow, and the team didn't appear to notice the weather at all. I wanted to wear my goggles for protection, but they made it too dark to spot the trail markers. I wondered if the dogs were able to see much or if they were just feeling and smelling the trail. They seemed to be making good speed despite the conditions. Speed . . .

. . . *Oh no, let's go crazy* . . .

I kept watching for the Twenty-Eight-Mile Creek, so-called because it's twenty-eight miles from Nikolai. I knew that at some point we'd move into thicker woods around the creek, close enough to see even with the snowstorm. But the miles were long and it took a minor eternity to reach the woods.

Finally I saw trees close to the trail, and the going became much easier. I relaxed. Suddenly the trail took a curve through the trees and the front end of my team disappeared. As I rounded the corner, I saw water. Most of the team had already crossed the small creek. The dogs made it easily, but the sled's brushbow caught under a ledge of ice on the far bank and slammed to a stop. I had to wade into the water to pull the sled out. Now it was time to really go crazy. Mumbling unprintable words, I sat on my sled and dumped the water out of one of my boots.

"That was a heck of a place to put a trail," I told the dogs. They all looked back at me, wondering what the big deal was. After all, I let them get wet all the time. The little bridge we had crossed in other years had apparently collapsed.

The dogs shook the water from their fur and

rolled in the snow, trying to dry off while I dug out a dry boot liner and socks from my sled bag. It was a relief to have a break from the wind-driven snow in the shelter of the trees. But we still had a couple of hours on the trail between us and Nikolai, and I was anxious to get out of that wet snow. At least it was warm enough that my wet boot wouldn't freeze.

Not much farther up the trail I ran into Terry Adkins again. Tim Osmar was still moving ahead of us, and as we picked up the trail again I began to see faint traces of his tracks. The snow finally began to lighten and the trees helped block what was falling.

The trail to Nikolai from there blended into a memory of snow and darkness and music. The last fifteen or twenty miles involved scanning the woods for cabin lights, a sure sign the checkpoint was near. We ran past signs the school kids had made to encourage their favorite racers. Many of them were covered by the deep snow, but I could read several of them as we passed: "Go Herbie Go," and "Go Emmitt." The village had to be close.

Nikolai is the first real village on the race route, and the residents always give the racers a grand reception. The kids collect autographs and interview mushers as part of a school project, and the rest of the people mill around watching the racers and looking at the dogs. It's a smaller village than Teller, but I heard there were as many as ten dog teams there. I'd like to think the Iditarod has helped bring dogs back to some of the villages.

The snow continued falling, but the farther we went the less blinding it became. We passed out of the woods and down onto a river, turned a corner and then saw the lights of the village. I could hardly wait for the chance to rest in a warm house, if I was lucky, and maybe find a hot bowl of soup. Chores first, though.

I checked in just after one-thirty in the morning. Over the course of the day we'd gained a few places. The field was settling out again and we came into Nikolai ninth, just three and a half hours behind the leader. Despite the lateness of

89

the hour, plenty of people were out to greet us. I asked the checker to send the veterinarian to me as soon as possible. I wanted to get some medication for Inca, Bugs, Binga, and now Brownie, too, who were all experiencing digestive problems.

Some locals came by, and I had to struggle to hold up my end of the conversation. I was too tired to handle anything more straining mentally than the automatic preparation of the dog food. I tried. I hoped I sounded at least halfway normal. When one of the racers invited me to come over to a cabin right across from my dogs, I was more than pleased. I took along my extra dog food for my hosts' animals—a small token of appreciation.

On my way, I stopped to look back at the dogs two or three times. There was nothing to tie the front of the team to. They could swing around and get tangled or fight if they were so inclined, but it seemed that they had settled down. They were probably too tired to cause any trouble.

I entered Willie Petruska's house somewhat sheepishly. It was, after all, three in the morning. Willie and his wife were up, though. Two other racers already had passed out on the couch and floor. I peeled off a few layers of clothes and tried to arrange them to dry. Willie's wife gave me a hand and insisted on drying my boots with her hair dryer. The warm air in their house was like a narcotic. Even the desire for food faded under the druglike temptation to sleep. I poked at the food placed in front of me, almost forcing myself to refuel. Whenever I came indoors my cold symptoms flared up, leaving me flushed and shaky and my stomach queasy.

They offered me their son's room to sleep in. I was asleep in a second.

March 9, 1985

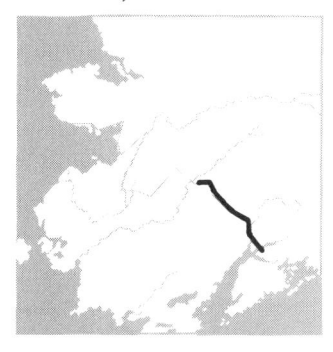

Nikolai to McGrath: 48 miles

Blowing snow, high 33° and low 28°, with winds from the south averaging 10 knots and gusting to 28.

Four dogs have lost their appetites, and the day grows too warm for the team. Riddles travels slowly and rests the dogs often; she herself is exhausted.

It seemed moments later that someone opened the door and told me an hour had gone by. To sleep another hour would have been so fine, but races aren't won by sleeping. I sat up in the bed feeling sick and dizzy, trying to pry my eyes open. I forced myself to walk out into the main room, then sat on the floor for another ten minutes just trying to get my bearings. I wondered what made people so abusive to themselves as to run the Iditarod.

I found the Alka-Seltzer Plus and had myself a cocktail. I didn't have the stomach yet for coffee.

The two drivers who'd been asleep when I walked in were gone. That gave me incentive to get a move on. I stumbled along and collected a big sack of extra gear from my sled to mail back home. The first village on the trail also had the first post office on the trail. Willie and his wife said they could box my stuff and mail it. They were so nice, really gave everyone the treatment. I still couldn't believe they'd dried my boots with a hair dryer.

Inca had perked up a little, seemed happy to see me, but she turned her nose up at breakfast. Bugs, Binga, and Brownie were down in the dumps still, but they were no less willing to hit the trail than the others. Since they would get dehydrated fast if they weren't eating, I would have to take it easy on them. That meant moving slower.

The snow had just about stopped and daylight had broken by the time we got started again. It turned out to be the warmest day of the month, reaching a high of thirty-three degrees at McGrath where we were heading, twenty-six degrees above normal. I tried to forget the rumors I'd heard about rain, but the sky wouldn't let me. The possibility existed. The light was bright, diffused through the gray overcast and reflecting off the snow, but over toward the horizon it looked super dark, and everybody was passing the word that it was raining in McGrath.

I enlisted the aid of a villager in turning the dogs around and leading them over a huge snowbank. On the downhill side he released his grip and I was on my own, in motion again, almost too sleepy to realize it. I had signed out of Nikolai in tenth place, a bit farther back in the pack than I would have liked, a little more than three hours behind the leader, Lavon Barve. But with a few sick dogs and another warm day, I was planning on taking it very, very easy. Here we were in the eighth day of the race and not even halfway. In other years the front runners had reached McGrath in a little more than three days.

The trail was no picnic. The dogs were used to running through deep, drifting snow at home, but at home, just a few inches down, there was firm, hard-packed footing. Here we were constantly sinking into the barely packed four feet of snow. Bottomless trail. Step off the trail and you were up to your waist.

In my sleepless haze my thoughts tended to drift. This deep snow made me think of my old dog Specs, one of the few dogs I'd had who actually enjoyed breaking trail. He raced to Nome with me in 1980 and 1981, and sometimes I'd used him for a leader. I could picture him in training at Nelchina, leaping through the clean unbroken snow, practically smiling. He just loved to go someplace new.

I had given away or sold Specs and his brother Phantom, and Savage and Blondie and the other retirees. I hoped they were happy in their retirement homes. The only one of my original dogs left at home was my faithful Bane. I'd bought him when he was six months old from Rod Perry. The dog was out of Jerry Riley's breed, a line that could be traced to dogs that ran the original Iditarod Trail in the early part of the

From Puppy to Sled Dog

While a racing team is in training, a new supply of dogs must be trained and conditioned to take places in next year's team. As soon as sled dog puppies are old enough to run around and explore, their education begins. They need first to be socialized, to become accustomed to working with people. Each day the driver must spend time handling them, talking to them, teaching them their names, discouraging fights, and taking them for walks to develop their muscles. All the while he watches for signs that the pups might grow into top-flight sled dogs. In addition to speed, stamina, and conformation, he wants to see a desire to run and a willingness to please. A potential leader may show a spark of intelligence or be exceptionally eager to cooperate.

As the dogs reach nine months to a year, they are trained to harness, most often with older dogs to show the way. As the driver calls out the commands, the experienced leader may even throw a shoulder into his disciple to push him one way or drag the youngster by the neckline to turn the other way.

Puppy runs start with lightly loaded sleds and distances up to five or ten miles. Then the young dogs' conditioning begins. Those that fail to meet the musher's standards are sold or given away for recreational sledding or as pets.

century. Bane was the son of Puppy, one of Jerry's leaders when he won the race in 1976. Donna Gentry kidded me that if I ever broke my sled, I could saddle up Bane—he was that big. Bane was the father of two dogs in this team: Minnow and Tip. He had been in so many races with me, it was odd not having him race this year. Though powerful and fast, at his age he couldn't quite keep pace with the younger dogs. Instead, I'd been using him on short fun runs training puppies. That kept him in good shape and happy. He deserved some special treatment while I was on the race, so I'd asked Ray and Carla Lang to keep him in their dog yard at Nome. Sort of a vacation. My neighbor Steve Olsen was taking good care of the rest of my dogs at home. I wondered how the young dogs would do in their spring training once I returned to Teller.

I saw a lot of teams between Nikolai and McGrath, passing them when they were resting and watching them pass me when my team was taking a rest. The weather was uncomfortably warm, too close to thawing temperature. The gray sky threatened and nasty wet snowflakes fell from time to time, but the glare of the sun through the clouds onto the snow-covered ground still made sunglasses necessary.

The heat wasn't good for the dogs, especially those sick ones. I rested them often, giving them small frozen snacks to cool them down and trying to tempt those sick dogs into eating. Everybody else appeared to be going easy on the dogs, too. That's why we saw so many teams that day. The trail offered few turnoffs to park the dogs, so I ended pulling them off into the deep snow for their breathers.

During one break I worked up a healthy sweat from tromping around in snow up to my armpits. A mild wind was blowing but it wasn't enough to cool me. I had stripped off my outer layers and was down to a sweater. Hot and wet and several days into the trail, all of a sudden I felt very grubby. To treat myself to a little cleanup, I decided to start with trying to brush out my hair and rebraid it.

93

Just getting my hat off and shaking my hair loose felt good. I started brushing, but my hair had been under that hat for such a long time that the handle on the little brush broke before I'd made much progress. I could imagine telling my sisters how my hair had been so tangled it broke the brush. I started the braid high on my head and worked the bothersome wisps and strands of hair into it so that they wouldn't hang loose and gather frost. I was hustling in case one of the guys rounded the corner and caught me fixing my hair. It would have been more than slightly embarrassing: we were supposed to be tough Iditaroders, out roughing it on the trail, and here I was, out in the middle of nowhere fiddling with my stupid hair. But then some of those guys shaved on the trail.

I had the idea that if I could find time while racing to spoil myself occasionally without costing myself the race, it would pay off in the end. I had to take care of myself so that I would have the energy to take good care of the dogs. And if I could keep myself happy, the dogs would pick up my attitude.

A happier me and I hoped a happier dog team pulled back onto the trail to continue our journey into McGrath.

Despite the competition I held my patience that day and let several teams get ahead of me. My dogs needed the extra breaks. The trail alternated between woods and river, crossing and recrossing the meandering Kuskokwim and several tributary creeks. Noon passed. I was too tired to pay much attention to my surroundings until I caught a glimpse of two moose on the edge of the river. That shook me alert.

I listened to several tapes that day, trying to pass the time and stay awake: Bruce Springsteen, the Pretenders, Bob Marley and the Wailers. The miles passed slowly, even to the beat of reggae in the wilderness.

We passed some fish camps up on the river banks, with small cabins and drying racks for the salmon that came up the river in summer, and I knew we had to be getting close to McGrath. That trail between Nikolai and McGrath seemed like a long way, even though it was only forty-eight miles. It had seemed even longer on my first two Iditarods.

Then, I had taken my twenty-four-hour layovers in McGrath. Most of the racers favored the Rohn checkpoint for a layover, maybe because it was a good quiet place for the dogs to rest. I didn't like the idea of resting the dogs there and then having to negotiate the Farewell Burn. The trail was so tough in there, I thought it would be better for the dogs to rest on the far side of the burn. In those two races, I'd arrived in McGrath with the top few drivers, but they had passed me while I was stuck there taking my twenty-four. It's probably better strategy to take the layover earlier, particularly because those first few days are so tough on the dogs until they become accustomed to the racing routines. But this year the weather had decided for us and everyone had taken layovers at Rainy Pass during the freeze.

As the sun started to dip into late afternoon, the temperature cooled just a little and the snow stopped falling. I tuned into KSKO radio station in McGrath and listened to *A Prairie Home Companion*. "Lake Wobegone, where all the women are strong..."

Just before dark we pulled into McGrath. A good crowd was out on the main street watching the racers, and a few familiar faces in the crowd greeted me, mostly race officials. Some of the people commented on how good the team looked. I guess the sick ones didn't look all that bad to everyone. I was still tenth, after about ten and a half hours on the trail.

Joe had tried to describe to me the most strategic site to put the dogs, somewhere where it was quiet but where I could keep an eye on the outgoing trail. I shanghaied a couple of handlers to help me get there. The main street in McGrath is also the taxiway and parking lot for airplanes. Just across the airfield from the town, the river bank drops down to the Kuskokwim, and that was where I was headed. We weaved around the Cessnas and Supercubs to a spot just over the lip of the bank.

I picked up a different sled. Now that we were across the sled-busting mountains and the burn, I could switch to something a little lighter. From here on the sled wouldn't take nearly the beating I'd expected between Anchorage and McGrath. A new sled saved the trouble of attaching new plastic to the damaged runners. Also, this one had a seat.

With the straw I had shipped to McGrath, I made beds for the dogs, stamping down the snow and filling the depressions with straw. The dogs loved it. When they saw me coming, they all rose to their feet and stood aside in anticipation, ears pricked. As soon as they got their rations of straw, they went into their habit of circling round and round, scratching, rearranging until they had found just the right position for comfort.

Sister had a peculiar habit. She always dug around a little with her front paws, then grabbed some straw in her teeth and placed the pieces just so. Stripe seemed to have inherited the same trait.

"Hey, Stripe," I said, watching him go through his routine. "How's that Sister-pup? Think you're pretty tough, don't you, big guy? You're ugly, Stripe. Ug-ly."

Once the dogs had arranged their beds and settled, I pulled their boots off, then left them to tend to their feet. They licked them dry and smoothed the fur, nibbling any pieces of ice that had collected.

A small crowd had gathered to watch me go through my dog food performance. I had to move deliberately through each step, tired as I was. While the food cooked, I changed the lines from one sled to the other, moved the sled bag, and arranged the equipment for quick packing. Then the old sled had to be prepared for shipment back to Teller. Barb Knapp from Bethel agreed to ship it for me. I had known her when I raced the Kushokwim 300 and I knew she'd be reliable. I could at least eliminate that from my list of worries.

One of the village kids was running around on a three-wheeler helping the checkers and pitching in. When he found out I had been invited to stay with Nora Baker, where Donna Gentry was staying, he volunteered to take me on his machine when I'd finished my chores. Nora's house wasn't far away, maybe half a mile or less, but the way I was feeling, if I'd had to walk, I might just have spared myself the effort and snoozed on my sled instead.

Del Carter, the veterinarian, recommended a blander diet with less meat until the dogs recovered. He gave me some more medication and suggested I add some rice to the sick dogs' cooked feed. The Alaska Commercial Company store already was closed, but my little buddy on the three-wheeler rounded up the manager, and he opened the store just so that I could buy the rice. The folks along the trail are great, offering that sort of hospitality to us crazy dog drivers.

Only Inca, who was still the sickest, didn't eat anything, drawing away almost disdainfully from my cooking and ignoring all the other treats I tried to tempt her with. The way she looked at me, I could almost tell her thoughts. She wanted so badly to please me, to do her best in this race, and she couldn't understand why she didn't feel like her old self. She knew she could do it. I knew she could do it. And in fact she had done it, in Joe's team the year before when she was just two years old and he finished third. It really hurt me to see her so sick.

Some of the simplest things in life become some of the greatest luxuries on the trail. As I rode to the Bakers' house on the youngster's machine, I couldn't believe how pleasurable it was just to sit down. More luxury was coming.

I spent about fifteen minutes in the Bakers' hallway just climbing out of my heavy clothing and Walkman wires. Nora polluted her clothes dryer with my damp, dirty clothes. Inside the warm air hit me with such force it almost pushed me right to the floor in my fatigue.

Food was offered, but I thought it might be best before I sat at table to perform my own paw-cleaning ritual and remove the dog food, foot grease, charcoal soot, and everything else from my hands.

I slipped into the bathroom, a real bathroom, with hot running water and clean towels. Such things are not a common sight on the Iditarod Trail. Very carefully avoiding the mirror, I scrubbed my hands, letting the warm water soothe all the aches and pains in my fingers. I splashed some on my face, ran my hands under the stream some more, and then reluctantly turned off the tap. But even after all the scrubbing, soot and grease rubbed off on Nora's nice clean towels. I supposed the skin itself would have to fall off before my hands came really clean again.

The combination of the almost oppressive heat and near exhaustion dampened my appetite again. It may have been that I was picking up an attitude from those sick dogs. They had responded to my moods, and I began wondering whether I wasn't responding to theirs. I picked at the food in front of me, a bite of this, a bite of that, and drank glass after glass of juice. Everything around me intensified this feeling of growing depression, and I was so tired I almost fell asleep at the table. I was much more tired than I felt I should have been. I needed a lift.

I reached Joe on the telephone but could hardly hold up my end. After each sentence I had to take a long breath. Taking those long pauses, fighting sleep, I told him my worries about the dogs. I suppose I ranted and raved a bit, as much as anybody could rant and rave in my condition. There was nothing he could tell me that I didn't already know: not to drop any dogs until I gave them a good chance to recover, to take it real easy on them, but not to fall too far behind the front-runners, to know I had his support.

I felt better just hearing someone tell me things would get better, even though I didn't believe a word of it. Later I almost wished I hadn't called Joe because I'd made things sound so bad, probably worse than they were. After the race I found out he'd stayed up all night worrying about me.

Nora showed me to a bedroom upstairs. I asked her to wake me in an hour, then I hit the bed. My years in Alaska have left me with a keen appreciation for the small comforts of life, those taken for granted by most Americans: a warm room, a hot shower, even electricity. Since I've been here, I've never been able to afford a house with running water. After being on the trail, those little comforts seemed even more alluring. I really wanted to spoil myself. But such comforts are dangerous in a race, and I even thought for a second of sleeping on the floor so that I wouldn't get too comfortable. I resolved instead to sleep as well and as deeply as I could for my hour. I dozed off immediately.

March 10, 1985

McGrath to Ophir: 61 miles

Blowing snow, high 37° and low 21°, with winds from the south averaging 7 knots and gusting to 21.

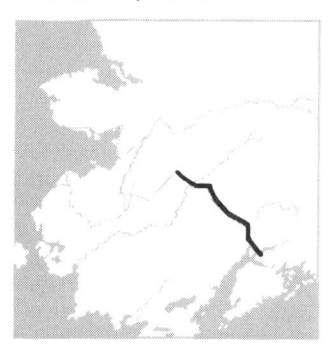

Running in the cool hours of the night, Riddles sings to keep herself awake, still going easy on the dogs. Her position slips, from sixth to fourteenth.

When they woke me and told me the hour was up, I sat on the edge of the bed shivering and had to give myself a little lecture. "There's plenty of time to sleep after the race," I told myself. Barve's words came back: "It ain't very important to you if you can't even wake up for it."

Plenty of time to sleep later. I picked my way down the stairs and gathered my gear in a drugged state. An hour of sleep in the warmth was harder on me than being on the trail. I was nauseated and light headed.

Plenty of time to sleep later. Outside the terrific kid on the three-wheeler was waiting for me. I left reluctantly, my mind still in that warm bed.

Before I zipped the sled bag shut, I booted the dogs, stuffed some snacks into my pocket, and changed the batteries in the headlight. I located fresh batteries for the Walkman, too, and picked out a tape.

By now the dogs were eager to go. As they pulled out onto the main trail, I discovered my mistake. My heart roared into my throat and an icy thrill of adrenalin raced through me. The dogs were not attached to the sled. Somehow, when I'd changed sleds, I'd neglected to fasten the gangline. All that was holding them was the snowhook. I had a vision of dogs tearing down the Kuskokwim River in a beautiful lope while I stood on an immobile sled.

John Barron came running when I hollered, as fast as anybody can run through deep snow. He held the dogs while I wrestled the sled into position and manipulated the clip through the loops

101

of the sled bridle and gangline. Another disaster averted. By the time we were out on the snow-covered ice of the Kuskokwim River, it was after two in the morning. But the hour didn't matter. I was with my dogs. And I was wide awake.

Darkness took away the scenery. I turned on a tape—the upbeat Creedence Clearwater Revival—for some distraction and kept an eye on the dogs and what trail I could see in the light from the headlamp. A big moon, almost full, rose behind the heavy cloud cover, not quite shining through but producing just enough light to keep the night from total darkness.

I rode through the night, up and down hills on the way to Takotna singing along with the tape at the top of my lungs. I could hardly fall asleep singing. It was accidental, but I'd picked appropriate music: "Bad Moon Rising."

I hoped no one was close enough to hear me. I had to worry about the dogs, too. If they weren't used to my singing, they would think I was talking to them. As long as I sang at a steady level for a while, they'd grow accustomed to the noise behind them. When one of them turned his ears back, I had to quiet down so he'd know I wasn't giving him any kind of verbal abuse. Not deliberately, that is. Back home, people have to gag me.

After a while I turned off the Walkman and just sang to them:

As I rode out one morning for pleasure,
I spied a young cowboy just riding along;
his hat was pulled back and his spurs were ajanglin',
and as he rode on he was singing this song:
Whoopie tie yie yay, git along little doggies. . .

Even without the machine, I had ear-to-ear stereo going in my mind, a residual from music I'd heard.

Music was a big part of my growing up. My father was always singing lots of silly kid songs for us. Folk songs, too. In his younger days he'd played saxophone in some of the big-name big bands and also in a Hollywood studio orchestra.

My mother saw to it that I took piano lessons in the second and third grades. I did learn to read music some, but it wasn't my type of music

The Harness

*A*t the turn of the century a sled dog's harness was made of leather. Today's material is inch-wide woven nylon, padded where it fits around the shoulders and under the forelegs. The harness rises along the rib cage into a diamond pattern down the dog's back. At the base of the tail, a rope loop attaches by a snap to the polypropylene tugline, whose other end is attached to the main gangline. All the power from the dog's pulling comes through the tugline. A neckline, connecting the dog's collar to the gangline, serves only to keep the dog facing forward.

Harnessing a team of fifteen dogs takes approximately half an hour. Mushers therefore let the dogs sleep in their harnesses along the trail, but the harnesses come off for long rest stops, and they are removed when wet or frozen so as not to irritate the dogs' skin.

Mushers may buy harnesses or make them to their own specifications.

even then, and it was too easy for me to cheat. If I could persuade my teacher to play the piece of music once, I could play it back by ear and not have to learn the notes and rhythms from paper.

I discovered my own type of music at age eight right in our living room, the Sunday night when Ed Sullivan introduced the Beatles to the world. I sat there with my mouth hanging open. It was like nothing I'd heard before. I was hopelessly addicted. Then I took up my father's old Goya guitar. Seven of us kids were raised on it. My brother Mike got pretty good, and when we were teenagers in St. Cloud, I used to yell at him for playing his electric guitar at eight o'clock on Saturday mornings in the room next to mine. Then he'd yell at me for singing along with the radio. It's a habit that still bothers some.

Once, when I was working for Aatco Trailer Company in Anchorage, my boss came over to turn off the radio. He couldn't find it. The noise he wanted to turn off was my singing. But the dogs wouldn't complain.

I had to stop singing when we climbed one long hill, a tough scramble, and I ran most of the way up it to give the dogs a boost and also to get my circulation going and stay awake, rolling along under that "bad moon." Then the trail leveled out. My thoughts drifted back to McGrath. The first time I'd raced and taken my twenty-four-hour layover there, I had been so exhausted that someone had to lead me to a chair and set me down. Patty Friend had pulled my boots and socks off as I sat there in a daze, too tired to move. She had raced the year before and knew what it was like.

Approaching Takotna on one of my earlier races I had seen a big football-shaped orange light. I convinced myself it was a flying saucer. That really had me spooked for a minute. Then I remembered that there's a small Air Force installation at Takotna. The lights were on some sort of gear up on a hill. It had been so dark I hadn't realized the hill was even there, and the lights looked like they were up in the sky. So much for my UFO.

With the lack of sleep and crazy diet and extreme physical effort, a lot of the racers suffer hallucinations. Racers have tried to knock on the doors of houses that aren't there, and seen naked ladies lurking behind trees. On the Kuskokwim 300 race, where the windblown river surface alternated between glare ice and patches of snow, I saw a sled, a packed toboggan sled, right in the middle of the trail. I thought, "Aah, those jerks, leave their sled right in the middle of the trail." I hawed my dogs around it, but when I passed, there wasn't anything there at all.

Sometimes I worry about sweepers—tree branches that hang across the trail and can knock you off the sled. When I wake up, I mistake the line of the horizon for a sweeper and flinch. Sometimes I even duck.

But at night it feels like the team and I are going through a tunnel in the darkness because all I can see is in the narrow beam of light from the headlamp.

When I figured we were approaching Takotna, I put the Walkman away. I heard some dogs barking, then caught a whiff of wood smoke. Two sure signs of a checkpoint. The dogs picked up a few rpm's when the village dogs barked. The sick dogs picked up right along with the others.

We'd been on the trail less than three hours since McGrath. That wasn't long enough to warrant a long rest, but I thought an hour would be all right. Besides, I couldn't pass through town without a stop at the Takotna bar.

People have asked me about the loneliness out on the race. But the race is when you finally have some social contact after a long winter of training alone on mostly empty trails. On the race you meet people at checkpoints, and you mix it up with other drivers, people from all walks of life who are bound together once a year by their miseries on the Iditarod Trail. The race was where I had met Joe, in 1980, when we both stopped for a rest outside Takotna and shared some tea. I had thought, "He has a nice smile."

On the way through town we cruised past the

Takotna school. Under the lights I could see the bright colors of bigger-than-life portraits of children—work of my friend Susan Ogle. She'd done a portrait of each one of the eight or nine students in the school in their winter clothes. The effect was cheery, with all the bright primary colors and especially because a friend had done it. When Susan was planning the mural for the school, she had to solve one of those typical Alaska problems. The mural had to fit inside a small, single-engine aircraft. Instead of painting large boards, she had cut each figure so that it interlocked with the next—a sort of gigantic jigsaw puzzle. Piece by piece the artwork fit into a Cessna 185. Then the pieces were joined on the school wall.

A few teams already were parked near the bar. I didn't want the dogs too far away while I was inside, so I parked as close to the bar as I could. The only thing to tie them to was a snowmachine. Later I had to come out and move the dogs when its owner wanted to leave.

The checker came out and declared me officially in the village. While I fed the dogs out of the cooler, the old appetite returned with a vengeance. Just the thought of a hot bowl of soup made my knees weak. I knew I could drink gallons of coffee.

My hunger had picked the right place to return. As soon as I was inside with my coat off, there was a bowl of something hot in front of me. A few other racers sat in the bar, but conversation was sparse. Everyone was attacking the chow seriously. Seems I wasn't the only one who found her appetite that night. The Takotna women who had put up the feast asked only that we all sign some race annuals, a sort of Iditarod program, that were piled on the bar. They even sent us off with a bagged lunch for the trail—not bad service for five in the morning. Some of the checkpoints you leave with a little reluctance, some you are glad to leave behind. I left Takotna almost inspired, fired up and ready for anything.

It was still dark at six forty-five when we pulled away and started a long uphill climb. In those first few miles house dogs barked out of the darkness at our passage and wood smoke floated above the trees. Soon enough the world fell quiet again, with only the whispered shush of the runners and the breathing of the dogs as the sky lightened a world we had to ourselves.

The rolling hills between Takotna and Ophir are one of my favorite sections of the trail. When we've climbed up the hills, I can look back across the miles and miles of countryside that we've traveled, the dogs and I.

We had an incredible distance still to go. I tried not to let myself think of the total mileage left and concentrated just on the next checkpoint. Up in those hills, looking all the way back across the broad expanse of the Kuskokwim River valley, the burn, and the long trail we'd already run was somehow reassuring. I could see all the way back to the Alaska Range and its Ptarmigan Pass. Seeing all that back trail gave me a thrill of accomplishment.

We were heading into gold country now, first Ophir and then the district that gave the trail its name, Iditarod. When the gold miners made their way through this country, some pulled the sleds themselves and broke their own trails on snowshoes. Others had only a handful of dogs pulling thousand-pound loads. Some, wanting to move faster, actually left the dogs at roadhouses and snowshoed alone because they could make better time. Now, those guys must have been tough. With all our checkpoints and air support and each other, we had it pretty easy.

The sun rose into a bright morning and the day seemed full of potential. I was feeling frisky and tried to run up all the hills. The muscles around my hip were stiff and sore, still giving me trouble from the wrenching they'd taken at Finger Lake, but as long as I took short steps, everything worked all right.

Later that morning dark stratus clouds overwhelmed the sun and the temperature rose. I rested the dogs every hour—that also helped the ones who were sick. At each stop I tossed them some *quaq*, Eskimo for frozen meat or fish, and commented on their fielding abilities: "Good dog!" if they caught their fish on the fly; if not,

"What a turkey." I wondered if it didn't particularly please them to eat those Salt Lake whitefish popsicles from back home. Occasionally I took a couple of slices of the whitefish for myself. But with all those stops, I fed them too much, and that only made them more sluggish.

Nevertheless, they seemed to be responding to the easy pace that day. I picked up some hopeful signs from the sick ones. I knew Brownie was feeling better when I saw him dive for a chunk of frozen meat someone had left on the trail. I usually tried to discourage my dogs from grabbing discarded meat and snacks—a change in diet could make them sick—but the sick dogs I would gladly see eat anything. I let them amble along at their own pace. Pushing wasn't going to help.

Swenson passed me that day, and so did a few others. Swenson's team looked awesome, as good as the rumors I'd been hearing. It was the first time I'd seen his team in action during this race. It turned out to be the only chance I got on the whole race to check my team against his, and it had to be when my team wasn't a hundred percent.

He ran behind me for a while as I looked for a good place to let him pass. The snow off the trail was pretty deep through that area. While we looked, we shouted back and forth, chatting about the pups he and Joe had traded the spring before. At a bridge over a little creek, the trail widened enough for him to pass. I let the dogs have another breather and watched Swenson move on down the trail out of sight. I looked at my dogs and then at his until he disappeared and wondered. I didn't particularly like being passed, slipping in position, but I figured on seeing him up the trail sometime, somewhere.

Rick and Sonny Lindner and several others who raced almost every year always remembered the details of the trail. I could recognize some spots from my past two races, but when I was tired and out of it, I couldn't tell where I'd been. Sometimes I camped in a poor spot and then found out that just half a mile down the trail was a real beauty. Even over a thousand miles it seemed these guys could remember every tree. They had resting places between checkpoints that they used year after year, places where they'd be out of the wind or have water.

I had to grit my teeth as I watched a couple more teams pass me. Duane Halverson told me the race was probably going to be frozen again because snowstorms had kept the race people from flying dog food to the checkpoints ahead. As the early brightness began to fade and the sky grew gloomier, I didn't think many planes would fly that day, either.

The exuberance I'd felt at dawn faded to dismay as more teams passed. I couldn't let on to my hounds just how bad I was feeling, for they would pick up the mood and get depressed, too. Anybody who's ever been in a foul mood and watched a pet dog either hunker down or slink away knows that the dog picks up the master's mood.

On top of everything else, the wet, warm snow on the trail was sticking to the runners like glue, adding to the drag and making the dogs' burden worse. My sled felt like it weighed a thousand pounds. Traveling that slowly takes a lot of the fun out of racing.

More teams passed and I had to restrain my urge to pick up the pace. The dogs were not at their best. I had to be patient, keep giving them enough rest, keep the strain on them to a minimum. To cover the thirty-eight miles between Takotna and Ophir we took almost four and a half hours; Swenson did it in three and a half. I had been sixth into Takotna; now I was fourteenth.

The old town of Ophir is strung out along the trail. At one time it served as the center of a major gold mining district, and people lived and mined there well into the 1930s. A few people still worked claims in the area. My mood started to perk up a little as we saw some familiar landmarks. We passed an old gold dredge, caved in on one side, a ghost that lay quietly, unworked in the trackless snow. Soon we encountered a few more scattered, abandoned houses. A log

Refreeze

*D*espite the reports of bad weather that night, the race judges in McGrath thought the supply planes might yet make their drops in Ophir, Iditarod, and Shageluk.

"We decided we wouldn't say anything to anyone about a possible freeze," said race marshal Donna Gentry, "and just hoped that by the time the first teams were in Ophir and getting ready to leave, the food would be in Iditarod and we wouldn't have to take any action. By nine the next morning we would know whether the planes had landed."

Flying a race official into Ophir was impossible. To make sure someone would be there when the first racers arrived, Gentry sent judge Dee Dee Jonrowe on a midnight snowmachine run to Ophir. But the airplanes could not make their drops, and Gentry stopped the race again—for the second time in the 1985 race, and for only the second time in Iditarod competition. Teams that had left McGrath were held at Ophir; those that hadn't stayed at McGrath.

"We held them at two checkpoints," Gentry said, "because we couldn't handle the logistics of supplying sixty teams at Ophir."

Race officials decided that mushers would leave the two checkpoints in order, according to their times of arrival, rather than in a mass restart, as at Rainy Pass. There, teams had been ready to leave for nearly thirty-six hours, and technically, every musher was equal. But the Ophir freeze was declared before any team reached the checkpoint.

Gentry acknowledged the

problem: "The freezes hurt the guys with money and gear. There's no arguing Rick Swenson's point, that it hurt those who were the most capable. But some of the people in the Iditarod just haven't done it enough, and as race marshal I had to look out for all of them."

cabin with red trim stood on a small hill with several bare birch trees. It reminded me of a cabin on Lake Michigan my family used to visit when I was a girl, and suddenly I felt homesick.

The gray, weathered boards and logs of the buildings, cast against the white of the snow and the dark leafless trees, made me think we were running through a black-and-white photograph. One last, long bend in the trail and the photograph exploded into a confusion of bright Technicolor nylon, the reds and blues and yellows and greens and purples and pinks of sled bags and dog food bags and parkas. I couldn't see where in the kaleidoscope to put the team. While I was deciding, the checkers ran out and confirmed the rumor: the race was frozen at Ophir.

Soon after I arrived at about eleven in the morning, fat, wet snowflakes began to fall. I pulled the team as far as I could away from the trail, off in the deep snow. That made for some tough going as I walked around the team to take their harnesses off. Here and there I could gain a foothold on patches of hard-packed snow, but just as often I'd punch through a couple of feet.

I took Bugs first and tied him with an extra drop chain up front where he could dig himself into a comfortable bed and not have the other dogs bothering him. Despite being under the weather, he was still snapping at the dogs next to him and making horrible faces. Whenever I started hooking dogs for a run at home, Bugs would stand at the end of his chain trembling, hoping to be chosen. One side of his face would curl into a slight smile, and he'd twist his head to hide the expression as if he were embarrassed to show his emotions. It worked, too. I never could bring myself to look at him on those days I planned to leave him home. Sometimes I took him along rather than shatter his expectations. He always wanted so desperately to run.

Stewpot and Stripe were now healthy and active, and I had to separate those two rounders or count on a fight. I tied Minnow across the trail, well away from everybody. She was still fragrant and the boys were taking a keen interest in her. Socks received a chain tied to some willows so that she wouldn't eat the towline.

The other two years I had raced there had been a checkpoint called Don's Cabin between Ophir and the next place, Iditarod. This year I had made up a drop for Don's Cabin and then found out it wouldn't be a checkpoint. I just relabeled the bags for Ophir. With four big bags, I wouldn't have the supply problem I'd had at Rainy Pass. Life occasionally disobeys Murphy's law.

Chuck Schaeffer helped me lug the sacks to my sled. Emmitt Peters, parked next to me, joked that Chuck was buttering me up just so he could borrow some of my extra dog food.

When I made my airdrops, I had tucked in little gifts for the people who had invited me to stay with them, especially the people I had met on my first two Iditarods. The hard work and hassle these people go through for us racers is truly incredible, and the hospitality shown us on the race assures me that the old Alaska spirit is alive and thriving. A small gift was the least I could do in return. When Audra Forsgren had finished checking me in, I dug through my bags, and in the last one, at the bottom (of course), I found a fat box of chocolates. I made Audra promise to hog them for herself.

Audra had been out there every year greeting mushers with hot stew and a ready smile, and her husband Dick had been a member of the race committee for many years. Their getaway cabin in Ophir had been built in 1936 by a miner. Dick had worked for the Federal Aviation Administration in McGrath. Even though they'd moved closer to Anchorage for their retirement, they still ran the Ophir checkpoint. Audra was keeping a journal of her days at the cabin during Iditarod.

The weather had been so bad for flying that Dee Dee Jonrowe, the race judge, had had to ride into Ophir by snowmachine that morning, arriving only a few minutes before the first mushers. The race officials said there was no dog food not only at Iditarod, the next checkpoint, but also at Shageluk, Anvik, Grayling, and

110

Eagle Island. As soon as the food could be flown to those checkpoints, we could leave, this time according to the time we had arrived at Ophir. I thought that was fairer to the racers than the mass restart we'd had at Rainy Pass.

However long it lasted, this freeze would be enough to bring around those few sick dogs of mine. They were almost there. The thought of having the team back to one hundred percent was exciting. One of the veterinarians resupplied my antibiotics and gut medicine so that I could continue the medication until they were over their illnesses.

The freeze took the edge off the racing pressure, and I could relax. Before settling into the routine of cooking dog food, I put a tape into the player to ease the tedium of the chores. Bob Marley and the Wailers provided a soothing background as I took the axe and chopped the frozen meat. The charcoal fire roared nicely and I went to fetch some of the water that Robbie Roberts, the "Loafer from Ophir," was so graciously hauling for the racers. He was the only full-time resident of Ophir. He had a yard full of sled dogs at his cabin just around the bend from Audra and Dick's place, and he had once made a run at the Iditarod. He spent a lot of time examining everybody's teams and equipment. I don't know why he was known as the Loafer. He seemed pretty energetic to me, hauling five-gallon buckets of water on his sled.

I noticed that most of Emmitt's dogs had uneaten food near them. My dogs had kept eating, at least a little, when they were sick. Again I was glad for the extended rest at Ophir. Emmitt probably was, too.

While the meat cooked, I took my jar of foot ointment and waded through the snow to grease the dogs' feet. They hated to see me coming to smear that distasteful goo all over their nice clean paws. Can't say that I blamed them, but it was quite the stuff when their feet were dry or sore. Like most of the other racers I used it occasionally to soothe my own sore paws—for burns from the charcoal cooker and the nicks and abrasions from ropes and sleds and trees. At

111

least I was smart enough not to lick it off.

By the time the food was ready, I'd finished with Bob Marley and was listening to Bruce Springsteen, but I turned off the Walkman to hear something I liked even more. There is no more pleasing sound to my ears than all my dogs drinking noisily out of their feed pans.

The ham operator told me I could dry as much stuff as I could find room for in the outbuilding where she was staying, but that was kind of tricky. I wasn't the first one there. I scrounged a couple of nails and used the heavy wire I'd brought from my airdrop to rig a line of sorts to hang the dogs' wet harnesses. I left some boot liners and gloves to dry, too. With everything hanging around the stove, there was barely room to breathe.

I was feeling pretty used-up by this time, and I sat down on my cooler, just watching the next batch of dog food cook and staring into the hypnotic flames. Giant flakes of snow were soaking my head and clothing. I was aware someone was walking toward me, but I didn't pay much attention until he laughed. It was Chuck Schaeffer. He told me I looked pathetic. I felt pathetic all right. At least it gave him a good laugh. The charcoal had burned down to some fine hot coals, and Chuck proposed a deal. A friend in McGrath had given him two big steaks; if he could grill them on my charcoal, he'd give me one. Sounded like an offer I couldn't refuse. In a short time the tantalizing aroma of steak began to bring me back to my senses.

After we ate and before dark, I went to Audra's cabin for a cup of coffee. The cabin was strongly built, with squared logs and an arctic entry, a small room with one door to the outside and one to the main cabin, designed to insulate the inner cabin from the cold outside. In the entryway I used a broom to dust the major bulk of the snow from my boots and coveralls. Then I opened the inner door. The warm air hit me like a punch. The little cabin overflowed with racers, officials, pilots, press people, everybody. Gear hung drying from every available spot around the stove. The commotion made my head spin and the

An Eskimo Treat

Almost every village in Alaska has its own recipe for kamamik, or Eskimo ice cream, and almost every Eskimo family has its own variation. Libby Riddles is not an Eskimo, but from her friends and neighbors in Alaska she has acquired a taste for the delicacy and come up with her version:

With a cheese grater, grate frozen reindeer fat into a large bowl (moose kidney fat is an acceptable substitute; the cheaters' version uses lard or vegetable shortening).

Alternating ingredients, blend in small amounts of seal oil (rendered blubber), sugar, and water, using your hands to stir (you may use a blender to whip the mixture until fluffy).

Add berries: blueberries and blackberries, and for special occasions, salmonberries (a kind of raspberry).

Boiled and boned whitefish or pike may be added for texture and more protein.

Kamamik *provides both quick and long-lasting energy, and it quenches the thirst. However, Riddles cautions,* "seal oil is not for everyone."

heat made me drowsy, so I put on my coat and headed back to my sled. Outside in the cool air I revived, and my concern turned to figuring out a place to sleep that night. I considered sleeping in my sled, but with all the thick, wet snow, I would get soaked. Chuck Schaeffer and Herbert Nayokpuk were eyeing an old cabin close to our teams. I was all for the plan and volunteered to help dig out the snow around the cabin and fix it up for the night.

On snowshoes we beat a path to the cabin and tried to shovel snow out of the doorway. The snow was so deep we had to walk down to a door that in summer was actually a couple of steps above ground level. Inside we found a dirt floor. The glass from the windows was long gone. I tried to imagine the people who might have spent their long, dark winters in this tiny cabin. Audra thought the cabin was once the quarters for a cook who worked for the little mining camp there.

We draped some old canvas over the window openings and Chuck started wrestling with the stove. Traveling light, I didn't even have a ground pad. Herbert had been smart enough to pack a lightweight reindeer skin, which I eyed enviously. But spruce boughs would work well enough. I slogged around on my snowshoes, taking just a couple of boughs from each tree to keep the damage to a minimum.

The heavy snow continued falling while the temperature hovered right around freezing, at least cold enough for snow instead of rain. Darkness was almost on us by the time I brought the last armload of spruce boughs home (home, after all, is where your sled is parked). The guys had a fire going in a corroded old barrel stove and the cabin was beginning to warm. This was much better than sleeping in a sled with all that wet snow. We even found a shelf for the important stuff: food, cassette tapes, headlamps. And among us we had three kinds of Eskimo ice cream, or *kamamik*. A neighbor, Cecilia Topsekok, had made my *kamamik* for the race because I had been too busy to do it myself. Herb had some tasty smoked fish to share, too. After we'd talked for a while and sampled each other's foods, I went outside for a walk.

In the radio shack I heard Del Carter, the veterinarian, saying there was a kennel cough epidemic at Ophir. Sixteen dogs were ill, and he wanted medicine. Sure enough, several dogs in the surrounding teams were coughing and hacking. I had vaccinated my dogs, but this was a supercontagious disease, and all the race dogs were packed together around the checkpoint. That scared me.

I stopped by my team for a minute and petted Tip. She had tangled in her harness earlier, and when I wasn't around she'd chewed through it in one place to free herself. The harness was one I'd designed especially for her and couldn't be easily replaced. Tip was a big dog with a narrow chest, and most harnesses tend to slide off to one side and rub her raw under her front legs. I had tried hand-making a perfect-fitting harness, tried putting extra padding where the harness rubbed, and finally ended up using an old leather collar that had belonged to Joe's grandfather. Her special harness pulled from the sides rather than the back, and the straps didn't even go under her legs.

One of my regular spare harnesses wouldn't replace that one, and I definitely had to sew a repair on it. I didn't scold her; she had chewed it only because she'd been tangled and uncomfortable. She was such a good dog, I don't think I ever had to get on her case about anything. Tip was just a big pet, almost always happy, especially when she could coax me into giving her some attention, which wasn't hard to do. That happy, expectant look was irresistible. She was fastidious, always grooming, keeping herself clean, even in the summer mud and rain. She had the softest, cleanest, shiniest pelt in the dog yard. Between her cleanliness and her desire for attention, she was always a candidate for coming into the house.

"How's that pretty Tip?" I said, sitting in the snow and running my fingers through her fur. "You big wolf, you. You've got good skin, don't you, girl?" Light and sound filtered from the

114

Two Canine Maladies

Canine parvo-virus was first diagnosed and identified in 1978. It is highly contagious. The virus attacks cells in the lining of the stomach and intestines, in bone marrow, in the lymph nodes, and in the heart. A dog whose gastrointestinal tract is affected loses his appetite and suffers severe vomiting, diarrhea, and pain. In puppies the virus often attacks the heart muscles, causing cardiac failure. A vaccine is available, but once a dog contracts parvovirus, its chances of recovery are uncertain; mortality is especially high among puppies.

Acute tracheobronchitis, a respiratory infection characterized by a harsh, dry cough, is another highly contagious disease, one that can infect sled dogs along the trail. Commonly called kennel cough, it can lead to pneumonia. Although a vaccine is available, it does not prevent all cases, and infected dogs must be given rest; antibiotics are often administered to prevent complications.

Forsgren cabin across the yard. It looked so warm and comfortable, but I couldn't have slept there. Too crowded.

It's not just people noise that bothers me. Once at the Iditarod checkpoint in 1981, one of the dropped dogs from another team was barking constantly. I lay in my sleeping bag growing madder and madder until I was wide awake. All I could do was get up and get out. At home I don't allow my dogs to bark without good reason. The acceptable reasons are feeding time, hitching-up time, wild animal alarms, loose dogs, and another dog team passing by. Barking at shadows or tweetybirds doesn't count.

I also try to discourage bad-mouthing, where two dogs go to the ends of their chains and start trading insults. A lot of that goes on in our dog barn right after I walk out. Bugs was by far my worst, although almost any of Joe's dogs could outdo him. If a loose dog strutted by, Bugs would tell the interloper how sincerely he'd love to rip him to shreds if he could just get a little closer. But on the whole, my dogs were pretty mellow. After a run I could unharness most of them and they'd run for the dog barn without fighting. Even most of the bad-mouthing is all bluff. Still, when they are rested, a fight is possible.

My dog lots weren't always so peaceable. When I was learning to run dogs, using them to haul firewood and do other chores around the cabin, I had to deal with plenty of dog fights. Some of my dogs were giveaways, and a giveaway dog usually has something wrong with it: it's slow or lazy, or has bad feet, or fights. Like Yukon. Yukon was a sweetheart with people but would hold grudges against certain dogs, and if he could break away, he'd try to kill them. One time Yukon jumped his half-brother Dangit on the way home from hauling water. Dangit's leg had just healed after being torn up by Yukon two weeks earlier. I was trying to break up their fight with a stick when two more dogs started fighting in the back of the team. While I was separating them, another dog chewed through the line, and the front four dogs took off. I sat down on the sled and cried.

It's not just each other that the dogs can injure. Once, when I was standing between two dogs, one decided to rip the other's ear off; he missed and slashed my leg instead.

During the 1981 Iditarod, I had two or three dogs who were a little fighty. Most of the time they behaved, but along the trail the dogs got tired and crabby, just like humans. Two of the females were in heat and that didn't help. The males kept laying their ears back and snarling at each other. On the way to Finger Lake that year, Dave Monson was following me in the dark. I warned him we might have some trouble if he passed. He said he'd stay behind. Sure enough, the first time my dogs found a chance to bunch up a little, one dog jumped on another, and I had a five-dog fight going. Monson learned a few new cuss words as he waited for me to separate the fighters.

It wasn't worth keeping a dog that continually fought. Some day that dog was sure to cripple another dog. In this bunch of dogs, there were only a few bad-mouthers and no fighters to speak of—a pretty mellow bunch, all told. I looked them over and glanced back toward the noisy cabin. At least the tiny cook's cabin, however dark, was isolated from the general mayhem.

March 11, 1985

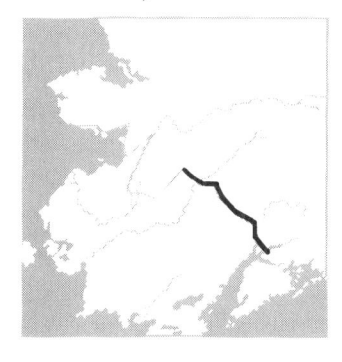

Ophir

Overcast and some snow, high 32° and low 15°, with wind averaging 6 knots and gusting to 30.

The race has been frozen again because pilots cannot drop food and supplies at the checkpoints ahead. The sick dogs have had a chance to recover, and the race begins again.

Overnight some snowmachines had made it in from McGrath hauling dog food, including some donated by Charlie Champaine, a sprint musher who had flown it into McGrath. This helped the others. I was still using food from the extra airdrops I'd sent to Ophir and didn't have to change my dogs' diet.

In Audra's cabin I found a cooking marathon in progress. Audra, Kathy Mackey, and Bev Schupp were all working on breakfast for fifty. Audra hovered over the wood-burning cookstove, making a dozen hotcakes at a time. I noticed a large jar with a wooden stick in it—sourdough starter. The very sight sent me into withdrawal symptoms. At home we have sourdough hotcakes or biscuits almost every day, and once you're used to sourdough hotcakes, there's no going back to any other kind. I ran out to tell Herb and Chuck—it didn't look like the hotcakes would be around for long—and finally got a plate of the golden-brown little beauties. I savored every bite.

The dogs were all healthy. I saw no signs of diarrhea, and they ate heartily. The threat of kennel cough still worried me, but there was nothing I could do about that. I could attend to my team's feet, though, so I went over all their paws again with foot grease. Their feet would stay in better condition if they were well oiled. I talked to each one as I massaged the oil into their pads, calling them by their nicknames. "Here you go, White-dog . . . the stuff is good for you, Bugs, you old Bug-bait . . . now don't go licking it off, Tipitina . . ." Then I tried to straighten my gear. It seemed that everything kept spreading out from the sled in an ever-widening circle.

117

Dewey Halverson said he had some dog boots to give away to anyone willing to dry them. We agreed that I'd dry them and then keep half, and he could have the rest. I was desperate for boots. I'd sent what I thought was a plentiful supply in my checkpoint drops, but I never anticipated using as many boots as I had this year. Drying Dewey's boots would be easier than booty pirating.

When I'd finished hanging them to dry in the radio shack, I dropped in at Audra's for another cup of coffee. Now that most of the racers were outside with their teams, there was a little more room in the cabin. After a good, hot cup of coffee, I borrowed a comb from Audra and tried to untangle my braid. When I had finally worked all the knots out of it, I left my hair down for a while and contemplated borrowing a bucket for a shampoo. As I thought about it, the whole process grew in my mind in to such a hassle that I settled for just leaving my hair down, a pleasure after having it braided for so long. I was starting to feel more than a little grubby, but I was going to be tough. I could handle it for two weeks. As long as I could wash my hands and face once in a while, I'd survive.

When I went back outside to check on my dogs again, a couple of guys with a movie camera asked to do an interview with me. So far the media had pretty much ignored me, which was fine. I still felt grubby, but I agreed to do it, and the interview was short and relatively painless.

An undercurrent of tension spread with the rumors about an epidemic of kennel cough. I didn't feel very reassured when I heard a dog coughing just fifty feet from my team. All I could do was hope the vaccine I'd given the dogs earlier would work.

Then word began drifting through the racers that the freeze would be lifted that night. That was enough to keep me awake, even though I tried to nap on my bed of spruce boughs. At least it felt good to lie down for a while and rest weary muscles. Official word finally came that the freeze would be lifted that evening. The first teams, Tim Osmar and Burt Bomhoff, could

The Logistics of Chaos

The Ophir checkpoint consists of a cabin, owned by Audra and Dick Forsgren. Besides the 26 mushers and 323 dogs, there were a dozen race support people and their helpers. People slept in the woodshed, the gas shack, the annex, and the Forsgrens' daughter's old playhouse. Wet dog booties, wet harnesses, wet parkas, and other wet gear were hanging to dry in every available space. At night anyone who stepped outside would return to find somebody else sleeping in his spot on the floor. Reporter Lynette Berger finally went down the trail toward the river, dug a hole five feet deep, filled it with spruce boughs, and slept there, confident that no one would roust her from this bed.

"It was fun," Audra Forsgren insisted. "I had actually planned for feeding a crowd and had taken extra food for soup and spaghetti. Beverly Schupp, Kathy Mackey, and I kept a pot of something going all the time on the stove.

"After four hours' sleep, we were cooking breakfast for everybody. There wasn't a lot of grumbling from the mushers. After so long, we all had to laugh to keep from crying."

But toward afternoon on the second day she started running out of food. Then the Supercubs landed. People in Takotna had sent quantities of bread, oranges, bananas, onions, carrots, tomatoes, potatoes, eggs, butter, lunch meat, frying chickens, and gallons of chili and stew.

"I was flabbergasted," said Forsgren. "I found a note with the food. It said, 'Stay sane.'"

leave at seven-thirty; I'd have to wait until after eleven.

The pace around the Ophir cabins picked up noticeably. Sleep, and even rest, became less and less possible as the noise increased with the activity. I hauled myself off those comfortable spruce boughs and began puttering around, slowly preparing to leave. I could feel the excitement grow.

As I walked around the teams, I saw a new sense of urgency. Everyone knew that after two freezes and a slow race so far, this was going to be the real race. From here on it would be all-out competition. All the dogs were rested, and in that yard that night were twenty-six teams, the best in the Iditarod. Competitive tension was high.

Shortly after dark the first team left. I was parked right alongside the outgoing trail, so I went up to the front of my team to make sure the guys didn't try any funny business with those first dogs passing. Everybody was rested and frisky, just the time for such nonsense. Bugs jumped up and made some threatening growls as Tim Osmar's team trotted past. Inca stood ready to back him up, but the other team glided past, barely acknowledging the threat as they disappeared into the darkness of the trail. My dogs seemed to know I wasn't ready to leave yet, so they weren't going absolutely crazy as the other teams drove by us. I organized my load and sorted through my remaining dog food to arrange snacks and meals for the ninety miles of trail to Iditarod.

I also had to pack my junk out of the homestead, stuff my sleeping bag back into its sack, box up the Walkman and other gear. As I packed my equipment, I felt a little sad thinking of leaving the place. I'd had a lot of fun there.

As the clock ticked toward eleven, the checkpoint grew quieter. A dozen more teams passed by, trotting out into the darkness of the low hills. It was time to harness the team. Axle moved right into position between my knees, practically begging to put his nose through the harness and putting his front feet through the

119

straps. Binga performed his usual act: show him a harness and he would transform himself into a frothing wild animal. They were all eager, excited to be going again.

Bev Schupp came by to visit while we waited for my official departure time. The night was now so quiet I felt I should whisper. It was also dark, with clouds obscuring the stars.

Bev stood on the snowhook while I unsnapped the dogs' lines from the bushes and put them into position on the trail. A few dogs barked to go as I attached them to the gangline. When I pulled the hook, I felt a surge of power and speed. The dogs lunged forward and the heavy sled lurched into motion. I was proud to have all fifteen dogs still in harness, and happy to be back on the runners, eating up the miles again. The cool breeze on my face felt grand.

March 12, 1985

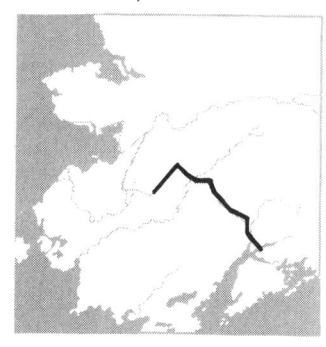

Ophir to Iditarod: 90 miles

Blowing snow, high 34° and low 22°, with winds averaging 9 knots and gusting to 30.

The dogs, now healthy, make a wild dash after a herd of caribou. After a seemingly infinite progression of hills, they reach the old mining town of Iditarod and press on through deep snow, breaking trail in the darkness.

What more could I ask for than to be moving again?

As the miles flew past, we emerged from thick forest into open country and the trees dropped farther and farther behind. Even in the darkness, with just the tunnel of light from the headlamp, I could sense broader, less confining country. The clouds broke up. We traveled up and down a trail over several low hills out into the Iditarod District, where the discovery of gold had stimulated the last major stampede in Alaska. Thirteen teams were ahead of us somewhere in the darkness. We moved right along, the dogs running easily and the sled gliding smoothly uphill and down, and we passed a few of those teams.

Most of the time we were out of sight of any other mushers. I could keep track of those we passed for a while until their headlamps disappeared behind the crests on the hilly trail. Jerry Austin was running somewhere close behind me after I passed him. I slipped a cassette into the Walkman, wanting to make a great night better. I was enjoying an easy night on fairly good trail. None of the dogs looked sick, and it appeared we'd escaped from Ophir without contracting the cough.

I coasted along on the sled, listening to tunes and trying to recognize what constellations were visible among the clouds, unaware that we were not alone. With no warning, a sharp jolt jerked the sled forward, almost out from underneath me. All of a sudden I had an atomic dog team blasting down the trail. I whacked the Walkman a couple of times until I hit the off

121

button and stood on the brake to dig it into the trail as far as it would go.

The dogs had sensed some animal and were giving chase. They pulled me so fast my heart was pounding. They were borderline out of control, and if I couldn't stop them, they would exhaust themselves. I lay on the brake again, but in vain. We whipped around the curves and flew headlong down the straightaway. At least we were staying in the trail instead of taking off into the bushes after whatever it was they were chasing. Probably caribou; there was supposed to be a herd in the area. I tried to scan in the direction the dogs were looking, but no reflections of caribou eyes answered my headlamp. They were nearby, though: the dogs don't get that jazzed up unless they're close to what they're chasing. I looked down the team at Joe's leader Dusty, who is notorious for chasing game. At least he was in the center of the team, and if the caribou turned off into deep snow, he couldn't take his teammates with him in hot pursuit.

All I could do was hang on, riding the brake and trying to slow them, but for all my efforts and unprintable yelling, they chased for about five miles until the animals either outdistanced them or turned off in a different direction. Only then did the dogs slow down and fall back into a trot. The chase put some excitement into the evening.

Despite my fears about exhaustion, they didn't seem any the worse for wear after the hard run. It was amazing how much energy they had. Now I knew they were healthy. After a couple of miles I stopped to give them a break, and Jerry Austin caught up with us. He said it had indeed been caribou we were after; he had seen a small group of them in his headlamp. I never caught the slightest glimpse of them, but the dogs had acted like they were just off the edge of the trail.

I checked all the dogs, especially their feet, and then hit the trail again, crossing the open hills toward the new checkpoint. A little farther on we approached a stand of spruce trees down in one of the valleys between the hills. The team wove through the trees until I saw where several teams had stopped. I spotted a cabin, Don's Cabin, the one I had mistakenly thought would be a checkpoint. A few years earlier some of the racers had stopped there in an old shelter cabin that might have dated back to the original trail. They had had such a miserable time that the next year one of them, Don Montgomery, donated materials, and Rick Swenson and Sonny Lindner had built a new cabin. It had been used as a checkpoint on a couple of races, but not this year. Nevertheless, several racers were stopping there for a break. My dogs could use a rest soon, but the area looked too crowded for us. I slowed to let Austin pass so that he could join the others and then waited while he and another racer parked their teams off the trail. As soon as the trail was clear I hiked the dogs up, and passed through the confusion. Shortly I was out of the trees alone and back out on the open trail.

The mild night began turning colder. The moon was distinguishable through the clouds by this time, so I had enough light to pick out the lay of the land without my headlight.

About four or five miles past Don's Cabin I hawed the dogs off to the left side of the trail, let them dig in for a rest, and fed them a good meal out of the cooler. With the dogs making their happy sounds of vigorous eating, I kicked back on the sled for a precious few moments of rest for myself. I wanted to give them an hour's rest, which wouldn't be so bad for me, either. But after only fifteen minutes of relaxing, hunger struck. I sat up and scavanged around in my sled for some goodies. I found my container of *kamamik* but had to continue rummaging in the sled until I found my plastic spoon. The *kamamik* really hit the spot; it's power food. I sat on the sled dipping my spoon until I noticed a headlight approaching along the trail.

The gang at Don's Cabin was on the move again. Swenson, Lindner, Austin—the fast teams in the race, the real competition. As they passed, one by one, I tried to take a good look. The race was now on, and all these teams were rested and in good shape. These were the teams I had to beat if I was going to win this race. I was checking for flying tails—a good indication a dog is not pulling his share—and loose tuglines and ears laid back or turned to the side. These teams were looking good, all dogs pulling, tuglines taut. But I looked back at my own team and decided I could give them all a good run for it.

My team was behaving well, too. The dogs were trail-smart by now, compared with the first day of the race, when they ditched me. They were content to rest and sit while other teams passed, knowing they would get their chances soon enough. Only Bugs had a little nasty language for the dogs that trotted past.

Despite my own urge to follow, I sat tight for a while. I wanted to let my dogs rest for as long as I had planned. Sometimes it was difficult to be patient, but I forced myself to go by my watch. When an hour ended, I put the empty cooler in the back of the sled and called the gang to their feet to move again. We left the little camp sometime between four and five in the morning.

Not too much later the sun came up to disclose a sky slightly obscured by clouds and a desolate country all around. A wildfire must have burned across that area at some time. The hills for as far as I could see were covered with dead, charred scrub trees. I'm sure if I were to return to those hills in summer I'd find live vegetation, green and maybe dotted with flowers, but in winter not a living thing was visible for miles and miles.

The day wore on and warmed. For a long time we traveled on one side of a narrow forested valley. Rivers and streams snaked around the bare hills, and thick, tenacious belts of vegetation clung to the waterways, but half a mile from the water the vegetation gave way to almost barren land. It didn't seem like we were making much progress because the ground we covered looked so much the same. The land there was what people might call big country. I've come to enjoy such areas of open country where you can see for miles and miles. It inspires a better appreciation for the vastness of the land and my own place within it.

The size of the land can be humbling. It puts my human existence into perspective, not in the

The Iditarod Trail

Long before white men came into the country, Athabascan Indians had settled the interior of Alaska. One group, the Ingalik, established villages along the Yukon River where it turns south in the west-central part of the state. Living largely on salmon from the river, the villagers also ventured inland to hunt caribou in a place they called Haiditarod, "the distant place." There, near the headwaters of the river, they camped and stalked the migrating herds of caribou.

On Christmas Day in 1908 William Dikeman and John Beaton discovered gold in a tributary creek and set off the last major gold stampede in Alaska. Miners founded a town at the Indians' hunting camp, which they spelled Iditarod, and began agitating for a trail from Iditarod to tidewaters both north and south. In the winters of 1910 and 1911 the Alaska Roads Commission brushed out and marked a trail from Nome through Iditarod and on to Seward, the major seaport in southcentral Alaska. Originally called the Seward Trail, the interior portions of the route, and eventually the whole route, became known as the Iditarod Trail.

By their nature, winter trails change from year to year, but the sled dog race still follows sections of the original, particularly in the Dalzell Gorge and Farewell Lakes areas. Some of the old roadhouses still stand, and blazes can be seen high in certain old trees.

The Iditarod Trail from Anchorage to Nome is approximately twelve hundred miles *long. Because the race is a marathon of more than a thousand miles, and because Alaska is the forty-ninth state, Iditarod organizers call it a 1,049-mile race.*

sense of feeling like a bug on the windshield of life, but more a feeling of belonging to something too big to comprehend. The times when I have a view of the broad vistas sometimes make me feel as big as the land. I love the size of the land, how it rolls on and on, untamed and for the most part untouched.

The sky grew heavier as we went along and the temperature rose. Before long snow began to fall and we moved down onto the floor of a valley and into trees again. After a few miles we caught up with the Don's Cabin bunch in a small clearing, resting and feeding their dogs. Again, I needed to rest my own dogs but chose to continue along the trail a way and camp by myself. As we passed by, the thought that we were moving at relatively the same pace was reassuring. My guys were right in there with the other teams.

But the snow was extremely deep off the side of the trail, about five feet. I waited to stop until I found an old snowmachine trail that branched from the Iditarod and pulled the dogs onto it. Again the dogs dug in for the rest. They needed at least a half-hour blow.

I walked along the team and offered an encouraging word here and there as I tossed them their snacks, big pieces of frozen whitefish. The dogs lay in the snow holding the pieces of fish between their paws so that they could bite chunks from it. I enjoyed seeing them all eating and healthy.

The Dugandog had been a little particular about drinking broth. "You don't like to get your whiskers wet, do you, Duke?" I said, going to the front of the line. I gave him an extra piece of whitefish. The fish contained a lot of moisture, and I hoped that would prevent dehydration in him. He was a hard-keeper anyway, not always eating and drinking as much as he should. And being shorter-haired than many sled dogs, he couldn't retain heat as well. Yet he was always digging in every inch of the way, giving all he was worth, and that took extra fuel. I always gave him a little extra something when I fed the dogs, to keep him from getting too skinny. I didn't want him losing water and weight ever, but especially now that we were in the race and competitive.

After they ate, the dogs dug around and made themselves comfortable on the clean snow while I sat on my sled bag sampling snacks out of my people-food bag. My mood called for popcorn. I worked on a bag of that and took small sips from the Thermos of juice. Roger Nordlum came out of the woods and let his team take a quick breather while we talked for a minute. He left quickly, saying he needed to take a longer break soon.

After our own break I stepped onto the runners once more and whistled to the dogs. They moved readily onto the trail and we set off toward Iditarod once again. Before long the trail moved higher out of the trees in the valley and onto the open hills. At the higher elevations and in open country the temperatures dropped and a wind kicked up, blowing strongly enough to drift snow over the trail. Guy Blankenship had passed while we were resting, and though he was about half an hour ahead of me, the drifting snow left only vague traces of his tracks.

At times in the monotony of the trail the boredom grew intense. The hours crawled. I wondered how my pups at home were doing. Handsome Sam, Slipper, Wags, the rest. I thought up puppy names for the coming summer's batch—brilliant, cunning, colorful names, which I had entirely forgotten by the time I reached the next checkpoint.

Somewhere ahead of me Burt Bomhoff and Tim Osmar were racing toward the abandoned buildings of Iditarod, battling for the $2,000 in silver coins awarded to the first musher to reach the official halfway point. I hadn't thought about trying for it myself. The fifty grand awaiting the first team on Front Street in Nome concerned me more. I listened to KSKO long enough to determine that Bomhoff had won their private race to Iditarod. They had had to break trail and find their way through drifting snow, and I didn't envy them. I was, however, envious of those slick pieces of silver. They make such a wonderful noise when they clank together. But nothing was worth overextending my team.

With Billy Joel's "An Innocent Man" in the machine, I went to work a little harder, kicking along and helping the dogs up the hills.

The weather began changing again. The temperature dropped and some of the clouds had spread out, allowing the sun to shine through whenever the wind hustled them out of the way. A ten- to twenty-mile-an-hour wind pushed loose snow around, continually obscuring the tracks left by Blankenship. Markers stood out of the snow every now and again, so I didn't have too much trouble locating the trail. With the snow filling the tracks, most of the teams that traveled across those hills that day would have to break their own trails. As the sun shone brighter, the glare began to bother me and I dug out my glacier glasses while I was moving along a level portion of the trail.

All day long I felt hungry and thirsty. I dove into my windbreaker pocket constantly for pieces of dried meat or frozen blackberries to quench my thirst. Every few hours I allowed myself to have a few sips of precious juice. It was partially frozen, even in the Thermos, and stretching one Thermos over ninety miles of trail took restraint. All this nibbling and sipping on the trail had to be done in silent stealth or the dogs would start looking back at me in jealousy while I stuffed my face. Crinkle a plastic wrapper and it was a dead giveaway.

I had known it was going to be a long trail when I left Ophir, but the fact struck home when I wore out a set of batteries in the Walkman. Where were the old buildings of Iditarod? I knew they had to be on that river somewhere. I strained to see the checkpoint so badly I convinced myself on several occasions that there was a building ahead, only to find just another clump of trees.

When the trail turned in the direction of some huge, barren rolling hills I gave up my wishing and quit anticipating. My natural stubbornness kicked in. I had to keep plugging away until we reached the town.

Mile after tedious mile. Seemingly endless hills, with no sign of the old town of Iditarod. I changed the batteries and listened to Billy Joel for the second and the third time, too lazy to change the tape. I wanted to step off the runners for longer than the short breaks we were taking. I sang along with the tape every once in a while, trying to liven up my spirits.

The dogs trotted along very well, going nearly the same speed up and down the hills. They showed no signs of needing to rest. They seemed to tick off the miles as effortlessly as I might draw a breath. I wondered whether they got as bored with this kind of trail as I did.

Each dog knew what its job was and seemed content—even eager—to perform it well for the mistress. I had a goal. I was trying to place well and trying to win some money. The dogs knew nothing of these goals. They didn't know about the $50,000 at the end of the trail or the personal satisfactions I might gain. They performed their duties just to please me. They were the real heroes of this race.

Running through those infinite hills, I was using Dugan in single lead with Penny and Axle behind him in swing. That didn't put too much pressure on Dugan because the trail was relatively easy to find, and all he had to do was keep the team strung out. If the trail became difficult again, a second dog next to him would help ease his mind a little while he sought the way to go. But he didn't need any help here. He had always been a natural leader—I had never had any doubts about that, even when his puppy flop ears made him look like the Jedi Master Yoda in *Star Wars*. Before I broke the pups to harness, I would take them running with an adult team. Dugan would easily outdistance his littermates and the older dogs in harness, trotting steadily ahead and stopping now and then to wait for the rest of us to catch up. He'd be sitting alongside the trail, but as soon as he saw us coming, he'd take off again, leading the way.

I gave the team a few short stops every once in a while to cool them down and snack them with whitefish popsicles or lamb. They were

Right, Anchorage: *Though less experienced than some racers, Libby Riddles has trained hard.*

Below, the start: *The excited dogs surge across the line; 1,200 miles lie ahead.*

Bottom left, Rainy Pass: *After several days of bad weather and illness, Riddles and her team are back on the trail.*

Bottom right, Iditarod: *Hauling water for her dogs, Riddles fights exhaustion.*

Anchorage Daily News

Anchorage Daily News

Anchorage Daily News

Jeff Schultz

Left, Grayling: *From here the trail follows the Yukon into the deep cold of the Interior. Riddles will shiver in the minus-forty temperatures and worry more about freezing to death than about winning the race. But when she reaches Eagle Island, she will be in first place.*

Below, Shaktoolik: *Riddles has made her decision to keep her lead in full awareness of the risks. A team that loses the trail in this whiteout will be pinned down, alone, until the weather breaks. But Riddles is confident of her abilities, and the dogs are rested and ready. Axle (left) and Binga obey her call as teammates shake off sleep and snow.*

Jeff Schultz

Douglas Van Reeth

Anchorage Daily News

Anchorage Daily News

Top, Shaktoolik: *Transformed into ghosts by the storm, Riddles and her team set out for Koyuk. They have only a few hours before darkness will force them to stop.*

Above, Koyuk: *Still wearing the dog boots that protected her face from the biting snow, Riddles guides her weary dogs to rest.*

Right, Safety: *". . . and then it dawns on me—I'm heading back to Anchorage!" Despite the error, Riddles's lead is secure, and she can relax with well-wishers while her dogs sleep.*

Anchorage Daily News

Left, Nome: *Riddles is enveloped in a cheering crowd under the arch on Front Street. The hewn spruce log, carved by "Red Fox" Olson, proclaims the end of the Iditarod race; the sponsoring cities of Anchorage and Nome—start and finish—are named in huge burls at each end.*

Below, the winner's circle: *With champagne and her two most consistent lead dogs, Axle (left) and Dugan, Riddles celebrates her victory. It is a victory not so much for her sex, she insists, as for her adopted hometown and her own self. But to Riddles, the dogs are the real heroes.*

Anchorage Daily News

Jeff Schultz

used to the routine, and when I stopped, they were quick to take the opportunity for a quick rest and sat or lay down almost immediately. It wasn't that they were so tired; they had just come to sense that every stop was time to prepare for the next leg of the trail. Even resting along the trail they looked alert; their ears were up and they were lively and attentive. Dugan and a few of the other dogs liked to scratch themselves a little nest first. Minnow, Tip, and Bugs rolled around on their backs in the snow. They got such a kick out of that.

Gradually the hills seemed to wear themselves down into flatter land populated by scrub spruce and willows. This was the broad valley and floodplain of the Iditarod River.

I kept looking off toward the horizon, again hoping to spot the buildings abandoned when the miners had left Iditarod. At last one of those mirages held its shape. I made out the high peak on the roof of the tallest building, the two-and-a-half-story remains of the Northern Commercial Company store on the far bank of the river. My energy level rose immediately. To maintain it, I started cramming more dried meat and blackberries down. I had to have enough energy to cook dog food on arrival.

We dropped off a short bank onto the river, then passed a small airplane parked on the ice. Bags of dog food were arranged in a row next to the trail. I winged mine into the sled, grabbed a can of Blazo, and turned the dogs up the right bank toward a little shed.

The checker was Darrell Olson, a big, burly guy who lived in the nearby town of Flat, also a mining town that dated back to the original gold strike. I had arrived fourth. I was right up there now. It felt good to have gained some positions, but I was conservative in my thinking and reluctant to accept that I was right up there with the leaders, with a good chance of winning. We were only half the way to Nome. We had so many miles yet to go, and so much could happen. I wasn't terribly exhausted, after the long rest at Ophir, but it had been a long trail—and fifteen hours—between checkpoints, and I was glad to get off the sled and move around. It was around three in the afternoon.

The buildings of the old town stood high on the left bank. When I crossed the river to get water and walked in their shadow, I felt a strong sense of the history of the town. The old weathered walls spoke for the long-gone inhabitants, the cold, dark winters they had endured there, far from families and the luxuries of life. Perhaps this is a common bond among most Alaskans.

The place had once been a busy, bustling gold rush city with stores and bars and social clubs. I wanted to go exploring but held my curiosity in check. The dogs came first.

While their food cooked, I took some of my wet clothes and dog boots to a small cabin the checkers had opened for the mushers. It was a jury-rigged job with a tarp for a door, but it had a wood stove, it was warm, and it was wonderful.

Burt Bomhoff, half awake, talked a little about winning the halfway prize. He and Osmar had trouble finding the trail much of the way. When he finally reached Iditarod, there was no big reception because the officials who were going to present the award hadn't reached the checkpoint. I congratulated him. He said he was going to give his dogs a long rest, and then he fell asleep.

My dogs had a good, hot meal and were resting well. I wanted to give them four or five hours and then hit the trail again. Dugan had a gunnysack for a bed. I had tried to gather a few handfuls of grass near the cabin for the rest of the dogs but couldn't find enough even for one dog. I promised the gang I'd give them straw at the next checkpoint, in Shageluk.

I walked across the river again for water for the second batch of food. The checkers had chopped a big hole in the ice for us. Having chopped a few holes in ice myself, I appreciated the work they'd done. The hole wasn't that far away, but lugging the heavy cooker back and holding it out to the side to keep the charcoal soot off my bibs, with the cooker and another couple of gallons on my other side—well, it seemed a lot farther than it was. I half carried,

Running by the Rules

Rules for the first Iditarod race called simply for humane care of the dogs, adequate survival gear, and fair play along the trail: rules designed for a wilderness trek in which one team would reach the destination first. As competition has intensified and racers have reached for advantage, the rule book has grown, and by the 1985 race it stretched ten pages.

But the rules still address those same three goals: that the dogs be well cared for, that the drivers carry equipment sufficient for Alaska conditions, and that no racer gain some unfair advantage.

Since the first race in 1973, when more than thirty animals died, organizers have been particularly sensitive about the dogs. Their efforts have largely succeeded, and in each of the mid-1980s races, with more than three times as many dogs running, only two or three have died.

Rules require padded harnesses, booties for the dogs' feet, and adequate dog food. A veterinarian is stationed at each checkpoint and has the authority to force a musher to drop a dog. Drugs that would suppress signs of illness or injury or allow an animal to be driven beyond its abilities are prohibited, and dogs are subject to blood and urine tests during and after the race. Starting teams must have a minimum of seven dogs (the maximum allowed is eighteen), and a driver must finish with at least half his starting dogs, with a minimum of five. To give the dogs at least one long rest, the driver must take a twenty-four-hour break along the trail. And the rules have teeth: officials have the authority to censure, fine, and disqualify a musher they believe has treated his dogs in a cruel or inhumane way.

Beyond the mandatory gear—sleeping bag, axe, food, booties, snowshoes—the driver makes his own decisions about equipment, weight being more of a limitation than the rulebook. The driver himself must be at least eighteen years old and have finished a two-hundred-mile race.

The rules designed to ensure fair play along the trail are based on the premise that the musher and team should operate without outside help. Otherwise—in the extreme—a driver might pull into a checkpoint and go to sleep while a helper fed and cared for his dogs, repaired his equipment, and performed his other chores. For a time the rules forbade any help, but this put mushers in the position of having to refuse the hospitality of villagers. The compromise: incidental help, such as water and assistance in handling the team, is permitted as long as it is available to all. No outside assistance is allowed between checkpoints, and no planned help is allowed anywhere.

Other rules prevent teams from interfering with each other. A driver must yield the trail to a faster team except in the last stretch between Safety and Nome. Campsites must be at least ten feet from the trail so that a resting team will not interfere with one moving past. The rule against littering keeps the trail clean but also prevents another problem: scraps of food left in the trail can tangle a team should a dog attempt to pick them up. (One half dragged the load back across the river. Somebody snapped a picture of me struggling across, just another beast of burden.

Only six teams arrived before evening. Lavon Barve, Guy Blankenship, and I talked about leaving together toward dark. We hoped to be out by the time Swenson and that whole gang arrived. But before we could pack everything and move, another eleven teams had pulled into the checkpoint.

Barve, Blankenship, and I finally left at about eight in the evening. Burt Bomhoff, the first to reach Iditarod, was still resting. Only Tim Osmar was out in front of us, about three hours ahead.

A man on a snowmachine led us down the river to where the trail turned off into the woods and west toward the village of Shageluk. Guy went out first, then me, then Barve. As soon as we turned into the woods, we began to understand how little fun we were going to have that night. The snowmachines had just put in the trail over deep snow, and as soon as we climbed off the river we began wallowing. Heavy, wet snow was falling, and the temperature was probably around freezing, too warm for both dogs and humans. The snow fell so heavily we were already losing sight of the trail. We saw only a few pieces of survey tape along the way and, once in a great while, a reflector.

The country between Iditarod and Shageluk was much like that we'd just crossed, mostly rolling low hills, some of them just above tree line. The trail was crazy. Sometimes we went up hills where it didn't seem necessary. We figured maybe the trailbreaker had gone up those hills to get his bearings and said, "Oh, what the heck," and left the trail there. Pulling the sleds up those hills was tough on the dogs, especially with the deep snow and disappearing trail. This could take a lot out of our leaders.

Wind blew the steadily increasing snowfall, and in places the trail was completely obscured. As the night wore on, the trail became impossible to find. The three of us had to take turns locating and then breaking trail. The big crew that had pulled into Iditarod when we were leav-

131

ing would probably stay three or four hours. We wanted to preserve what lead we had, and so we pressed on. It wasn't easy.

We took turns going first. The dogs were willing, and the problems we had that night weren't their fault. I could feel the frustration growing, though. If the dogs lost the trail, verbal commands would lead them back, but only if I could see enough to tell them where to go. After a while I could tell the pressure was affecting the leaders, having to take commands constantly to stay on the trail. They were tiring fast and getting a little edgy, not responding as well as they should have. Dugan did well, but he didn't like it when I had to wade out front and pull him toward where I thought the trail was. And it took me a long time to get to the front of the team through the snow—it was about four feet deep. Meanwhile the dogs would pull the hook, which couldn't be anchored in the soft snow, and bunch up. I had to wade around and untangle the fifteen dogs, still unable to set the hook and get it to stay. I could definitely remember having better times dog teaming.

Snowshoes were such a pain to use. Strapping them on and unstrapping them off just added to the time everything was taking. Then, at the next tangle or lost trail, I had to do it all over again. The three of us took turns leading, all having the same problems, all having to help the dogs.

That night tested our patience. For a while we seemed to be losing the battle. Tangles, deep snow, sweat, food-withdrawal symptoms—I was in sad shape. I was verbally abusing my dogs, the trail, the weather, and myself. I never laid a hand on my dogs, though, even when I lost my temper. It wasn't their fault. It didn't do them any good to be yelled at, either. I lost my sense of humor that night.

The trail passed through thick spruce forest in several places. The warm snow was extremely wet, sticking to everything and soaking all my clothes. All the sweating I was doing, stomping around in the deep snow, was soaking my clothes from the inside as well.

year a leading musher was rumored to have carried balls of frozen hamburger to drop on the trail in case a team came up behind him along the last miles into Nome.)

The rulemakers give the mushers as much leeway as possible and leave the interpretation to race officials on the scene. Most officials have either run the Iditarod or worked extensively with dogs, and their application of the rules has been commonsensical. In the 1985 Iditarod, despite a lack of precedent or explicit authorization in the rulebook, race marshal Donna Gentry froze the competition twice because weather conditions had prevented planes from flying food to the checkpoints ahead. The 1986 rulebook included a notation allowing the race marshal to do just that.

We came upon Tim Osmar sleeping in his sled off the trail; he joined us. We went on through the trees and hills, cursing, sweating, and floundering. No cassette tape, no music would have eased that situation.

The dogs were growing increasingly tired, too. They were tired of us hollering commands at them all the time. As soon as I'd stop to check the trail, they'd begin curling up to rest. They wanted to stop all that nonsense as much as I did.

I had only one pleasant moment that night. It happened after Osmar joined our procession, and I was taking my turn breaking trail. I was miserable and feeling sorry for myself, when suddenly I realized that after two complete races and no more than halfway through a third, for the first time ever, I was leading the Iditarod race. I was in first place. First place.

Of course, first place right there meant not glory but slogging for me and the hounds. So I pushed my delusions of grandeur out of mind and returned to the business at hand.

We kept inching our way down the trail. We hoped the guys behind us were going to have just as tough a time as we did and that they were maybe three or fours hours back; it had probably taken them that long to feed their dogs at Iditarod. We even considered the possibility that they hadn't left the checkpoint at all because of the darkness and bad weather.

Finally, defeated by the elements, we stopped. Swenson and Company wouldn't catch us—we knew that—so we parked right on the trail. I was glad to give the dogs a rest. They'd worked hard in tough conditions and I didn't want them too unhappy. We all needed a break.

No sooner had I tossed each of the dogs a well-earned frozen whitefish than I fell back onto the sled, beat and almost beaten, and fell asleep.

March 13, 1985

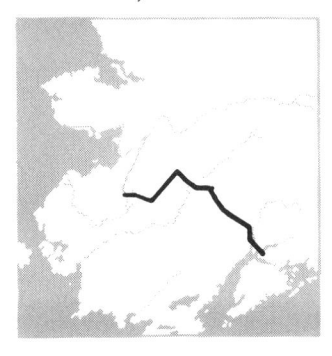

Iditarod to Anvik: 90 miles

Snow, blowing snow, and fog, high 16° and low 6°, winds averaging 10 knots and gusting to 20.

Riddles travels with a large group of her competitors, then prepares for the bitter cold of the Yukon River.

I was startled awake by a loud noise, a yell. "What the heck are you doing in the middle of the trail?" It was Rick Swenson. Hearing his voice was the most depressing way to wake up. We had worked so hard for that lead and it was for nothing. Swenson was hollering and behind him were an impossible number of headlights.

There was Mr. Swenson, standing in the trail we were blocking. Burt Bomhoff said it was like coming upon ptarmigans in the snow. We hustled as fast as we could to join the party, Big Rick in lead. I felt like a real jerk, caught snoozing in the trail like that. We had slept longer than planned. Swenson borrowed a brighter headlight from someone and gallantly led our bobbing pack of headlamps through the nearly trailless forest.

He was a real sport. People say a lot of things about Swenson, but somebody who will go out breaking trail in deep snow when there're a dozen and a half other drivers behind is a real pro. And his team was a real machine. We had had to slog our way down the trail, but his dogs sailed through that deep snow.

Swenson led the way for a couple of hours. The first part was tough going. Then we dropped down out of the higher hills into a valley with trees; the wind blew less, the trail was easier to find, and the snow wasn't quite as deep. We still had problems occasionally, and with that many teams around it was a hassle to stop for any length of time. And I had to keep from running up on the team in front of us. I hated traveling that close, but I liked it a whole

135

lot better than the slogging we'd done earlier. The dogs thought it was great, playing follow the leader.

The trail took a turn down into a creek bed. Swenson, the first one down the bank, took a gee turn when he should have hawed. We could all hear him yelling down in the creek bed where his team had tangled in the brush. He hollered up to us, and we waited until he was untangled. In time he shouted at us to keep to the left, and then the teams in front of me started down the hill. I could hear everybody cussing as they followed the first team down onto the creek. I held my foot on the brake waiting, trying to gear my mind to whatever lay ahead.

I gave the team ahead of us a good lead and then released the brake to follow slowly, being as cautious as I could. I saw the orange survey tape the trailbreakers had used to indicate the way not to go. But before I could react, the dogs took me right through it and down a bank. Remembering Rick's advice, I hollered "haw!" even though I had no idea what lay below. We whipped to the left and out onto a narrow creek. Perfect . . . except when I got to the bottom, orange ribbons were streaming from my parky.

After that the trail improved again. We started going fast again and it was fun. The sled went skidding around sharp bends in the creek. It was narrow and winding but nice traveling for a change. I wished we could have gone more miles like that. Our passage was a whole lot easier than the rest of what we'd seen that night.

Our caravan moved down the trail for a few hours more and then Swenson stopped. He announced that he was going to stay there four hours, and everybody stopped with him, planning to do the same. No one wanted to overdo it on the dogs. I pulled the team off along the edge of the trail in front of Osmar, who had already stopped and begun looking into his sled for snacks. Jerry Austin moved past us to park. He was all steamed, moaning about how everybody was too close to the trail. All our tempers were short, so I didn't pay much attention to him. I

The Program

On the trail to Shageluk, Burt Bomhoff passed Libby Riddles and noticed her perched on top of her sled, resting.

"I was aware then that Libby rested her dogs a lot," he said. "I had a very fast team, but when she later passed me going toward Shageluk, I began thinking, all that rest helps. It was obvious that her team was very strong. I didn't know yet that I couldn't keep up with her, but it did occur to me that her dogs were better than mine, and that I needed to get with the program.

"She didn't baby her dogs, though, or herself," Bomhoff continued. "Once I stopped with several other drivers to rest and warm up in a lodge alongside the trail. Libby drove up, and her dogs wanted to stop. She told them 'no' in a language they could understand. Real colorful language. And off they went.

"I had to admire her for that," Bomhoff said. "We were all relaxing and getting warm, but she never came in. She just told those dogs to keep moving down the trail."

snacked my dogs out of the cooler and then bedded down in my sled. I even went to the bother of crawling into my sleeping bag. I was almost asleep when I heard a voice. "You sleeping already?"

I recognized Austin. He had come to apologize for losing his composure and offer me a swig of blackberry brandy to patch things up. I don't drink much, but when I do, flavored brandies are my favorite. It was a great treat. We were both so tired, we didn't talk very long.

Activity around us woke me at daybreak. Reluctantly I started moving my stiff muscles out into the weather. The time had come to finish the next haul to Shageluk. We'd already been on the trail for twelve hours. In daylight the teams spread out and I took it easier on the dogs, stopping several times to rest, partly because it was warm and partly because the previous night had been so tough. A few teams gained some ground on me because I stopped so many times to rest.

Despite the night's work the dogs looked strong and healthy. I passed Bomhoff, who had passed me earlier, and lost him. Perhaps he stopped, but I thought I was faster then, and he was supposed to have a fast team.

Steep wooded hills filled the country we traveled through on the way to the Yukon River valley. Running and pumping, I helped the dogs up one side of each hill, then rode for a minute to catch my breath. Then we'd be going down the other side, the dogs loping and me carving a groove down the trail with my brake, trying to keep the sled from hitting Stewpot. The hills went on endlessly but we found the trail easily and a slight breeze kept us cool. It just seemed warmer because I had to work so hard going up all those hills. On the top of one a helicopter had landed and a crew had cameras out to film the mushers. They pointed their cameras at me as I passed, but I was intent on reaching Shageluk, and we never missed a step.

The terrain flattened, and we dropped out of the hilly country into a valley cut by the Innoko and Yukon rivers. Lowland and river and lake trail took us the last ten miles into the village.

Shageluk has a population of about 130. Several teams already were parked in the prime spots nearest the school, where the drivers hole up. After a minute or two of mulling, I commanded the leaders off into the deep snow just past the city building across the street from the school. The dogs jumped eagerly into the clean snow. They knew it was time to relax, and they set about digging little nests for themselves. But that snow was a real pain for me. After unsnapping the tuglines, I dug out my snowshoes to make the walking easier while I gave each of the dogs a little straw for bedding. I'd promised them.

The sunshine was making me a little sleepy. Several people came around to look at the dogs and I talked with them while I worked on the dog food. I was so thirsty. And I couldn't wait to change out of my wet socks and boot liners.

After running dogs, I'm always thirsty. When I was training at Nelchina by myself, sometimes I'd come home from a run so hungry and so thirsty that I'd have to run into the house for a few quick mouthfuls of fuel before I even unharnessed the dogs. I'd untie them and go in to eat a proper meal, and then, likely as not, pass out cold from exhaustion. It would be an hour or so before I could roust myself to go feed the dogs. But gradually I learned how to feed the dogs before having my own dinner; their needs have to come first.

The hot cooker began sinking into the deep snow around it and every once in a while I had to pull it up and balance the bucket. Stripe growled at Stewpot a couple of times until I told him to shut up. What a naturally crabby dog.

When the food was ready, I strapped the snowshoes on again and hauled the cooler up to the front of the team to deliver their nice, warm meal: lamb, seal meat, beef, and dry dog food. What more could any dog want?

The dogs' looks made me happy. The run that night had been tough for them and they were resting, but they were still alert and seemed in good spirits. Not a one was sick or looking like it was even remotely in trouble. Even so, I had my work cut out for me. Some good-looking dog teams were parked out in front of the school. I told myself not to worry about that. Worrying wasn't going to do me any good. We'd just do the best we could.

Hauling all my gear up to the school, even though it was just a short way, made me feel like a lead-foot. By the time I reached the steps up to the school, I had slowed to a crawl. The first matter of business was to start drying all the wet things. It looked nearly impossible to squeeze in one more garment anywhere. I tried working a deal for sharing space in the school's only dryer. Other groggy, wind-burned people were shuffling along doing the same things: ladling stew from a huge pot, drying their clothes, organizing equipment. I fought for a chance on the one phone in town to call Joe and give him an update. He wasn't home but I did get hold of Dave and Sue. When Sonny Lindner walked into the room, I felt a little awkward. I wasn't comfortable letting the competition know what troubles I was having. At least this time I didn't have many problems to relate, only how tired I was. I finished and left the telephone for Sonny.

Donna Gentry showed me where the school bathrooms were. She said we could use the hot showers and offered to lend me a towel and shampoo. That sounded so enticing. A warm shower, clean body, relaxation. Not having running water, much less a shower, at home, I am seriously into hot water worship. Actually, my favorite sport is not dog racing but showering. But I had to tell her, no thanks. It would have made me too comfortable, too sleepy, and I would have had to crawl back into my grubby clothes. I had a hard enough time staying awake as it was. I had to stay tough. Plenty of time for showers in Nome.

We were heading toward the Yukon River and almost 150 miles of what could be the worst traveling in the whole race. On the river the wind might rise to fifty and sixty miles an hour and the temperature drop to fifty and sixty degrees below zero. When it blew, that wind would come straight at us. And I had reached the point in the race where I had to keep up. Just an hour lost and the race could be lost. Shower and sleep were tempting, but I was determined not to succumb, so I went into the gymnasium and settled down on an exercise mat. No one was there. It was quiet, but I didn't dare fall asleep. My chores had taken longer than I'd planned, and I was anxious to limit my stay in Shageluk to five hours. Just laying my bones down on that mat felt fine. I let my muscles go slack and thought of the hot shower I'd take after I crossed the finish line. I'd go to Ray and Carla Langs', into the shower with the stained-glass window and the ivy plant in the corner, and I'd stand under luxurious streams of hot water. It was all waiting for me, in Nome.

When my watch alarm went off half an hour later, I struggled into a sitting position and then wrestled with my exhaustion. The showers still beckoned from the back of the restroom. I ignored them. Two Alka-Seltzer Plus, cold water for my face, warm water for my hands—a real bathroom was such a luxury. It was nice of the people in Shageluk to let us stay in their school. The schoolchildren had posted dog team drawings in the hallway. Some of these junior artists were hanging around and showed me the picture done by a girl who had elected to write a letter to me when the class sent letters to the racers.

Then the trail called. My aching body responded, willingly but slowly. I gathered all my stuff from the drying room and swigged down a couple of cups of coffee. It tasted awful, but I couldn't have cared.

The less I had to do, the better, so I found a boy who would clean up my straw for $5 hard cash. I left him a bag of trash and charcoal, too.

"Okay, you hounds, let's hit the trail," I called out to the dogs. "Let's get a move on. Let's go to Nome. The boss wants a shower, guys." They seemed rested, everybody looking good and up and ready to go. Bugs and Stripe barked and leaned forward into their harnesses. I went down the line and gave them all a few good words and a rub, then pulled the hook. We were on our way, the second or third team out. We moved through town at a good clip and careened down the steep bank onto the frozen Innoko River. At the bottom the trail turned sharply to the left and led us too close for comfort past a few airplanes. I was too tired to pay much attention to where we were. I knew only that we were on the trail. It was time to let Dugan take charge.

The sun was setting and it was a beautiful night. The sky was clear and the temperature dropping from the heat of the day. I stood on the runners trying to make myself lively, but without much luck. After the trail turned off the river and into deep woods, it narrowed and began snaking around trees, never going in the same direction for any length of time. As the dogs moved in rhythm under the trees, I drifted off into dreamland, fighting a losing battle with sleep. If I had glued my eyelids open, it wouldn't have helped; I would have dozed anyway. It was out of my control.

The rhythmic paddling of the dogs' feet didn't help either. It reminded me of the chugging of a train. Dreamland was shattered when my shoulder bumped a branch hard enough to threaten my balance on the sled. I maintained the grip, and we continued through the woods. The team twisted through the trees, sometimes dropping down onto frozen sloughs and then back up into the woods again. The trail crossed a marshy lowland that separates the Yukon and Innoko rivers; at times the land floods and people can take boats between the two rivers.

I knew I had to be on my toes for this ever-changing trail, but even bumping the branch didn't help me concentrate on staying awake. I kept dozing on the back of the sled, two or three minutes at a time, occasionally waking to tighten my hold on the sled again.

We were doing about ten miles an hour winding through the trees. Sleep was overpowering. I knew it was crazy, nodding off with all those trees around, but I was too tired to help myself. The dozing felt so good, and it became more tempting as we went along. Even thinking about a shower had made me sleepy, I guessed. I was taking my chances, indulging however briefly in the luxury of sleep. I nodded off again.

Wham! And then sudden darkness, and pain. I had hit a sweeper, a branch hanging over the trail. The impact had smashed my headlight down onto my nose. When I had recovered from my surprise, I took stock. First, my headlight. If I had wrecked it, the rest of the night's traveling would be in the dark. But when I switched it on, miraculously, it worked. Next, my nose. It hurt but was still in one piece. I dug some tissue out of my personal bag to wipe the blood that was streaming down my face, dabbing at it every once in a while until the bleeding stopped. After that I had no trouble staying awake.

In time we came out of the trees and sloughs to cross the mile or so of frozen Yukon River. A short run up the Anvik River from where it joins the Yukon and we trotted smartly up the bank into Anvik, a little after one in the morning. It had turned colder. The dogs were silver with frost—a perfectly matched team—and their breath surrounded them in a surrealistic fog. They looked strong; they had been ticking off the miles almost effortlessly. They stood for a while as if they wanted to keep going.

Only two teams had arrived ahead of us, Tim Osmar and Lavon Barve. I must have been quite a sight, all frosted and blood caked on my face, but I was too tired to care. I had food in my cooler and just needed to bum some water to mix it down. After the dogs were fed, I made my way up to the lodge where they were offering food and bunks for the mushers. I felt a little better about needing to sleep when I spied Roger Nordlum passed out on a cot. I lay down for a minute, but after a few minutes of shivering and shaking in the cold room, I walked back into the main room and picked up my pullover from where I'd been trying to dry it by the stove.

All my dogs needed was an hour of rest, if that, before heading to Grayling, just eighteen miles away. This rest was for me. I knew I'd fall apart unless I had an hour of sleep. It was three in the morning and I set my alarm for one hour.

March 14, 1985

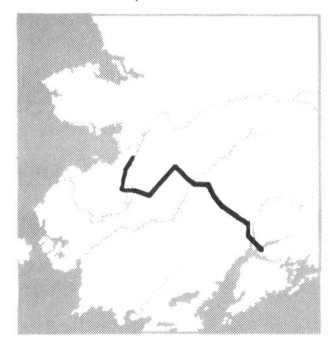

Anvik to Eagle Island: 78 miles

Clear skies, high 4° and low − 40°, with winds of 5 to 9 knots.

The trail is fast and easy, but the cold is intense and Riddles's rookie dog is having trouble. Riddles fears she has missed the turnoff to the checkpoint.

When I woke up it was after five. I shivered and shook my way into the warmer main room. I tried to eat but couldn't. The lodge workers seemed to be eyeing me with some measure of concern. Maybe it was the blood on my clothes.

I learned that Swenson, Lindner, and several others had been there and gone while I was sleeping. I moved as fast as I could to get us out of town quickly and down onto the Yukon River. Maybe it was my imagination but my dogs seemed to think it was about time I showed up. They'd probably become a little jealous of those other teams leaving them behind. We left about six in the morning. We'd spent more than five hours in Anvik, more than I wanted. At least it was a short trail to Grayling, so we could take a break there and not run in the heat of the day.

The trail stayed on Yukon River ice all the way to Grayling, another small village. It was fairly easy that morning and I even rode part of the way sitting on my load. I didn't see any other teams. We pulled up off the river into the village at about nine. My rest in Anvik had not done much good, but I kept telling myself this was the Iditarod, and if I wasn't tired, I wasn't doing things right. I'd been third into Anvik but was fourteenth into Grayling, positions I barely noticed signing the check-in sheets. Swenson, Lindner, in fact almost all the fast teams had passed during my Anvik nap. The rest were close behind. Herbert Nayokpuk pulled into Grayling shortly after I did.

Herb's experience running the race almost every year paid off even at the checkpoints. He knew where to stay and invited me to stay with

143

the village minister and his wife—something to look forward to after tending the dogs. At a nearby building, where I had been told we could get water, the water pressure wasn't high enough, so I just melted snow to cook my feed. I was used to being sleepy by this time, and the task of making dog food was as automatic as breathing. In short time it was boiling. Herb, parked next to me, kept saying, "I sure like your cooker."

As the sun rose higher, the day grew hot—at least by Alaska standards. The dogs stretched on their sides to soak up the rays. It was a good day for a sunburn.

Some local ladies invited me to come stay with them. A nice offer, but I'd already agreed to join Herb at his friends' place.

The minister took all our gear downstairs and hung it to dry around their furnace. His wife fed us salmon strips and other good snacks, and I enjoyed one wonderful hour's sleep in their daughter's bright, colorful room. It was difficult waking, but I had to keep going. I wanted to be traveling now that the heat of the warm day had passed. So did everyone else. Only seven teams got out of town ahead of me, but a big bunch was all ready to leave. Herb and I left at about the same time, right around three. According to the forecast, the temperature would go down quickly and it might be intensely cold that night. I almost accepted a pair of heavy wool pants the minister and his wife offered when I was doubting out loud the value of my Thinsulate pants. I should have taken them.

With the sun still shining the afternoon looked warm but was actually cooling rapidly. The long rests at Anvik and Grayling had done us all some good. The dogs looked great and were traveling easily and fast. The care I had given them to bring us this far had paid dividends. I caught up with Herbert within a few miles of the checkpoint. He stayed ahead of me, though, because I stopped fairly often to check feet and put on more dog boots. With the temperature dropping, the snow was becoming more abrasive, crystallizing and grinding away like sand between the dogs' toes. I had to keep boots on their paws.

Stewpot had been worrying me a bit. His tongue had been hanging out, and all day he had kept dipping for little bites of snow. The heat of the day seemed to have affected him more than the others, and he had been listless and careless about keeping his tugline tight. But as the temperature dropped, he went right back to business.

"That's the way, Stew-bones," I said to him, softly, so as not to disturb the other dogs. "You're no beauty, are you, you old pot-licker? But you've got that goofy dog-smile and you're a sweetie, right, Stew? You're looking good, you big wheelie."

The great river showed some of its faces as we flat-tracked in a northerly direction. Narrow sloughs lined with dark bushes and tall dead grass cut away from the main channel into the surrounding land. Birch mingled with deep green spruce on the river's edge. We came out to the main body of the river, more than a mile wide. Islands in the river and tributaries and sloughs opening along the bank could make choosing the right trail difficult. If there hadn't been a marked trail, I would have needed a map.

Afternoon turned to evening and then into one of those beautiful winter nights. The sun left a tinge of color where it had settled into the hills. Venus and some of the brighter stars already were showing. This was the time of day when I peaked. I was alert and feeling frisky. The steady motion of the dogs felt good.

Stewpot now seemed fine, but I began to worry about Stripe. This dog, who had amazed me so far in the race with his supergood attitude, was not feeling very happy. His ears were held off to the side and cocked back and he wasn't pulling very often. He wasn't used to wearing the dog boots, and they annoyed him. He was a big, heavy-boned dog, and his front feet were a little swollen, mostly from his own weight pounding on them. I could sympathize; my paws were pretty sore and swollen, too. I had accumulated dozens of cuts and nicks on my hands, and most were infected. The muscles in my hands stayed sore through the race from constantly gripping the handlebar, chopping frozen meat, and just being cold. My feet were bruised and sore, too, but at least they were better protected than Stripe's.

Just before the sky turned dark, I picked out the end of a long ridge about five miles ahead as a place to stop. By the time I got there, others had beaten me to it. Jerry Austin and Dewey Halverson were scavenging wood for a campfire. They invited me to stick around and use the fire. I usually like to camp alone, but it was starting to turn cold and the ridge had been farther than I first anticipated. I didn't want to make the dogs go farther yet for their break. Herbert decided a fire sounded pretty good, too.

The main object of the whole operation was to make hot coffee and thaw some people food—tasks that proved tricky. The bottom of the fire kept dropping out, melting down into a big pit. It was difficult to keep the fire burning hot enough to boil water, but it sure smoked like crazy.

Already my legs were near freezing. I tried to cuddle up with that fire and thaw out, but it just added a smoke flavor to my clothes. Roger Nordlum came along in time for a mug of our wicked brew. He wasn't particularly happy about how his dogs were doing—he'd been dealing with sick dogs, too. Austin snored in his sled while the rest of us swigged coffee and tried to eat. Dewey passed around some fancy vegetable stuff in tinfoil. I stayed there for more than an hour and a half, letting my dogs sleep while I tried to thaw out in the smoke. By then I was kicking myself for not borrowing the heavy pants the folks in Grayling had offered.

We finished our snacks and continued into the night. The clear sky meant deeper cold, and it was getting colder all the time. I passed Bomhoff dozing on his sled. He picked up right away and followed.

The miles ticked away as we worked up the river. At one of my stops to check feet, Burt Bomhoff passed me. After a few more miles, we saw some signs announcing food for the drivers.

Hidden Dangers

A common ailment along the trail is frost nip, *which occurs most often in damp cold at temperatures around the freezing point. It leaves a firm, white, cold area on the surface of a person's skin. If the spot is rapidly rewarmed, there will be no serious aftereffects. Not so with* frostbite.

Fingers, toes, ears, and nose—parts of the body around which air can circulate—are particularly vulnerable to frostbite. *The tissue freezes and turns cold, hard, and white. The victim may feel initial pain, but once the flesh has frozen, there is no feeling at all. A quick warming of the affected area is recommended, provided there is no danger of refreezing. A frostbitten area can turn gangrenous.*

Most serious of all is hypothermia, *a lowering of body temperature. At a drop of one or two degrees Fahrenheit, the control centers in the brain reduce the flow of blood to the extremities, where heat is being lost. A person's fingers become cold, and even the effort of putting on more clothing becomes difficult. A drop of another degree and violent shivering begins as the brain activates muscles to try to raise body temperature. After the person's temperature falls another degree or two, mental processes suffer. Behavior may be lethargic or irrational; the quality of the voice changes; exhausted muscles stop shivering. The body may begin to stiffen.*

At a core temperature of ninety-five degrees, a person is considered to be suffering from hypothermia. Temperature continues to drop as the body loses its ability to generate heat. Below ninety degrees, irregularities in breathing and heartbeat begin, and the victim may lose consciousness. Below eighty-five degrees, cardiopulmonary functions may cease altogether.

The symptoms can occur quickly and go unrecognized if the victim is engaged in intense activity or dozing during the long, lonely hours on the trail. More than one Iditarod driver has been found dazed, suffering from the first stages of hypothermia.

Unlikely as it may seem, problems develop most often when the musher becomes too warm. Working hard in the heavy clothing of the trail can leave clothing soaked with perspiration, a situation conducive to rapid heat loss and the beginnings of hypothermia. Drivers often strip to their shirtsleeves in ten- or twenty-degree weather, trying to stay cool enough to keep their clothing dry. Winter in Alaska brings with it the constant chore of adding and removing clothing as the situation demands.

Sounded tempting, but I'd just stopped for almost two hours. My dogs weren't thinking that way, though. Maybe they envied the other teams resting, or maybe they smelled the moose stew. They tried to cut up the bank to Blackburn Lodge without my consent. I might have thought about going in if the leaders hadn't tried their little trick. I wasn't going to let them get away with it. I pulled them away from the bank with nasty words for all of them. I finally forced them past the lodge and got back on the trail.

At least I thought I was on it. The trail turned out to be ski tracks from an airplane, and they ended abruptly where the airplane had lifted off the river. By turning out across the river, I got lucky and found a trail marker. We turned north again. A slight wind was blowing snow around and in time I found faint remnants of a trail, just parallel to a set of almost indiscernible ridges. I thought Burt or Herbert might be following, but I never saw any lights. I didn't know who was ahead of me because I didn't know who had gone up to the lodge. After a while the drifts diminished, making the trail easier to find even though we still had to break through a few inches of snow. We traveled mostly along the east bank of the river. There wasn't much wind, just enough to keep depositing a little snow in the trail. It was a tailwind, so once we turned north, it didn't drift snow on the trail as badly as where we had crossed the river coming out of Blackburn.

The Yukon River had a presence that night, cold and dark and silent. The stars were out, along with the northern lights—green and yellow with a little bit of red. I watched them for a long time, entertaining my mind in the night. It was about as cold as it was ever going to get, far too cold to stop. I pumped and kicked and ran behind the sled for all I was worth, trying to keep my feet from freezing in my damp shoepacs. At times it seemed the night would go on forever and never be light or warm again.

For some reason the cold was invading my right parka sleeve, and nothing I could do tightened the cuff enough to keep it out. My legs were freezing. I was wearing polypropylene expedition-weight underwear, thick wool pants, my high-tech $300 Gore-Tex and Thinsulate expedition suits along with my big blue parky insulated with Tuscany lambskins; good gear, but woefully inadequate in that kind of cold. My legs were cold, and despite all the running, my feet were cold, too. I had reindeer mukluks in the sled, but it was too cold to stop and change.

I had come close to freezing my hands on the Yukon when I raced in 1980. My hands had been nearly numb, but it was too cold then as well to dig out heavier mittens. Besides, the lights of the next checkpoint had been in view. But they were farther away than they seemed, and after I got there, more than an hour later, I had to stand for ten minutes with a frozen paw in each armpit before I could move my hands well enough to park the dogs.

There was a bit of wind chill now, from the breeze generated by the dogs' motion and the slight wind that was drifting over the trail. Every degree mattered.

As I approached the Eagle Island checkpoint, I gained a healthy respect for the situation. I was in danger of frostbite, so I kept those feet moving. I worked and worked behind the sled, trying like crazy to get to the nice, warm checkpoint somewhere up the river in the darkness.

Fear kept my adrenalin pumping all night. I was pushing my luck a little and I knew it. I was too close for comfort to that fine line between being okay and being in one heck of a lot of trouble. I'd never frostbitten anything, and I wasn't anxious to start that night. I shuddered, imagining what I would do if there were no warm cabin ahead. I could handle it, I knew. But sleeping out in minus forty wouldn't be fun.

I was a little frustrated, too, when I thought about the folding seat Joe and I had built on the back of the sled. All along I had been referring to it as my "Yukon River seat," and here I was on the Yukon, where the trail was flat and made for sitting, and it was too darn cold to sit down.

The Jack London story "To Build a Fire" came to mind, the story of a man traveling in this kind

148

of weather, wet from a dip into overflow. He fumbles with frozen hands and his few precious matches, struggling to build a life-saving fire. With the cold affecting his mind he battles the elements until they overwhelm him and the deep cold takes him. Cheery thoughts. I ground my teeth as I pedaled. I'd kick with my right leg five, six times, then change to my left. The cold invaded every seam in my clothing.

In my headlamp the dogs looked like ghosts, glistening with frost and half obscured in a cloud of their own frozen breaths. The clinking of the hardware on the collars and harnesses made music in the quiet of the night.

I tried thinking warm thoughts. Hawaii. I had never been to Hawaii, or anywhere else tropical for that matter, but I drifted into images of lying on a sandy beach with the sun beating down on me and the sound of waves at my feet. I promised myself a trip to Hawaii.

But sunny beaches didn't work. I was still an icicle. My feet would freeze if I stopped moving. I kept pumping and working. I didn't want to frost my lungs or work up a sweat that would make me even colder, so every so often I rested for a few moments. I kept shifting my weight back and forth on the runners to keep the blood moving up and down in my toes. Every once in a while the shivers would have me doing a little dance.

The long hours on the river began working on me. My mind wandered. I was a particle in space, magnetically homing in on the checkpoint. What lay in the beam of my headlight was my whole world. There was no future, no past, just present, gliding along behind my string of dogs, somewhere in Yukon River limbo, trying to keep from freezing to death.

We had traveled for so many hours I began to worry. Had we passed the turnoff to the checkpoint? Oh, mercy, I didn't even want to think of it. I turned off the headlight to move along in total darkness, hoping to catch the lights of a cabin, but only the northern lights flashed wickedly ahead of us. If I couldn't find the checkpoint soon, it was coming time to smarten up and stop to make us a fire. I had one chemical hand warmer down the front of my shirt, one down the back, but what little heat they had to give just dissipated into the surrounding cold.

When I was sure we had missed the turnoff, the trail started cutting across the river. Checkpoint ahead.

We still had to cross the river, though, and those last few miles were the worst. The wind blowing up the river obscured the trail with drifting snow, and I had to hunt as we moved toward the far bank. I turned the headlight off every once in a while, looking for the shore and maybe the twinkle of cabin lights.

But the farther we went in that direction, the harder the wind blew, and the harder the wind, the more snow obscured the trail. We must be approaching the checkpoint, I assured myself. We didn't go more than a mile or two before I came upon a series of cardboard signs. Eagle Island. We had made it.

The team had begun to climb the hill to the checkpoint cabin when the last of the signs suddenly registered in my frostbitten brain. It read: "No teams beyond this point." I had to back everybody down and do a one-eighty. Once turned, we followed the trail back into a big loop until we came to the best-looking parking place I'd seen. Another sign marked this place: "Dump trash here." I told the dogs to ignore the insult; it was the best, closest parking place and we were going to take it. Frozen and weary, I stood at the bottom of the hill and looked up. The hill seemed impossibly steep and long. I struggled up, my calf muscles mutinous from all the pumping and running I'd had to do just to stay warm, just to get to the bottom of the hill. This was the last straw.

I knocked on the cabin door several times before I got a response. A man opened it, looking surprised. The checkers hadn't been expecting anyone yet; they were all asleep. Someone said he was amazed the first musher was a "girl."

March 15, 1985

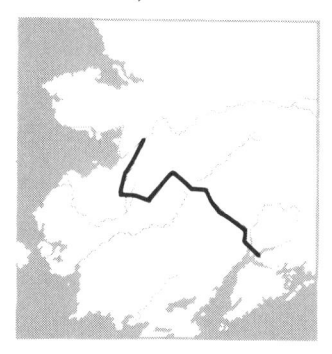

Eagle Island to Kaltag: 70 miles

Skies overcast, then clearing in the afternoon, high 17° and low − 40°, with winds up to 20 knots.

After resting during the day, Riddles sets out again into the night. The temperature drops to minus fifty, but the dogs make good time.

First. And this time I wasn't first just because it happened to be my turn to break the trail. To the press, I'd been just another Iditarod Nobody. That was all right. I wasn't in the race to be famous. I just wanted to show what my dogs could do. Joe and I had gotten fairly used to obscurity up in Teller. Even though Joe had placed third the year before and we had ARCO for a sponsor, we never drew much attention. It wasn't until now, at Eagle Island, that some of the reporters, as well as the other drivers, began to take me more seriously, when they noticed how well my dogs were holding up in the weather.

Ralph Conaster, the checker, said he'd be down in a minute, so I hiked back down the hill, this time concentrating on balance as I skidded toward the team.

I immediately lit into the routine. Soon a wonderful roaring fire blazed in the cooker, fed by several pounds of charcoal briquettes mixed with about half a gallon of Blazo: instant bonfire. I held close to the heat for a while, warming my hands. Later I noticed that the gas stoves weren't holding the heat, and it was taking other drivers a lot longer to cook in the bitter cold. I melted snow to start water while I chopped the frozen meat from my airdrops.

Austin rolled into the checkpoint and had driven almost up to my team when I told him most of the parking places were behind him. He was half crabby again, especially after I told him he'd have to turn around, too. We were both a bit near the edge.

Everyone in the cabin was up and moving by

151

the time I had fed the dogs, provided them with spruce boughs and burlap sacks for beds, and trudged back up the hill. The house was a piece of art, formed of hand-hewn wood. Several stout-looking structures stood arond the main house.

Then I discovered one of the best advantages of being first. I was first to the stove and had the choice positions on the drying rack. I had my parka and hat to dry, felt boot liners, and a few strings of Velcroed-together dog boots.

In quick time I emerged from my frozen clothing and began picking the frost off the strands of hair that had leaked out from under my lynx hat. With hot coffee I started warming from inside out as well as outside in. As drivers rolled slowly but regularly into the checkpoint, the general consensus was to stay there for a long blow. With everybody thinking that way, I allowed myself to relax. I soaked my hands in a basin of hot water. They were stiff and raw from the extended cold, and my knuckle was still swollen from the crash at Happy River, the ring still locked in place. The hot water was a real treat. I tried to borrow some lotion from Ralph's wife Helmi; instead, she gave me a little bottle of my own to take along and told me to sleep on her bed.

By this time I wanted to sleep more than anything and accepted the invitation gratefully. Austin already was snoring on the far side of the bed. I slept for half an hour until the smells of breakfast made me think more about food: moose steaks and fresh chicken eggs, two for every driver, provided by the chickens the Conasters kept in a heated coop. There we were in the middle of the Alaska Bush, on an isolated stretch of Yukon River at the only home for miles and miles; it certainly seemed bizarre to be eating fresh chicken eggs. Just keeping the coop heated when it was forty below zero outside must have taken a tremendous amount of energy. There were muffins, too, and endless cups of coffee. The checkers, Ralph and Helmi Conaster, had to be an example of the finest in Bush hospitality. Their son, Steve, had raced the

Deep Freeze

The severe cold at Eagle Island helped sort the champion teams from the also-rans. A team that is tired will fade in such cold weather.

"You can tell when dogs are uncomfortable," said Donna Gentry. "They look like they'd wrap their arms around themselves if they could; they look hunched up, like the whole body is contracted. Some of the teams were bothered by that sudden cold, but Libby's team was strong. I think the other drivers underrated her."

Iditarod in 1980. Maybe that was why they put up with us.

After that breakfast I returned to the bedroom to sleep. Bomhoff had the floor on one side, Swenson had a pile of his gear on the other. Sonny Lindner was sleeping at the end. I settled in and was almost asleep when I jumped up with a yell, waking everyone. A merciless pain had shot up my right leg. This was pain beyond my experience, and it frightened me. It must have been a bona fide charley horse, my first ever. Bomhoff told me I was lucky: "Get to be my age," he said, "and you get them all the time." I was not eager to experience a second one.

I snoozed a little while the pace at the checkpoint remained relaxed. In midafternoon Barve started making motions to leave. Swenson told a newspaper reporter he thought that was a mistake, that anybody going out in this cold would end up parked somewhere between Eagle Island and Kaltag "with the hood up." That didn't stop Barve. He left around three-thirty with Herbert and Emmitt Peters for company. Slowly I began my own preparations. The sky was what they call severe clear in that country, and that meant a night at least as cold as the previous one. Just the thought brought the chill back into my legs. I worked up enough courage to ask Helmi if she had some old overpants I could borrow. I hated to ask. I knew she'd never be able to replace them this winter before I could return them, but I had to ask her or risk another night on that fine line. Helmi found me a pair of orange down pants. At least this night I'd have a little more protection.

The press figured they'd better check me out, seeing as I'd arrived at the checkpoint first. Some cameramen interviewed me as I was organizing to leave. They seemed impressed by all my junk food.

I tried to take a picture of the hounds by the "Dump trash here" sign, but the temperature was just too cold for my camera. It sounded awfully sick when the shutter groaned to a close.

Dugan and Axle were still doing well in lead, so I left them there. The rest of the dogs were bearing up under the cold. Their weight was staying good, a prime concern in severe cold, when they tend to dehydrate into skinniness quickly. They were happy and frisky, leaning and jumping into the harnesses, ready to go. I heard Austin sigh as I rolled past him out of the checkpoint, mumbling something about how he wished his team looked that fresh. Actually, he had done a good job of keeping his team in good shape, and his dogs were still pretty lively.

We ran down the hill and stopped where the trail turned to go north upriver. Several drivers had parked at the turnoff, Raymie Redington among them. He'd promised me some of his wife's seal oil. This was something I'd come to appreciate in Teller. The stupidest thing I'd done for this whole race was not taking any. I had worried about a jar breaking in the sled and the oil soaking everything. I had been eating the little mixed with the Eskimo ice cream, but now I wanted some straight. I actually craved it. When it's forty below, I need the extra fat to burn for heat. Everyone and his brother recommends against a high-fat diet these days—and seal oil is awfully rich—but I don't know if any of those experts has ever been working his tail off in minus-forty weather with minimal sleep. Seal oil hits the spot then.

I dug out a container I had kept handy, and Raymie poured me some of that high-octane fuel out of his pint jar. I took a long swig. This was some of the clearest, freshest seal oil I'd tasted in a while. I felt indebted to the Redingtons for life. Now I could face the weather.

We hit the trail for Kaltag close to six in the afternoon, after an eleven-hour rest with the Conasters. Six of us left at about the same time, following the three who'd left a couple of hours earlier. Swenson and Lindner stayed longer, eventually taking off in the early hours of the morning. This is where I got the jump on them. After several disappointments back down the trail, this time my lead was going to hold.

Not too long after we left, maybe only three or four miles, I caught up with Tim Osmar. He was not looking pleased. "Want to sell me your dog

Clothing

The most common footwear along the trail is the shoepac, a laced boot that is rubber up to the ankle and leather above. A wool felt liner slips inside to provide insulation and can be changed when wet. For extremely cold weather many drivers wear "bunny boots," double-layered rubber boots with an insulating dead-air space between the layers. Developed by the military for its cold-weather operations, they are effective in extreme conditions, but the rubber prevents air circulation and can leave the feet damp and uncomfortable. Some mushers therefore favor the traditional mukluks, with hard sealskin soles and caribou fur or moosehide uppers. In wet snow mukluks can soak through, but in very cold, dry snow they provide good protection.

Because the mushers constantly fight dampness—wet snow and their own perspiration—down parkas and sleeping bags, which are useless when wet, have fallen from favor. Synthetic fabrics and wool, which retain heat even when damp, are therefore the clothing of choice. But many drivers, particularly Native mushers, still prefer the skin and fur clothing of old. These garments have no buttons or zippers or other openings that the wind can penetrate, yet they are loose enough to permit bodily movements and air circulation. A hood lined with fur keeps the head warm; its fur ruff protects the face without itself frosting up.

Underneath are layers of underwear: fishnet, polypro-

pylene, cotton, and wool shirts and pants. A musher may carry several pairs of gloves and mittens—fingerless, wool knit, sealskin, polypropylene, Thinsulate—each allowing some combination of warmth and dexterity. A waterproof poncho and glacier goggles, sunglasses with leather eye protectors at the sides, complete a driver's Iditarod gear.

team?" he asked. Funny guy. I just smiled at him and turned the Walkman's volume back up again.

With the sun, the first miles up the river were pleasant. As usual, I took it easy on the dogs, giving them lots of short breaks and checking their feet. They looked so good, it blew me away sometimes. This was the kind of dog team I'd dreamed about driving since I'd started, and here I was in the front pack with a charging team and not a dog dropped yet. It was worth every ounce of suffering it had taken to get there. The flat-tracking demanded only a minimum of effort from the dogs and me. I liked being out in the open again where I could see the sky. Whenever I stopped for a moment, Dugan stood with a northbound lean into his harness while Stripe barked to keep going. Everyone was eager to go.

We caught up with Herbert and from then on we traveled together much of the time through the night. The temperature kept dropping. Herbert carried the high-energy Eskimo snacks, smoked salmon and *muktuk*, and hot coffee— just what I needed to keep going in that cold. In turn, he was always a perfect gentleman on the trail; he let me and my team go first. Nice of him. But that little strain of leading wasn't such a bad trade-off for the snacks.

After the sun went down, the cold on the river became merciless, slipping below minus forty toward minus fifty degrees. Herb and I stopped after a couple of hours of traveling to snack the dogs—and ourselves. We talked a little as we sat on our sleds. I was much better prepared for the cold that night. I was happy with the pants Helmi had so generously loaned me, and I was wearing my mukluks. I'd tried putting the chemical handwarmers in the mukluks but they had croaked, gone out from lack of air.

John Cooper drove into sight. Enough of Herb's coffee was left to give him a taste, for which he seemed grateful. Like me, he was wearing a pullover parka and not suffering so much from the cold as some of the other drivers. He lived north and east of us in Ambler, at the

155

western end of the Brooks Range, so he knew something about cold, too. Herb, of course, had the good Eskimo gear. It made a big difference in the cold.

Cooper had passed me earlier that afternoon with his dogs loping. Since my dogs had come back from their illnesses, not too many teams had passed me, so when he did, it stuck in my mind that he was definitely faster than my gang. He had a good team and they looked strong on the river. Everybody liked Cooper. He never seemed to lose his cool out on the trail and didn't take himself so seriously as some of the others. The closer we came to Nome, the more intense the race was becoming. I would have to keep an eye on Cooper, too.

At least the cold weather didn't seem to bother my dogs much. I wasn't sure, but it seemed that some of the guys behind us were starting to wilt a little in the cold. The trail was still tough on the dogs' feet, and I had to be more careful than ever. It wasn't much fun messing around with dog boots in my bare hands with the temperature at forty below. No fun at all.

We finished Herb's coffee and plunged into the night again, continuing our battle with the still-dropping temperature. I kicked on the back of the sled and pumped like mad to keep circulation going in my legs and feet, but no matter how hard I worked, I couldn't keep the cold at bay. Every little opening in my clothing, even between the weave on the tightest of cloth and fur, became an enemy letting in that numbing cold. It was colder than the night before—I had on warmer gear and yet I was colder. I couldn't remember ever being so cold. For a while I was too cold to move, to pump and push. I just stood on the runners shivering uncontrollably. After several long minutes of that, I realized that I'd have to do something or I'd be in bigger trouble. I had some handwarmers down my shirt again, but it would have taken fifty of them to do the trick that night. I got smart and stopped to pull my sleeping bag out of the sled. I wrapped it around me as best I could, using it as a cape as we proceeded up the trail. The clumsy bag was awkward, a real problem if I needed to do any fancy steering, but it staved off some of that intense cold.

Even with the sleeping bag for added warmth, the Yukon River seat on the sled was useless. It had been a lot of work and a good plan, but it was just too cold to sit down for long. No sooner would I begin to feel comfortable, sitting with the weight off my legs, than the cold would start creeping in and I'd have to move or lose it.

Over the long, flat miles along the Yukon River my mind began to wander. The optical illusion of sweepers, branches like the one that had smashed my headlight down onto my nose, kept plaguing me. I'd look down for a while, or turn away from the wind, or drowse for a time, and when I looked up and ahead again, my mind would read the far horizon as a sweeper and I'd automatically duck. I knew of one driver who ducked so hard he broke his nose on the drive bow.

As we pushed along hour after hour up the river, I kept anticipating the warmth in Kaltag. It was impossibly cold. Herbert dropped back on the last little way into the village, the last stop in the Interior and the relief point, the escape from river travel. Kaltag stood high on a bluff overlooking the Yukon where the river made a big bend to the south, and I could see the glow of lights several miles away. Those several miles seemed to take forever. At least relief was in sight.

In time the dogs turned up the bank and into the village and there we were, three in the morning, third team into Kaltag and off the Yukon River for the rest of the race. We'd taken nine hours to do the sixty-five miles, averaging more than seven miles an hour, including all the rest stops. The dogs were one hundred percent, as fast as they needed to be, and I still had all fifteen. Three hundred and fifty miles to Nome.

March 16, 1985

Kaltag to Unalakleet: 90 miles

Skies overcast, then clearing in the afternoon, high 17° and low −40° (unofficial), with winds up to 20 knots.

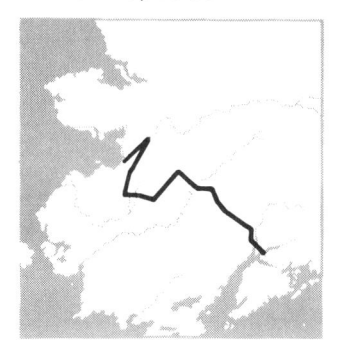

Strategy is becoming important as the racers draw closer to Nome. After a day of fine weather and good trail, the wind begins to pick up, spelling trouble ahead.

In the village I learned the temperature was fifty-two degrees below zero. In a way I was relieved. I was not turning into a lightweight after all—my misery had been for real.

I was supposed to meet Bobby Nikolai, who'd given Joe a place to stay the previous year. We had written to him earlier and even mailed him some straw for the dogs. As it turned out, Bobby was out of town, but his brother and cousin met me at the checkpoint. The two men gave me directions, but in my cold, weary state I couldn't follow and they had to guide me across town. Meanwhile, Herb's team trotted up the bank without him. Somehow he lost them just below the village and came running up the hill not long after the dogs. So I wasn't the only one to lose my team.

I gave my dogs their straw right away. Then I cooked up a quick batch of food, taking a pyromaniac's delight in the three-foot flames roaring out of the cooker. After they ate, the dogs curled into their comfortable nests of straw. Warm bedding was a special treat for the dogs, who were undoubtedly missing their nice, warm dog barn at home, especially in this kind of cold. Maybe they rested so easily because they knew they were on their way home.

By the time I finished the chores it was after four in the morning. My two hosts were still awake, watching a movie on a VCR. I caught glimpses of some bizarre character with purple or green spikes of hair . . . or maybe I was hallucinating.

Emmitt Peters had parked his team right across the way from me; I intended to keep an eye on him, old Foxy. I couldn't let anyone sneak out on me. With more than eight hundred miles behind us, the race was going to be faster, the competition more intense, the time for rest less and less. Emmitt's was just one of the dangerous teams I had to watch.

There was a room where I could sleep, and I took advantage of it as soon as I had finished eating and hanging my gear to dry. I asked the family to wake me in an hour and a half, but earlier if they saw any action over at Emmitt's camp. If he moved, I would.

Over a breakfast of hotcakes I had a chance to chat with Bobby's mother. One of her friends was visiting and they talked about their sewing projects for a big spring potlatch. It sounded like everyone in the village was making something for the get-together. I listened to them talk, but my mind was somewhere else, and I was heading into an automatic-pilot phase, just putting one foot in front of the other and maintaining the routine. One thing I did remember was to give them some candy and dried moose meat I'd sent in my airdrop for gifts. After picking through my people food, I found lots of juice and other extras to leave for them as well.

Emmitt managed to slip out ahead of me, but only by less than an hour. Barve also left, just a few minutes ahead of Emmitt. There was not much talk or kidding anymore. Everybody was focusing on Nome and keeping an eye on the competition. I was in third place and holding.

I was somewhat apprehensive the first few miles out of Kaltag because of the threat of moose on the trail. My thoughts passed to my good old .41 magnum back home. The first part of the trail rises to a thousand-foot pass through the Nulato Hills—spruce forest interspersed with clearings. It was hard to see ahead, so I stayed alert for a surprise moose. Herbert had been preparing to leave Kaltag right behind me and told me that if I had any trouble with a moose, wait for him and his old leader to detour us around the moose. I had put Joe's Dusty well back in the team to prevent him from chasing if we came across one. About six miles out of the checkpoint the trail opened out into a clearing. I stood on my toes trying to scope it out; it looked like an especially moosey place. When the dogs were halfway through the clearing, I saw it, and smelled it. My heart started to pound—a moose. When my adrenalin was up to full, I realized the moose was no longer all that lively.

This moose was cut into six large pieces and piled in a heap by the trail. Blood and stomped snow all around indicated a recent skirmish, but I didn't stick around to read the signs. The dogs cruised past the pile of moose without missing a beat. A few heads turned to sniff and then we were back into the trees past the clearing. Slowly I got my nerves under control again, but the scare was enough to make me impatient to climb higher into more open country, where there would be less chance of a surprise encounter with a more lively moose.

I wondered if Barve or Emmitt had shot the moose defending a dog team. But the kill wasn't fresh enough to be their work. Moose chew tender willows in winter when their other browse is covered with snow and the leaves have fallen. If it had been a fresh kill, I would have smelled a sour willow odor emanating from the gut pile; since I didn't, this one had been there for a while, and it must have been shot by the trailbreakers.

The dogs pulled toward the pass with me almost on my tiptoes, constantly on the alert for the slightest movement ahead. I kept a sharp lookout for the dogs, watching for some telltale movement of their ears, which would tell me quickly if they smelled or heard anything ahead.

After the bitter cold of the river we had a beautiful, sunny day. The cold from the previous night was nearly forgotten as the team trotted along a trail worn into deep snow. This part of the trail was one of the most beautiful along the way. The trip is about ninety-two miles across what's known as the Kaltag Portage. It's a natural trail through the hills that takes a traveler from the river and forest country of the Interior to the Bering Sea. Used for centuries as a trade route between Eskimo and Indian villages, it also was a supply line when the white men came into the country and the obvious route when telegraph wires were first strung from Fairbanks to Nome.

The trail generally followed the meandering path of the Kaltag River upsteam until the forest opened into the broad low pass at about one thousand feet, then dropped gradually from the divide along another serpentine river, the Unalakleet, toward the sea and the village named for the river.

As we climbed a gentle incline, the larger spruce trees gave way to a scattered population of scrub spruce: more of those foot soldiers climbing mountains and pushing north. The snow off the trail was deep and pure white and unmarked except for shadows. The squat little trees carried big loads of snow in their branches. The sun beat down generously, and I knew we'd have to stop for a lot of short rests.

The dogs trotted along easily at a medium speed. The day was too hot for them, so I let them set their own pace. I also stopped frequently to snack them and let them cool off.

The one I was worried about was Stripe, the only rookie dog in the team, the only one who'd never made the trip. He had held up surprisingly well, considering it was his first Iditarod. He could be sporadic with his pulling, sometimes leaning into the harness, sometimes resting back on his neckline, but he had a good attitude and would bark and lunge to go on every time we stopped. That helped keep up the spirits in the rest of the dogs. But Stripe still hadn't gotten used to wearing the dog mukluks on those big feet of his. He kept tugging at his booties and trying to shake them off. The conditions all along the trail had demanded the use of boots to protect the dogs' feet from irritation and injury. The other dogs were accustomed to boots, but Stripe lowered his head and put on an unhappy look every time I brought them around.

I tried letting him run barefoot from time to time to give him a break from the boots and improve his spirits, make him happier. But little by little, the skin between his pads grew in-

Racing Through History

As soon as there were dog teams, there were races. It was inevitable that freighters, miners, and trappers would brag about their dogs and run a race to settle the issue.

Races were an integral part of the life of many mining camps during the long, dark winters. The town of Iditarod held its first competition on New Year's Day in 1911, just half a year after its founding.

The Nome Kennel Club sponsored the best known of the early races, the All-Alaska Sweepstakes. Held annually from 1908 through 1917, the race followed a 408-mile trail eastward from Nome, north to Candle on the north shore of the Seward Peninsula, and then back to Nome. Interest in the race was high. When the telegraph reached the distant gold camps, the first subscribers—mostly saloons—bought hourly reports on the racers' progress.

Many of the sweepstakes teams were owned by businesses in Nome and run by drivers who made their livings hauling freight and mail. Other teams were sponsored by remote camps, which gathered the best of a settlement's dogs and chose the best driver from among their number. Scotty Allen won three sweepstakes with his famous lead dog, Baldy. John "Iron Man" Johnson won twice and holds the record for the event, covering the 408 miles in seventy-four hours, fourteen minutes, and thirty-seven seconds. For the seventy-fifth anniversary running of the sweepstakes in 1983, Rick Swenson harnessed the best of his and Sonny Lindner's dogs but could not match Johnson's time.

Leonhard Seppala won the last three sweepstakes, in 1915, 1916, and 1917, as well as several other races in the territory. Seppala continued racing his Siberian huskies after moving to New England and even entered the Winter Olympics' only sled dog race, in Lake Placid, New York, in 1936. In the two-day event, which consisted of twenty- to thirty-mile heats, Seppala was edged out by Emil St. Goddard, of Quebec. A name familiar to many who follow the Iditarod finished last in that competition: young Norman Vaughan. Half a century later, Vaughan was still racing, and in 1987, at eighty-one, he completed the run from Anchorage to Nome.

As Alaska's towns settled down from their rowdy gold-rush days, winter carnivals became popular. The first sled dog races of the Fur Rendezvous in Anchorage were run in the 1930s; they became an annual event in 1947. Today's Fur Rondy, as it is known to Alaskans, features heats of twenty-five miles run over three days; it is called the World Championship Sled Dog Race.

In 1927 the U.S. Army Signal Corps in Fairbanks sponsored the predecessor to today's North American Championship. The first race stretched fifty-eight miles from Fairbanks to the Chatanika gold camp and back. By 1946 it had become a four-day event with heats of eighteen miles, with a twenty-mile heat on the last day. Today it is run in three heats of twenty, twenty, and thirty miles.

Mostly Alaskans ran and won these races, but in the

flamed until he had to wear the boots a lot more than he liked. His spirits had begun to sink. He was pulling back.

"Hey, Stripe," I called out, trying to cheer him up. "How's that funny-looking dog, that Sister-pup? You're a tough old scrapper, aren't you, Stripe? Even if you are ugly, right, Stripe?"

But climbing up toward the pass on the portage, I decided I'd have to drop him once we reached Unalakleet. That would save his feet. Besides, I didn't want an unhappy dog affecting the rest of the team. I was glad he had made it that far. And if I dropped him at Unalakleet, he would be shipped to Nome rather than back to Anchorage. Nome was much closer to home, and shipping would be cheaper.

Several miles past the dead moose we were winding around trees again. In a clearing ahead I saw something large and brown and moving. The adrenalin pumped on full alert and I was up on my toes. But this killer moose was packing a large camera, and it had friends. A crew from CBS television was there with their helicopter and a tricky little camera setup that was planted down in the trail with a protective globe over it. I didn't realize what they were up to and stopped to chat with them for a moment, ruining their film footage of my team. Too bad. I saw their setup another time down the trail and I kept moving, trying to help them achieve the desired effect.

Everything went smoothly for the rest of the day, one foot after the other, mile by mile up into the pass. At one point we pulled onto an old snowmachine trail where I could rest the dogs without wallowing around in deep snow. Wolverine tracks headed off into the high country. Working comfortably on the hard-packed pull-off, I snacked the dogs, passing out whitefish and enjoying the warmth of the day. I had just finished feeding the dogs when Herbert rolled up. He also took advantage of the packed trail to stop and snack his dogs while he let them cool down.

When he'd fed his dogs, he shared some of his great trail snacks with me. I pulled out my camera and made him sit for a picture. I should have taken more pictures of the drivers and dogs and spots along the trail, but I'd been too preoccupied with racing and caring for the dogs. My photo album from the 1981 race includes ten rolls of film, pictures that help me share a little of the Iditarod with others—even if they do complain about too many dog shots. By this time it was too late to catch up. This year I was a racer, not a photographer.

Herb pointed out Old Woman Hill ahead of us. Old Woman had long been a rest stop for travelers on the portage. When the telegraph went through, the men had built a relay station in the shadow of the mountain. In 1980 someone had told me there was a tent set up in the same area, so Harold Ahmasuk, a Nome driver, and I had gone looking for it. We never found it. It was dark and forty degrees below zero and the tent would have been a welcome sight. Instead we built a huge bonfire, and I managed to burn several holes in my nylon parka from standing too close to the flying sparks. I had crawled into my sleeping bag for the few remaining hours until daylight, still wearing my mukluks, parka, and everything else. As I warmed in the bag, everything began to thaw and in time I was soaked. Then I really was cold and miserable.

This year, Herb said, there was a shelter cabin. I had just snacked my dogs, and stopping so soon again didn't seem to make a lot of sense, but I started daydreaming about how nice it would be if someone had come out from Unalakleet and set up camp there. I pictured a stove warming a cozy room, maybe some good hot coffee brewing. I could even smell it. A snowmachine tore out of the woods and through my daydream, swerving off the trail at the last minute to avoid colliding with my leaders. The machine came so close my first reaction was shock at realizing how very near disaster we had come, to losing the dog team, the race. Shock swiftly gave way to exhilaration. The machine meant that perhaps someone was staying at the shelter cabin. I bet they'd have coffee on the stove, too. The snowmachine made a big

early 1960s Roland Lombard left New England, where he had learned sled dog racing from Leonhard Seppala, and began racing in Alaska with dogs bought and bred from Seppala's Siberians. Lombard won eight World Championships and six North Americans. His chief competition was George Attla of Huslia, later of Fairbanks. The rivalry was intense, and several of their races were decided by seconds; eventually, Attla surpassed Lombard's record of wins.

In the mid 1960s the idea of a return to long-distance racing surfaced. Enthusiasts in Knik, near Anchorage, began dreaming of a race more thrilling than even the long courses run by the old trappers and freight haulers: a race from Anchorage to Nome. The group included Joe Redington, Sr., called the father of the Iditarod, and Dorothy Page, its mother. In 1967 they first organized a two-day race along a section of the Iditarod Trail to honor the centennial of the Alaska Purchase. Leonhard Seppala was invited to be race marshal but died before he could accept the honor. His wife officiated in his stead, and then spread the ashes of this most famous of the old-time dog drivers along the trail.

Encouraged by the interest of some, and pricked by the skepticism of others, Page and Redington in 1973 organized the first Iditarod Trail Race for the full distance. Financed by contributions, twisted arms, and the occasional mortgaged homestead, thirty-five racers left Anchorage on an adventure few had thought possible. Twenty-two reached Nome. Winner Dick Wilmarth, of Red Devil, covered the distance in

164

just over twenty days; the last-place finisher took thirty-two. The organizers had proved the race could be run.

one-eighty and roared back the way it had come.

We continued winding through the trees. There it was, just as I'd pictured it, a little plywood cabin, smoke coming out of the stovepipe and several faces peeking through the doorway. It all looked so good, in my hurry I left my dogs parked right in the trail; Herbert was the only team close behind and he'd probably stop, too, or at least not be too put out to find my team blocking the way.

People from the cabin came out and introduced themselves. These folks had decided to come out to the cabin and watch the first racers pass. It was pleasant to visit, but I didn't want to stay long. The closer we came to Nome, the less time we had for anything but moving. I situated myself next to the stove while they tried to locate a clean cup for coffee. I told them not to worry about how clean the cup was—by this time I was immune to everything. One of the women made a joke about saving my cup, now that a famous musher had used it. I joked with them; they really couldn't wash it now.

Looking up from my coffee mug, I spied a bag of jelly beans in a box. I don't eat a lot of sweets, and I hadn't shipped much out to the trail with my food, but for some reason the sight of those jelly beans raised a craving I hadn't anticipated. They became an obsession. I gazed longingly at them, in hopes someone would notice and offer me a few. It worked, and quickly, too. I sank my teeth into what turned out to be a watermelon-flavored jelly bean. These, they told me, were gourmet jelly beans, Ronald Reagan's favorites. They had two bags of them for St. Patrick's Day, they said. I tried to figure out the connection. I think they tried to explain it to me, but I also think I'd been on the trail too long.

When I realized I wasn't tracking very well, I figured it was time to hit the trail. The folks forced about half a bag of jelly beans into my hands. They must have seen in my eyes that I would have traded diamonds and gold for those fancy sweets. Once again I was indebted for life, and probably addicted for life, too.

I was just about ready to leave when John Cooper arrived. He must have passed Herbert—John was traveling fast again—and there was my team parked right in the trail. The problem resolved itself when he heard there was hot coffee. As soon as he had another "famous musher's cup" in his hand, he decided he might as well park for a while, too. The folks said they would be heading back to Unalakleet before long; I hoped Herbert would get there in time for some coffee. I picked up the hook and started down the trail, greatly refreshed and thanking everyone for the comfortable stop . . . and the jelly beans.

Just an hour or two of daylight remained. The traveling was good and I felt on top of the world. Maybe it was a sugar high, but I felt great. Or maybe it was the good company. The dogs seemed to pick it up, too, moving along easily and happily, even Stripe, although by now my decision to drop him was firm.

Soon enough the night came down on us as we descended the last of the hills onto the open coastal plain. The temperature dropped with the elevation and I had to reach for warmer clothing.

Moving along in the darkness, I used my headlight, now and again swinging my head from side to side to scan the snow near the trail. At one spot, the light sprayed shadows across a wide area where the snow had been disturbed just off the trail. I stopped to examine the churned-up snow and found fresh wolf tracks. They looked larger than possible, so much bigger than the prints my huskies made on the trail. They rambled all over alongside the trail, and as we worked our way across the flats, I stopped frequently, interested and curious about the wolves. I tried to figure from the tracks exactly what the wolves were doing. My dogs exhibited the same faint unease I always noticed in them when the air smelled of wolves: hasty glances, ears up, noses occasionally testing the wind, sometimes even a quick look back at me. The wolves must have been traveling, hunting as they went, digging in the snow for small animals. But we never heard them or saw them.

A few miles past the wolf tracks, we hit the Unalakleet River, and I knew we had to be approaching the village. The Unalakleet wound out of the pass toward the Bering Sea. Sometimes the trail followed the river; at other times we climbed the bank. By this time in the race the ninety-mile sections between checkpoints didn't seem so impossible, but toward the end of this leg it felt like an awfully long way. The last few miles were endless.

In one of the river sloughs we passed Emmitt Peters, snoozing on his sled and resting his dogs. That left only one racer in front of me, Barve, and we were coming into the critical stretch. With all the dogs pulling well, I felt good about where I was and how strong the team was. As it turned out, that was the last time I saw Emmitt before Nome.

We followed the river until sometime past midnight, when another snowmachine came bombing around a corner. I stopped as quickly as I could and set my hook, in case the operator didn't see me in time, and to prevent my dogs from turning suddenly into the path of the machine. The superbright lights on those things can be blinding.

Fortunately, the driver saw us. He said we had about six or seven miles to go; then he turned back toward town and soon was out of sight. In the darkness I could see the lights of a couple more machines, but when they saw my team, they turned back for town. The last machine headed off the river to the right. That helped. It would have been easy to miss that turnoff in the dark.

Those last miles into Unalakleet were tiring. After ninety miles on one trail we had to choose from a million snowmachine trails crisscrosssing everywhere. Making all those decisions, trying to pick the right trails, wore us down little by little. Here on the coast the wind was stronger and the temperature kept turning colder. In time I could see the lights of town, and I gave up looking for the trail and just made a straight line for the biggest lights. I was still trying to figure

167

out where to go when the buildings of town loomed out of the darkness. It was two in the morning.

People came out to meet us. Many of them knew I was from Teller, and they made me feel like family with the warmth of their greetings. I was the second team into the checkpoint— Barve had pulled in about an hour earlier. The dim world of the village brightened almost to daylight as the TV cameramen activated their lights and pushed the darkness away. The dogs stood up, looking around; a couple of them rolled in the snow. Watching the team stand alert after a ninety-mile run across the pass, I felt my confidence growing. They looked like they were going to be strong the rest of the way. None of them seemed very tired.

It felt good to be back in Eskimo country again. An older fellow stayed around and tried to make sure everything was running smoothly for me. His face was familiar. I'd seen him when he'd worked in Teller for a few months. Some time later I remembered his name was Oscar Koutchak.

I pulled the dogs in toward Jean and Kevin Buttons' house and proceeded to round up the Blazo, dog food, and water. With at least a dozen people milling around watching, I chopped seal meat, using a chunk of frozen beef for a chopping block. Then I went after the chicken and a few little whitefish. I took a small knife and shaved liver into the simmering pot for a little flavor. The last bit was chopping the beef, each swing of the axe driving it deeper into the soft snow.

After I had arranged for Stripe to be shipped out and tied him off, Jean directed me to their table, and in quick time I could see that some serious cooking was going on. Kevin and Jean had shanghaied one of their friends, a chef at the lodge in town, to cook me a meal. Everything looked and tasted so good, but I was too tired to be hungry.

All my gear was now hanging around their oil stove. I looked it over, selecting. Everything I could possibly do without went into a pile, which the Buttons kindly offered to mail home. Every bit of weight was going to count now that we were entering the last dash, Nome was only 269 miles away and, at most, two days of hard traveling. Every extra ounce I could take out of the sled was going to help. At four-thirty I asked my hosts to let me sleep just an hour and a half, no matter what. I think I fell asleep while I was still dropping toward the bed.

March 17, 1985

Unalakleet to Shaktoolik: 40 miles

Blowing snow, high 16° and low 0°, with easterly winds gusting to 37 knots.

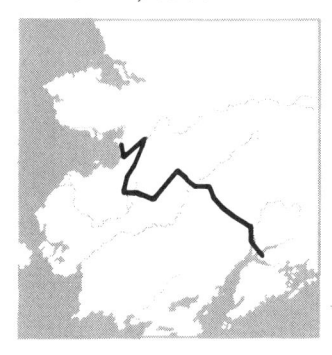

Riddles is in first place but knows her rivals are right behind. A fierce storm is howling down the coast. Having decided to risk going ahead despite the blizzard, Riddles must face the consequences.

A t six in the morning Oscar came by on his three-wheeler to make sure I was awake. He seemed intent on my doing well. The Buttons offered me breakfast, but I opted for an aspirin. As long as I stayed outside I felt fine, but a few hours in a heated house had me flushed and stuffy, my stomach in chaos. I had a glass of cold water and then started booting my way along the team. It was a slow task. With the temperature around zero and a breeze blowing out of the east, I could boot only a couple of feet at a time before I had to thaw my hands. The most convenient place to do that was on the belly of a complying dog, so every few feet I stuffed my hands under a dog's leg to warm them for a minute. One of the people who were watching me said Barve had decided that his dogs weren't ready yet and had gone back indoors. I would be first out of Unalakleet. The rest of the drivers—Emmitt Peters, John Cooper, Herbert Nayokpuk, and Dewey Halverson—who had come in during the night wouldn't be leaving, either. Rick Swenson arrived just about the time I left.

"That's the way to do it," I told the onlookers, "keep racing out of checkpoints when those guys are checking in."

Some cameramen, looking as half-frozen as I was, asked if they could film the team as I left. I tried to barter permission in return for one of their bright lights, to show the way until the sun rose. It would be hard going out there in the dark, especially working our way through town. Too bad it wouldn't have worked.

Somebody told me the weather was supposed to kick up. I didn't care for that news, but I had

171

to listen to the people who lived in the area. They knew the weather a lot better than some of those fancy instruments. A reporter from the *Anchorage Daily News* asked me about the nasty forecast. "Right now," I told him, "I have to go for it."

I was ready to go. We were in the last stretch, the place where the race is won or lost, and I was heading out in first place. The television people fired up their lights and started the tape rolling. In the blinding brightness I couldn't even see where my dogs were heading. Once we had passed out into the darkness, Oscar was there on his three-wheeler to guide me through the houses to the edge of town. Along the way I managed to catch the sled on a stop sign and wrap the team around it. With both of us struggling, we managed to free the dogs and sled, and I headed out onto the trail north to Shaktoolik.

It was a beautiful morning. The hills around us and the ice alongside the trail reflected an icy pink sunrise. Even Sister's dingy-white coat had a glow. All fourteen dogs strained into their harnesses, pulling the sled easily as we approached the first series of hills. To the east, a progression of low mountain ridges called the Whalebacks rose into the Interior of Alaska. To the west lay the Bering Sea. It looked deceptively placid.

We were leaving the rest of the teams behind, either on the trail to Unalakleet or resting in the village, but for how long I didn't know. They had to be coming sometime soon.

It could be tricky getting onto the trail leading up the first series of hills. And it was a little scary being in the lead. There was no fresh scent for the dogs to follow, so the risk of taking a wrong trail was greater. I had an advantage in that I had covered the trail in past years and could help the dogs find the way. Also, there had been a race from Unalakleet to Shaktoolik earlier that winter, and the markers were still there.

The sun took its time rising behind the Whalebacks, but as it got lighter, we hit the Pumphouse Road, then caught sight of the familiar, fluorescent pink flagging and turned off into the

Strategies

*I*n the first Iditarod races, when little was known about long-distance sled dog racing, strategy meant getting the dogs to Unalakleet on the Bering Sea in decent shape, then sprinting for Nome. But as experience and knowledge about racing have grown, strategies have become more sophisticated.

Some drivers decide to get as far out front as they can right from the beginning. These racers set timetables specifying so many hours of running and so many hours of rest, hoping to put enough miles between themselves and their competitors that when they approach Nome, no one will be close enough to catch them. If storms delay the pack, the race is won. Using this plan, and abetted by the weather, Joe May of Trapper Creek, Alaska, won the 1980 Iditarod.

A second strategy is to key the race to the pace of others, staying within striking distance of the leaders but letting them break trail. Being out front puts extra pressure on lead dogs, since the trail is difficult when there is no scent of other teams for them to follow. But dogs will chase the team ahead of them. Having thus conserved his dogs' energy in the early going, a racer only two to four hours behind the leaders can call up reserves and increase speed as he nears Nome, passing those teams that have been working harder out front. Rick Swenson of Eureka, Alaska, has won four races this way.

Drivers with experience in training, dog care, and nutrition can push harder from the start. Operating on a schedule but with refined food and rest

172

programs, these racers can ask more speed from their dogs earlier. And their schedules are precise. In 1986 Joe Garnie aimed to reach Nome in eleven days and eleven hours. He came close, finishing in eleven days and sixteen hours, but Susan Butcher came even closer to the mark and won. It was no fluke. In 1987 she won in eleven days and two hours—despite all the variables of twelve hundred miles of Alaska wilderness and Alaska weather.

Weather can make or break any strategy. Each year trail conditions favor certain teams because of where or how they have trained. Fast, hard-packed trails and warm days but cold nights benefit a team like Swenson's. May prefers "dirty" weather, which his big dogs can slog through; heavy weather in 1980 forced several of his big competitors out of the race. Warm, wet weather and even rain in the 1984 race favored Dean Osmar, who had trained in one of Alaska's warmer climates, the Kenai Peninsula; he ran the last five hundred miles without seeing a competitor.

Besides using sophisticated strategies, experienced drivers have refined their rest stop routines. So much work is involved in maintaining a team on the trail that any trick a driver finds to ease the load helps. For every minute he doesn't have to work with the dogs, he gains a minute to rest himself. Carrying a cooler in the sled, for example, means that the driver can cook two batches of food in checkpoints, where water and fuel are accessible, and feed his dogs a hot meal on the trail.

Racing at this level of competition leaves little room for alders. There was a steep bank on one side, and I chuckled as we passed the exact place where my toboggan sled had completely flipped in 1981.

About ten miles out we went past other familiar landmarks, including a large two-story building. On an earlier race I had driven the team up the bank to the building, just to take a quick look around. This was a different race. I was in a little more of a hurry this year. We'd already come 900 miles over some pretty hard trail in sixteen days, but now we had only something over 250 to go. At this point in the race, a single hour could mean the difference between winning and losing. No time to explore old buildings.

As we climbed and climbed, I kept thinking I had made it to the top, only to see another hill just a little bit higher beyond. But once we got into the hills, it was easier to find the way. It was fairly warm, too, between ten and twenty degrees. And I was making my own heat, huffing and puffing to help the dogs and push the sled up all those hills.

When I figured we'd gone almost half the forty miles to Shaktoolik, I fed the dogs from the cooler. We took a good rest.

I tuned in one of the Nome radio stations on my Walkman to find out what was happening behind me. The announcer reported that Rick Swenson was said to have checked out of Unalakleet that morning. But nobody knew for sure, and even the newscasters were speculating as to whether he'd really left or was just trying to fake us out. They thought he was still there, but then, nobody had seen him.

Swenson's ploy was good for me because it made me hustle to Shaktoolik. I wanted to hang onto that lead and gain as much advantage as I could. I figured he could be coming at any time; Lavon Barve, too. I was taking no chances: no extra stops, and no stops longer than absolutely necessary. I was just concentrating on putting as many miles as possible between myself and Swenson and the rest.

We pushed until we reached the crest of the last ridge. Two by two the dogs disappeared over

173

the top. Then the trail dropped out of the hills onto a peninsula of frozen marshland. The descent was steeper and more exciting than I had remembered. I had to dig into my brake for all I was worth to keep the sled from running over Stewpot. Going down those crazy hills was almost as much work as going up. The only time I could let off the brake was going around curves, and this was only to maintain some kind of maneuverability. I was glad when we got to the bottom. So were the dogs, I think . . . at least until we realized what we were in for.

As soon as we got down into the flats, it turned nasty, cold, and windy. The wind drove snow into every little opening in my clothes, even between the teeth of zippers. I had to stop and dig around in the sled for warmer gear. I changed into my big pullover parky, pulled the cuffs up tight, and put on my sealskin mittens. Everything had to be tight against the wind.

I looked the dogs over. "Sister, you old battle-axe," I said, trying to decide which dog to move up into lead with Dugan, to give him some moral support. Any dog, even a great lead dog, would get discouraged with the wind always in his face. "How's that sweet Sister doing?" No, not Sister. Things were bad, but I would need her if things got worse. "Axle-man, you're my man. Up you go with Dugan."

When we got down to sea level, I lost the radio station on the Walkman and slipped in a tape, Madonna's "Like a Virgin." What the radio station might have said wouldn't have changed anything. I had to stick to my strategy now, keep moving regardless of what was happening behind me. An hour or two were all I had, as far as I knew.

We still had almost twenty miles to go to Shaktoolik. Some years before, the village had moved about three miles north from its original site. Some of the old houses and stores still stood along the beach, and a few trail photographers and TV people were waiting there to take their pictures.

The weather was deteriorating. Wind whipped and swirled the crystals of snow into

error. In 1986 Joe Garnie missed a trail sign early in the race and went forty miles and six hours out of his way; despite a valiant effort to catch up, he finished second, less than two hours behind the winner.

The 1985 race was run through dirty weather, conditions familiar to Libby Riddles and her team. The willingness of both dogs and driver to brave those storms, combined with expert care of the animals, gave them the edge to win.

our faces in abrasive gusts. I pulled my hood down for protection, but the dogs, especially Axle and Dugan out front, had to muscle into it. Yet there was so sign of quit in any of them, despite the weather. For the two sisters, Minnow and Tip, this was almost a homecoming. A couple of years earlier, when I'd worked as a fish buyer in Shaktoolik, they had spent some of their puppyhood running and playing on the summer beaches. I was proud of them now, all of them, how tough they were.

By the time we got to Shaktoolik, the ground storm had grown into a full blizzard. I had mixed feelings as I approached the village. I hadn't seen many of the people there since I'd been working in the village during summer 1981. The race checkers in Shaktoolik, Lynn Takak and his family, had let me stay with them when I bought fish in the village; they were like a second family to me. I looked forward to seeing the Paniptchuk family also, and lots of other faces. But as much as I wanted to see everyone, and as good as the warmth would feel, this was not a pleasure trip. I had to steel myself to the business end of it and not lose any time.

All of those thoughts blurred in my mind when the dogs finally pulled me out of the frozen marshes onto the higher spit that fronts the sea at Shaktoolik. The leaders went through their usual antics, trying to take me to the houses that looked to them like good places to stop. Even though the weather was nasty, many familiar faces came out to welcome me. They even cheered. Franklin Paniptchuk, Sr., called out, "Did you learn how to cuss any better yet?" He always told me if I was going to get any better as a dog driver, I had to learn how to cuss. Between the force of the storm and the strength of the welcome, I would have loved to stay a week.

I tried to park the dogs somewhere out of the wind, but by this time there was really nowhere out of the wind. Huge drifts of snow, higher than houses and packed hard as mountains by the wind, blocked the only street in town and funneled the wind as it curled and twisted through

175

the village. I finally parked them where I wouldn't have to climb those drifts walking back and forth, and behind a building where the gusts didn't hit them quite so hard. Even resting, the dogs would use precious energy staying warm in that cold wind. I had shipped some straw to this checkpoint to give the dogs something to rest on, but I couldn't use it. The wind would have blown it away.

It was a little past two in the afternoon, and we'd been on the trail from Unalakleet for just about seven hours.

For once breaking my dogs-first rule, I went into the Takaks' for a cup of coffee. I felt pretty guilty about it, though. I kept my pullover on and chugged the coffee down so that I could get moving. I had to thaw out a little bit before the work. The storm was growing all the time, and the wind pounded the village so hard you could feel the house walls shake. Few people ventured out, and the ones who did either leaned into it or flew before it. The guilt won and I finished the coffee to go back out into the fierce wind and snow.

Flames swept several feet from the cooker in the wind. I was anxious to get a good hot meal into my dogs, one they really needed and deserved after the last tough miles. I had to watch them closely and hustle to grab their empty dishes before they blew away in the wind.

After they had eaten, the dogs curled up against the storm as tightly as they could, tails covering noses. It was frustrating to have straw for them and not be able to use it to make them more comfortable. But they were more in their element than I was.

Sixty miles of trail lay ahead. The first ten or fifteen miles were across the same sort of frozen marshland we'd crossed coming into Shaktoolik. Then the trail left the beach to cross thirty miles of sea ice to the village of Koyuk on the northern shore of Norton Sound. But because there wasn't as much ice as usual, the trail made a more circular route to the east, adding ten or fifteen miles to the distance. The wind would be in our faces the whole way. The lead dogs would have a tough time going into the wind, besides the difficulty of staying on the trail. No dogs had gone before us to leave a scent, and the way the snow was blowing, visibility would be minimal; I might not even be able to see the trail markers.

Lynn helped me change sleds. I took a good look at the finishing sled Ray Lang, our friend in Nome, had lent me. It was a beauty, long but light. It would be a pleasant change from my toboggan sled, which is a good sled, but not the greatest for handling and steering. Everything came out of the old sled. The new bag was smaller, so it was a tight squeeze getting it zipped.

Finally, weary from chores and the constant battle with the wind, I walked back to the Takaks' place. I took a huge bunch of things to dry, along with my people food and presents: chocolates and dry moose meat, which I made them promise to hoard for themselves. Hannah had a huge spread on the table, as usual. Year after year Lynn and Hannah had opened their home to the race, with the mushers sleeping all over the house and a table loaded around the clock with goodies. They didn't have loads of money, and they used reindeer meat from the village herd, but I saw food from the store, too. They always found enough to feed the race as it came through. They had received the best checkpoint award several times because of their hospitality.

Their place was crowded. It had been four years since I'd been there and I almost couldn't recognize some of the kids, they'd grown so much. I peeled off my pullover, hat, bibs, and what felt like three quarters of a ton of other stuff and then found a seat at the table. Right away Lynn and Hannah tried to spoil me with lots of food, but I had a somewhat queasy feeling. I felt a vague sense of urgency. It was time to come up with a plan of action.

The first person who had mentioned what he thought I should do was Dick Mackey, almost as soon as I got into the checkpoint. Mackey had won the race in 1978. This year, while his son Rick was racing, he was working as race manager, taking care of the logistics of flying the food drops to checkpoints and making sure the trail was marked and broken. He had come up all excited and told me he had just flown over the bay ice. He said there was just a big patch of fog up there, on the other side, toward Koyuk. "You should get going out of here," he said. "You can make it over there, no problem."

My home was only a couple of hundred miles to the northwest, and I knew a little about the weather here. The only reason for fog out there is if there's open water, and I knew that had to be farther offshore. I figured his fog was a blowing ground storm, which can look like a patch of fog from the air. Maybe Mackey was just trying to give me the incentive to get it in gear, to keep going and hang on to my lead.

The weather, especially the wind, was getting worse. Other racers surely would be reaching the village soon, and there was no time to waste. Leaving the checkpoint was a huge gamble. Was the chance of losing my life a fair gamble? I allowed a part of myself to swear I'd never take any chance that foolish, while the rest of me proceeded to make plans.

I wanted to talk with Joe. It would have to be my decision in the end to stay or leave, but I at least wanted to hear what he thought. Since the Takaks didn't have a telephone, Lynn, Jr., offered me a ride to the game arcade, where I could use a pay phone; Hannah Takak lent me a pair of boots and a jacket while my clothes dried by the stove. I had to hold my hands to my face to keep from freezing as the snowmachine skirted around the house-sized snowdrifts on the main street. Inside, in the bright lights of the arcade, I found the phone and called Ray and Carla Langs', where Joe was staying in Nome. But Joe wasn't there. I told Ray about the weather. "Just go for it," he said. Which was easy for him to say.

I had to keep in perspective that a storm usually seems scarier when you're inside a house, with the walls shaking and the chimney wailing, than it is if you're outside and properly dressed. Still, this storm looked like a killer.

Then I thought about the other racers. I'd already been stopped in the village for more than an hour. Any time now they'd be pulling into Shaktoolik, and whatever lead I had would start dwindling.

Time was becoming an important factor in another sense, too, as afternoon was passing toward evening. I'd have more trouble finding trail markers in the dark, and in the blowing snow the headlamp wouldn't be any help at all because the light would just reflect off the snowflakes and all but blind me.

According to the race checker, the weather was bad on the Koyuk side of the bay, too. I talked with Franklin Paniptchuk, Sr. He had lived here all his life and raised his family in the village. He had hunted seals out on the ice and caribou up in the hills. He had fished from boats and from shore and had lived through the best and the worst of it, and had stayed alive. He understood the weather and the ice.

I said, "Franklin, you think I can make it?"

"Oooh, yeah. You can make it."

He thought the chances were pretty good that the weather might clear up or be a little easier past the hill. Lonely Hill, as it's called in the area, or Little Mountain on the maps, is fifteen miles north and a little east of Shaktoolik, right on the shore of Norton Sound, and if nothing else, it might be something to hide behind if the storm got too bad. And if I could get halfway across the ice, I might be able to see the lights from Koyuk and head across without a trail.

Three years earlier a storm had stopped the race here at Shaktoolik. The leaders spent about forty-eight hours resting and playing basketball, waiting out the weather. Only one racer, Herbert Nayokpuk, had ventured across the ice. Herb lived farther up the coast from us, at Shishmaref, and knew the country and the weather. But after a night on the trail he had returned to Shaktoolik to wait out the weather with the others, saying he was the coldest he'd ever been in his fifty-some years in the arctic.

My dogs were fast, but not so fast that I could outrun all the others if we started together after the storm had passed. Swenson in particular was known for his fast team. I had a jump. But by

179

waiting, I might lose the lead, and the race, to faster dogs. Still, I kept thinking, "You're not really going to do this. You're not."

There was another voice in the argument, too: "You must. You must try for this. This is the most important thing in your life." Here was one part of me saying, "You fool, this is crazy," and another part was saying, "Well, for first place and $50,000, it would sure be worth it, wouldn't it?"

I finally reached Joe on the telephone. He'd been out on that ice in five races and he knew what the weather could throw at me. He knew this dog team, too. These dogs had run the year before, when he finished third in the race, so he knew they were tough and capable.

"Get going," he said. "Get your butt out of town."

Even so, I had a lot of reservations because I knew him. With forty-mile-an-hour winds, with eighty-mile-an-hour winds, he'd still tell me the same thing: "Go."

Wind gusts began to clock sixty and seventy miles an hour, driving walls of snow before them. Turn your back to wind that hard and it actually pulls the air out of your lungs—a sort of vacuum effect. The temperature dropped below zero as the sun began its dip into the Bering Sea. With the wind chill factor, it was minus fifty-six degrees. And darkness was fast approaching.

A decision had to come soon; no decision would be a decision. I had set a process in motion, just by thinking about going and making the plans. That motion gathered a momentum of its own, despite the warning signals flashing in my mind. At some point the possibility of departure became the answer instead of the question.

I made myself get ready to leave, not believing I would. I packed the new sled and got all my dried clothes from the Takaks' and booted the dogs, all fifty-six paws. When everything was done, there was nothing left to do but leave. Still I hesitated. Then Barve rolled into the checkpoint. The wind whipped snow around him and his boots crunched on the cold snow as he walked up. His face was raw from the wind.

"What are you doing?" he asked. "If it's anything like what I just came through, it's impossible."

That set me. "Impossible?" This was the whole point of all the work and energy I'd put into the past five years. Everything aimed toward one thing: Iditarod. I lifted the snow hook. "Okay, gang. Let's go."

I allowed only one thought: to keep my lead at all costs, taking it inch by inch if necessary. Winning the Iditarod was the dream that had driven me since I first raced. It was the dream that had rousted me out of a warm bed on many a dark, cold winter morning and dragged me over the tedious miles of training. My goal was attainable now, and so long as I was capable of putting one foot in front of the other, no storm was going to prevent me from achieving it.

Lynn, Jr., was giving me a start onto the staked trail out of town, but visibility was so grim I lost sight of his machine twice. Both times he stopped to wait for me. When he found the first markers, he stopped again and wished me luck. Then I whistled the dogs up and we took off straight into that north wind.

For a while I wondered whether I'd ever find the next marker. Then it materialized in a field of white, a single wooden slat sticking out of the snow. The visibility was something like you'd find in a blender full of powered milk, only this powdered milk was frozen and sharp and cut your face. We found the next marker, and the next, but progress was tediously slow. The dogs just walked. Those many miles in training that had taught me patience served now; otherwise I'd have been going out of my mind. The trail was marked well and that helped. Several of the markers were tripods, which were a little easier to locate than the slats. They were spaced a hundred to a hundred and fifty feet apart, but I'm poor at judging distances and even worse when I can't see. Moving from one marker to the next took total concentration. I had to ignore cold and wind and what they were doing to me in order to focus on that next precious stick of wood. I could only see thirty or forty feet ahead, which wasn't much beyond the front end of the team. I kept each marker in sight while searching for the next. I had to stop, set the hook, and walk ahead to look for the next trail stake. Once I had found it, I walked back to the team, which waited for me with great patience. They'd learned, too. Then we drove past the marker until it almost dropped from sight and began the process again.

Each time we stopped, as I walked along the team, I wiped the glazed snow off the dogs' faces. The wet snow plastered their fur, especially around their eyes. I could feel the dampness, too, but for the time being I didn't pay much attention to it. Out of necessity the scope of my thoughts was limited. All I could think about was finding those markers. I couldn't lose that trail or I might never find it again. Leads of open water sometimes cut into the bay ice, and if we found one by mistake, some of my dogs might get wet. At the least. Just the cold and wind could overcome us if we spent too much time here. More than one person had lost a life out here in storms like this. Hypothermia was a major consideration, the creeping cold that overwhelms both body and mind, driving out common sense and logic.

Nothing else existed in the world, just the team and me in this sea of a storm. When my mind could wander for just an instant, it didn't go far. From concentrating completely on finding the next marker, I went to arctic survival. I had to think about protecting myself and my dogs from the cold and the wind. Danger existed just a few feet on either side of the trail, a few feet from those precious markers, and my senses were on alert.

My concentration was so intense, I was aware of individual snowflakes. It was exquisitely uncomplicated. Nothing else mattered. Life had been reduced to its simplest form. All I had to do was find the next marker and direct the dogs to it.

The storm pounded us unmercifully, battering the dogs and me without discrimination. The wind forced snow into every little opening in my

The Race for Life

The first Iditarod race was run not in sport but in deadly earnest. In late January 1925, Dr. Curtis Welch diagnosed three cases of diphtheria in Nome. The seventeen hundred people in the community were largely Eskimos, who had not been exposed to the white man's diseases and had not built the necessary immunities. Dr. Welch feared an epidemic.

A call for help went out through the Army Signal Corps' radio relays, and a doctor in Anchorage found enough units of diphtheria serum. But more than one thousand miles of winter lay between that serum and the endangered Eskimo children of Nome.

Airplanes were considered. Just a year before, pioneer aviator Carl Ben Eielson had flown mail from Fairbanks to McGrath, marking the beginning of the end for the sled-dog mail carriers. Two airplanes were located in Fairbanks, both disassembled for winter storage. Pilots were ordered to make them ready, but territorial officials decided the risk was too great. A plane would have only three or four hours of midwinter daylight to fly, and if it were lost, the serum would go with it. The next supply would have to come from Seattle, months away.

Dogs and sleds would be safer for transporting the precious cargo. Through the network of the Northern Commercial Company, a relay of twenty freight haulers and dog teams was organized. The serum was wrapped against breakage and freezing, then loaded aboard a special Alaska Railroad train for the

two-hundred-fifty-mile trip north to the railhead at Nenana on the Tanana River.

By the time the train reached Nenana, the temperature was fifty degrees below zero. A Northern Commercial dog puncher named Wild Bill Shannon took the twenty-pound package of serum, wrapped it again in fur, and turned his team down the trail. Over the next five days drivers carried the serum through Nine Mile and Whiskey Creek, Bishop Mountain and Old Woman, places whose curious names make light of the inhospitable landscape.

As Shannon was leaving Nenana, Leonhard Seppala drove his team of twenty dogs out of Nome into a blizzard, planning to meet the serum at Nulato on the Yukon River. He dropped dogs at villages along the way to ensure a supply of fresh animals for the return to Nome. While he pushed through blizzards on the sea ice, dog teams in the Interior trotted on in the silent cold of the Yukon River. Temperatures seldom rose above minus forty. At each relay point, drivers took the serum indoors to warm it on Yukon cabin stoves.

From Isaac's Point east of Golovin, Seppala turned south across the sea ice toward Unalakleet, hoping to save time. He knew the ice could break loose from shore, carrying him and his dogs out to sea. Still expecting to run all the way to Nulato, Seppala met Harry Ivanoff on the ice, driving north and carrying the serum; organizers in Nome had not expected a relay driver at Shaktoolik.

Seppala took the medicine and turned back toward Isaac's Point. The temperature

clothing. Several times I had to adjust the Velcro holding my cuffs closed, strapping it tighter and tighter to keep the snow out. Snow plastered my face, then melted. The wetness on my cheeks and forehead made the cold and wind even more unbearable.

I longed to wear my goggles, anything to break the wind in my eyes, but the visibility was so poor anyway, the tinted shade in the lenses and snow melting on them made seeing that much more difficult. Instead, I turned my head slightly and peeked out of my hood, one eye at a time, resting the other for a moment or two.

Axle and Dugan were doing a super job together, taking the incessant commands, keeping the lines tight when we were moving and then waiting patiently, holding the rest of the team when I had to walk ahead to find markers. Not only did they have to lead the team into the wind without even another dog in front of them to break the blasts, but I had to command them often to direct them to the next stake. All those commands put extra pressure on them.

From what I remembered of the two previous times I'd raced, the trail crossed swampy lowlands for ten or fifteen miles before reaching the bay ice. The marshland had been relatively flat in my memory, but as the sky gradually darkened I had the feeling we were climbing a hill—an illusion created by the wind and the dimness.

The thought of turning back never occurred to me. For one, it would have been just as risky returning to the checkpoint as going forward. And after fighting for each hard-won mile in that storm, I didn't want to retreat even one foot. It would have been tough mentally on the dogs, too, leaving a checkpoint only to return to it and leave again. On top of that, they would pick up my feelings, and since I would have been downhearted for giving up, they would have been as well. I knew when I left the village I wasn't going to turn around. If I had to dig in and camp, so be it.

We pushed through the storm marker by marker until darkness overtook us. I had very little perception of time and I wasn't going to dig

183

out my watch. But we'd left Shaktoolik around five, with about three hours of daylight to work with. I didn't even want to think about how pitifully few miles we'd come in that time. This was it. I didn't dare go for even one more marker or I might lose the trail in the dark. I stopped the team next to a trail marker to camp—I didn't want any questions as to where I was when we started up again. This time I figured no one would come along and complain about our camping in the trail. I had to lean into the wind while I pulled a bag of snacks for the dogs out of the sled. They had already curled up in the snow, backs to the wind, noses under their tails. I stumbled forward against the wind through the drifts to toss a frozen whitefish to each of them. The wind pushed me back to the sled. With the dogs hunkered down, all I could think about was finding some shelter from that raging wind for myself. I threw all the gear out of my sled except for the sleeping bag and the big pullover. Then I yanked the sled crosswise to the wind and piled my gear along the leeward side with heavier stuff on top, hoping nothing would blow away. The last I saw of my dogs before I jumped into the sled bag, they were already half buried under a protective layer of snow.

Lying on my back in the tiny sled bag, I wrestled with the two zippers I needed to close, nearly freezing my bare hands while I worked with the sticky, cold metal. I silently thanked Ray Lang for lending me a sled with a bag more stormproof than the toboggan sled bag I'd left behind in Shaktoolik. The zipper proved tricky, though, and I had to quit and thaw my hands several times before I managed to close it. When I finally accomplished that little feat, I felt such a grand relief. For the moment I couldn't think of anything more in the world I wanted than to lie there and relax, free from the wind at last. For many minutes I enjoyed the comfort, happy as a clam in my little shell. I had survived so far, still had my lead, wasn't lost and, for the moment, had the wind out of my face. I didn't need anything else.

was minus thirty but warming in the blizzard, and at times he felt the ice moving beneath him. Trusting his lead dog Togo, whom he could see only intermittently through the blinding snow, Seppala crossed the ice, then turned at Isaac's Point for Golovin: in all, ninety-one miles on the return trip.

At Golovin, Charlie Olson took the serum out into fifty-mile-an-hour winds on the twenty-five-mile run to Bluff. There, Gunnar Kaasen picked up the serum and, using a team of dogs Seppala had dropped on his way south, headed for Port Safety. Another driver was supposed to meet him, but when he saw no lights, he passed the roadhouse and completed the last twenty-two miles to Nome.

At five-thirty in the morning Dr. Curtis Welch opened his door, expecting notification of yet another case of diphtheria. Instead, he saw an arctic apparition. Kaasen, covered in frost and exhausted from eight hours on the trail in winds that had hit eighty miles an hour, staggered into the room, handed Welch the package, and collapsed into a chair. The serum had arrived, 127½ hours after it had left Nenana. It was frozen but still vital.

I closed my eyes and swam in a rotating darkness. There on my back I felt half-giddy, so pleased was I with myself for having foiled the north wind. It ripped and howled, shaking the sled, but it couldn't get to me inside my walls of nylon.

"Ha! North Wind, you've tried to get me ever since I moved up to the coast, made my life a hell."

And it had. I had seen the north wind whip up big breakers for the cold to freeze. The waves turned to slush and then froze solid. But that was nothing compared with how the north wind treated the people who lived in the North. Every year Joe and I had to tighten our yard against the blowing snow of winter and seal all the miscellaneous buildings—the dog food shed, the tool sheds, the steam bath shed. Any openings were an invitation, and if a slit went unrepaired, the shed would fill up with snow and have to be shoveled out.

The north wind would blow snow as high as thirty feet above the ground; back at eye level it would sandblast exposed skin. Still the dogs had to be fed, which meant going out to the dog barn and digging out the door—the barn had two doors, so if snow buried one, maybe we could reach the other—and they had to be let out, which meant digging out their chains and raising them to the new snow level. There were times when we had to leave the dogs in the barn for three days.

If we'd left anything lying around, we could kiss it good-bye. Lighter things just blew away. Heavier ones stayed put until they were buried, and then they were lost till spring. One year the camper door blew off our truck; we never did find it, not even after the last patch of snow had melted.

"But now, North Wind, now I've got you. I can be as stubborn as you."

I rambled on, feeling deliriously smug and secure until a chill began to creep into the bag with me. This sobered my mood considerably. There I was, out in the middle of nowhere in the worst storm I'd ever seen. It was dark. The tem-

185

perature was dropping. I was nailed down for the night. And now, despite my best efforts, I was beginning to feel cold. As these realizations came over me, the tingles of fear came, too.

Everything I'd learned during my few years in Alaska came into play. Everything I knew about cold weather and arctic survival applied *now*. Any little mistake could turn my tenuous position very serious very quickly. It was all up to me. It was the next thing to impossible for a rescue crew even to find me . . . if anybody even knew I was in trouble. No, I was on my own and responsible for my own mistakes.

Gone were the grand feelings of having defeated the north wind. My thoughts and fears brought a flood of adrenalin, giving me plenty of energy to deal with my predicament. The main task was to get myself out of my damp clothes and into my sleeping bag—the sled bag wasn't going to be enough in this storm. I was all too tempted to crawl into the sleeping bag still wearing my jacket and everything else, but I knew from experience that as my icy clothing thawed, it would soak everything.

I wriggled around inside the sled bag, trying to extricate myself from the jacket. I worked through the chore, talking to myself like a parent to a child: "Take your jacket off. Now stop. Blow on your fingers. Warm them. That's good. You're doing great. Everything's under control. Now take your pullover out of the bag."

My pullover is a long, Eskimo-style parka, without zippers for extra protection against the wind; I'd copied the design from Joe's parka and sewn it myself, patching together tiny pieces of Tuscany lambskin to economize and trimming it with wolverine. It would be hard to improve on the design the Eskimos developed, usually using caribou and seal skins: the parka is warm, light, durable, breathable, and comfortable. The only problem is that it's difficult to get on and off. Because it's tight around the neck and shoulders, I have to dive into it and wriggle and wiggle to get my arms into the sleeves and then squirm my way back into daylight. I always looked silly getting into it, but never sillier than

The Support of Friends

Joe Garnie was in Nome, where the same storm was raging, when he heard that his partner Libby Riddles had left Shaktoolik. Friends advised him not to worry, saying that Riddles would soon turn back and wait with the rest of the racers for the storm to pass.

"She ain't turning back and she ain't waiting for anybody," Garnie said. In his confidence, he told the race committee not to send out a search-and-rescue party "for at least a couple of days."

That same night, Garnie declined to venture out to feed the dogs. Everyone looked out the window into the blowing snow. "It's too stormy," they agreed.

when trying to do it in a five-by-two-by-two-foot sled bag. After a few contortions I realized I had to go outside in the wind. I unzipped the bag, quicker than I'd zipped it just a few moments before, and sat up into the storm. It was wicked. My hands went nearly numb before I could squirm into the parka. I pulled it over me and forced my head through, but before I could manage the sled zipper again I had to tuck my fingers into my pants next to the warm skin of my belly to keep them from freezing. When I could move them again, I zipped the sled bag and then lay on my back, exhausted by the effort but snug and warm inside the pullover. The next task was to crawl into the sleeping bag, but I was going to rest for a while first.

I was busy congratulating myself for the success of Phase I, the pullover, when the new realization struck me. I swore violently. I still had my bibs on, the Gore-Tex snowsuit, and it was damp. If that moisture soaked my sleeping bag, it might be tolerable for one night, but if the storm pinned me down for a second night on the ice, which was not impossible, I would have an iced-up sleeping bag. It's not without reason that an arctic sleeping bag is mandatory survival gear on the race, but it wouldn't help at all if it were wet or frozen.

To take the snowsuit off, I had to remove the cozy parky I'd just maneuvered into as well. There was no way around it. I had to repeat the whole process, beginning with unzipping the sled bag.

That went as smoothly as it could, and then I whipped off the parka, exposing my now sweat-soaked body to the elements. I ripped the zipper down the snowsuit, pulled out of the armholes, and thrashed myself back into the parka. Again I had to warm my hands on my belly to prevent frostbite before I was able to work the sled bag's zipper.

In the dark, the storm was even more terrifying; the land was so hostile, and I was so alone. I may as well have been on the moon. Again I snuggled down into the shelter of the sled bag to rest up for the next task.

I wasn't very worried about the dogs. They were much better adapted to this sort of thing than a mere human. They were well-designed for the arctic weather, even a storm of this magnitude, and were no doubt tucked into tight little balls with insulating layers of snow drifting over them. I was glad I'd gone to the effort to give them all a snack, though. That was all I could do for them. No way could I have given them a warm meal in these conditions.

Slowly I started working around inside the confines of the sled bag. I wrestled the snowsuit the rest of the way off my legs. I felt like a regular Houdini when I'd finally worked it over my ankles and feet in that tight bag.

Next and last came the sleeping bag. I had to unzip the sled bag one more time, lay out the sleeping bag, then hustle into it and zip up my shelter yet again. After a little more wrestling and a little more cursing, I squeezed myself all the way down into the bag, zipped it all the way up, and that was that. I was in business.

Now I could take my thoughts off the immediate. Maybe by morning, if I was lucky, the weather would have let up a little. I tried to drift off to sleep, but throughout the night I slept lightly, waking to squirm from side to side when I felt stiff from lying on the narrow slats of the basket. At least I was warm.

March 18, 1985

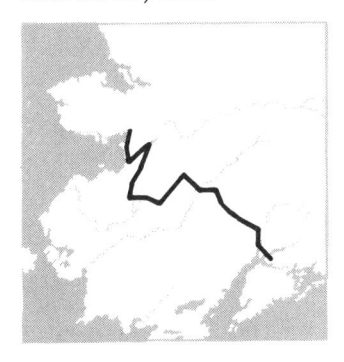

Shaktoolik to Koyuk: 58 miles

Blowing snow, high 20° and low 0°, with winds from the north of 60 to 70 knots (unofficial).

Uncertain of her competitors' positions, Riddles and her team fight their way through the storm. A veteran dog leads the team across a stretch of trackless sea ice.

Sometime in the morning I rolled over, half awake, and became aware that the haze of blowing snow was growing lighter. The storm howled as wickedly as ever, and I huddled down deep into that nice warm bag, pulling it over my head. Sleep came back so very easily and I dozed again for a while. Maybe an hour later, I awakened with a start.

"Holy smokes! I have to get moving."

It was a little before nine. If I didn't want to spend another night out on the trail in this storm, I had to get going, and fast. I hated to get out of that bag, but I ripped at the zipper, then dug around in the bag to locate a pair of gloves I'd slept with to dry them out. I felt a few moments of claustrophobic panic when at first I couldn't budge either zipper on the sled bag. Overnight the frost from my breath had frozen over them, and they were frozen stuck. In time, the warmth from my hands melted a little of the ice and one side loosened. Too quickly I was poking my head out of that warm, tiny shelter.

Everything was raging white; I couldn't tell where land ended and sky began. The freezing wind set me into motion fast. Standing sock-footed in the sled, I whipped off the pullover, climbed into the snowsuit, and wriggled hurriedly back into my parka. Then I fished around until I located my mukluks, which I had stashed under the sleeping bag to keep them from freezing solid. Pausing every once in a while to thaw my hands while I sat with my back to the wind, I laced the mukluks. Everything took so much more time with stiff, cold fingers.

My jacket and windbreaker were flat, icy

189

planks in the front of the sled bag, useless now. I had no dry clothing except what I was wearing. To keep moisture away, I pulled my rain poncho over the pullover. To keep the poncho from flapping in the wind, I used an elastic bungee cord for a belt. Stylish, Alaska chic, almost as good as big bunny boots with a dress.

As near as I could tell, none of my gear had blown away, but I did have to kick through a snowdrift to find everything. The packs I shoved into the sled as quickly as I could; the sleeping bag I crammed into a plastic garbage bag to keep it dry.

When I looked in the direction where the dogs should have been, I saw only a blank white expanse of drifts. The dogs were nowhere to be seen. I leaned into the wind and plowed over to where I had left them the night before.

"Brownie? Where are you, old boy? Come on, Sister. Dugan? Up you go, Duke." As I called their names, they began standing up through the snow, ghostly creatures rising out of the ground. They shook and smiled and stretched happily despite the weather.

They seemed especially glad to see their bag of snacks. Everyone got half a Salt Lake whitefish. I watched them eat hungrily and vigorously. They looked so healthy, if a little pathetic with big clumps of snow stuck to their fur. We'd been camped there nearly twelve hours, so they were well rested.

When they had finished their fish, I stood out front and called Dugan toward the next marker. All the dogs leaned into their harnesses eagerly, although it took a mile or two for them to shake out the stiffness from a cold night's sleep.

The wind allowed me no opportunity to be sleepy, but I'd had all that rest, too, and all my senses focused again on getting from one marker to the next. I didn't even think about Nome. I just wanted Koyuk, somewhere on the other side of this storm, the next checkpoint and some shelter from this fearsome wind. My friend Vera Napayonek would be waiting for me. She always wanted the women mushers to stay with her and had taken me in during my two other

The Storm

A group of teams pulled into Shaktoolik after Libby Riddles went out into the storm: Herbert Nayokpuk, John Cooper, Duane Halverson, Emmitt Peters, Rick Swenson, Sonny Lindner, Jerry Austin, Tim Moerlein. They and Lavon Barve, who had arrived as Riddles was leaving, stayed in the village that night, figuring that Riddles would not get far.

Race marshal Donna Gentry was in Unalakleet. "I was scared to death about Libby," she said. "But then, I knew Libby and had traveled with her. She has a good head. Once, when my life was in danger, I was so foggy I had to sit down and, in the snow, write out the steps to take, to get it all straight in my mind. I knew Libby could do the same. Still, it was dark and the wind was blowing, and I knew how hard that wind could blow; I'd been across that ice, too."

At daylight the next morning Jim Strong, the judge in Shaktoolik, called for an airplane. Rick Swenson had convinced him that Riddles was in trouble and persuaded him to have a spotter report on her location. Gentry called off the search.

"Libby hadn't had time to get into Koyuk," Gentry said. "She wasn't expected there until three o'clock that afternoon, and until then she wasn't overdue. Had we gone out, we could have been accused of guiding her across with an airplane, babysitting her. And if those guys in Shaktoolik had known where Libby was, it might have changed the race. They might have been out of there sooner."

The storm lasted three days.

Koyuk reported winds of fifty to sixty knots, but Koyuk is in a notch in the mountains and thus protected; winds on the marsh and the ice were undoubtedly higher. Many of the mushers were pinned down on the trail. Burt Bomhoff was among them.

"The snow was blowing like it was directed at us with a fire hose," Bomhoff recalled. The storm forced him and other racers to stop on the ice of Norton Bay.

"We went till the dogs quit," he said. "One after another, our teams quit. The dogs would do only so much in that wind."

Bomhoff, Raymie Redington, and John Barron spent more than thirty-six hours on the ice, much of it wrapped in their sleeping bags.

After a similarly difficult crossing, Duane Halverson reached Koyuk and stopped to talk with an Anchorage Daily News *reporter.*

"That darn Libby," he said. "I never thought she'd pull it off. I thought we'd find her piled up out there. If she wins, she deserves it."

races. I thought long and hard about her warm, cozy house.

The first few miles went fairly smoothly. I was able to keep the whole outfit moving with just a few directional commands to the dogs. They have a tendency to travel in a straight line, so in the light—what light there was through the storm—everything went a little easier. But I still could not lose sight of the marker behind me before I had found the next one out front.

The gray outline of a big hill at the edge of the bay ice appeared on my left. For a moment that caused a little concern. In previous years we'd passed on the other side of Lonely Hill, but the trail was different every year, and the stakes marking trail were clear, so after the first flash of panic I didn't worry any more about it.

I could feel the drop when we left land for the ice on the bay. The slight decline was all that told me I was leaving land. In the whiteout, everything looked the same.

Not even an hour after I'd broken camp, I heard an airplane droning in the distance and soon spotted it heading toward me. I guessed it was the mail plane out of Unalakleet, and when I saw the all-red paint job, I figured it had to be Ryan Air. I didn't know it at the time, but a friend and fellow racer, Clarence "Junie" Towarak, was the pilot. All I thought when I saw it was, "Damn. Now everyone will know how few miles I've really gone." At least it was flying away from Shaktoolik. Seeing it helped inspire me to kick up our speed across the ice. After having spent the night in such weather to keep my lead, I sure didn't want anyone to catch me. I thought about trying KNOM on the radio to hear whether anyone had left behind me yet, but with gloves and all the clothing I was wearing, a radio was just too complicated to deal with. Instead, we kept fighting every inch of the way, ever so slowly toward Koyuk. There was something to fight for, though, and the farther I went, the more tangible my goal became.

At more than one point I felt a strong surge of emotion as I watched those incredible dogs, moving out as smoothly as a machine through

191

the storm. I respected them tremendously for their fine spirit in that incessant wind.

Every once in a while I stopped to wipe snow from the dogs' eyes. "Poor hounds, all iced up," I said. "Here you go, Brown-dog. Give me your face, Inca." The leaders were always the worst—they took the blasts first. I decided to give Dugan a break, even though the going would be more difficult without him up front.

"It's okay, guy," I told him. "We're making it. No problem. Piece of cake, right, Axle?" I moved Dusty into lead with Axle. He wasn't exceptionally happy to be leading for me, but he seemed to head directly for the stakes on his own. The other dogs either couldn't see or just hadn't figured it out. The problem with Dusty was that he kept hanging back, letting the swing dogs run up on him and tangle his line. So I tried Penny, Inca, Binga, and Bugs. And then I decided I'd been saving Sister long enough. This was the bad stretch, this was the emergency that she could pull us through.

"Let's bring one of your girlfriends up here, Axle," I said as I put Bugs back into the team. "Hey, Sister, let's give you a try, old girl."

Locating the stakes became routine. The trick I'd used the previous day of exposing just one eye at a time helped. As soon as I spotted a marker, I could pull my goggles down over my eyes for a few moments of respite from the wind. The dogs, I think, didn't watch the trail much. They bore directly into the wind unless I commanded them one way or another.

As we followed the trail stake by stake, foot by foot, I became convinced the markers were leading us in a circle. I just knew we couldn't be going in a straight line. I expected to end up back at Lonely Hill at any time. We were going across, it was just the disorientation generated by the lack of landmarks, all obliterated.

Around noon I forced myself to take a quick break. I didn't feel hungry, but I knew it had been nearly twenty-four hours since I'd eaten anything. I'm usually the type to suffer food withdrawal within a few hours, especially while I'm working hard. In fighting this storm and cold, my body must have shut down some of its functions—fortunate, in that even eating in these conditions was a challenge. I never even had to relieve myself the whole time out there. With all the clothing I would have had to shed, it would have been close to impossible anyway.

I dug through my sled bag looking for the most high-powered stuff I could find: what was left of the seal oil, and Britt's big bar of Norwegian chocolate. Turning my back to the wind for a moment felt so good, a luxury. With gloved fingers, I tried to swig seal oil from the little plastic bottle without dribbling it all over my fur ruff. Then the chocolate. I chased it all down with a swallow of my nearly frozen fruit juice from the Thermos. While I nibbled, the dogs worked over their own high-powered snack, good-sized slabs of lamb. The lamb fat would give them the energy they needed. When I turned face to the wind and told the dogs, "Go ahead," they showed no hesitation. We were all anxious to reach the next checkpoint.

It seemed we'd come an eternity, with an eternity left to travel. All I'd ever known was this raging blizzard with winds ripping at my face and driving snow into every little opening, and all there was in life was finding the next trail marker. If I ever did find Koyuk, I was going to kiss the first snowbank.

My mind wandered now and again to the friends I knew were thinking of me. By this time they would know I was out in the storm. I was used to being out on the trail alone, but in a tense situation like this I drew on all my resources, including the faith those friends had in me. My friend Nancy Studer from Nome came to mind. Before I had even started training this season, she told me she just had the feeling this was going to be my year.

I couldn't imagine how long the day was going to be. I hoped to reach Koyuk before dark, but nothing around me suggested I could. Just when I was thinking the most pessimistic of these thoughts, the weather cleared—just for a moment, and just slightly, but just enough. I had to brush my eyes to believe what I was seeing.

193

Land ho! The unmistakable dark mass of mountains, barely to be seen, emerged through the veil of snow. I knew from experience that in large flat areas like this, distances could be deceiving, and it would no doubt be many hours before we made it to shore, but at least I could see it. We were closing in, and if I lost the trail now, we could aim for shore and not worry about ending up in Siberia.

I whooped and hollered. My dogs looked back at me like I was crazy. They had no idea what the big deal was and trotted on, unimpressed.

The storm closed in again until I could no longer make out the coast. The snow constantly pummeled the small patches of exposed skin on my cheeks. I tried to turn my face away from the direct blast as often as I could, but that was risky. Each time I looked away, I risked losing sight of the trail. Frostbite was a possibility. I had to do something, and quick. In a flash of inspiration I dug out a handful of unused dog boots. The soft bunting material of the boots is one of the warmest man-made fabrics. That wasn't why we used it; the material also was super durable and nonabrasive on the dogs' pads. I stuffed two or three of them on each side of the hood, being careful to keep the scratchy Velcro away from my skin, and that did the trick.

I must have cut quite a figure in my belted poncho and mammoth parka with purple dog boots sticking out of my face. More Alaska chic. But at this point I would have worn a clown's suit if it would have helped.

Actually, considering the conditions, I was comfortable. My mukluks were just starting to dampen, but my feet weren't cold. My hands felt a little cold from time to time, but just the thought that I still had one more pair of dry gloves warmed them some. With the dog boots my face was fairly well protected. All I had to do was reach that shore.

But I wasn't prepared for how long it would take to reach Koyuk. As we passed mile after indiscernible mile while I kicked and pedaled to help the dogs and maybe make us go a little faster, we didn't seem to be coming any closer.

As that first rush of sighting land faded, I had to draw on my patience again. I had no choice: no matter how impatient I became, nothing was going to get me across that ice any faster.

Then we ran out of markers. They just stopped. All of a sudden, there wasn't one where there should have been. I stopped the dogs and walked out ahead as far as I dared, making sure I didn't lose sight of the team, but I still couldn't see a trail marker in front of us anywhere. There I was, close to making it across, and I'd run out of trail.

Luckily, for a time the weather thinned again, and I could look back and see the last three markers behind me. I lined up on those three stakes and decided to strike out in a continuation of that line.

Sister was in double lead, with Dugan now, and as we proceeded out onto the unmarked ice, she kept pulling the team to the left, determined and persistent. We were on new ice, pale green with just a dusting of blown snow from the storm. The slick surface made stopping difficult, and Sister took advantage of that to have her own way. I knew we should be going more toward the right, away from the ice edge and toward land.

"Gee, Sister," I called. She kept going left.

"Dugan, gee! Gee!" But Dugan knew better than to cross Sister, and she was ignoring me.

"Aw, come on, Sister, give me a break. Gee! You stubborn old rattlesnake!"

It was no use. She bore on in her chosen direction, her ears back, listening but not heeding, and paddled along in a no-nonsense trot. She had me because I couldn't stop on that glare ice. When we found deeper snow I could stop and look around for the trail—and give her a piece of my mind. But the farther we went following Sister, the more tension I felt. That ornery dog. Why wouldn't she obey me? We had gone a couple of miles without markers over the new ice, always heading toward open water. This was dangerous.

"Sister, you airhead, you're going to get us lost. Gee, dammit! Gee! Please?"

Then I caught sight of something dark ahead of us. Could it be? It was. Sister had led us straight to a marker. Stubbornness can get you incredible places, I thought. And this time it was someone else's stubbornness. Sister knew where to go better than I did, and when we found the trail, I could have sworn she turned around with an "I told you so" look on her face. I stopped the team and apologized to her for all the nasty names I'd called her while she was dragging me across the ice. What a dog.

Apparently, a lead had opened up in the ice and carried a section of trail, with its trail markers, out to sea. The lead had frozen—that was the glare ice—and left a gap in the trail. How Sister found her way to the next marker, I'll never know, but thanks to her we were back on the trail again, finding the markers a little more easily in growing visibility. We finally were coming into the shadow of the mountains near Koyuk. As the day lightened, at last the shore appeared out of the mist and, better than that, looked like it was closer. I stopped and put Sister back in swing to give her a break and left Dugan up there by himself. Sister had proved herself again, always coming through in the tough going. Even with Sister, it would have been twice as difficult to cross that bay without Dugan. I was thankful to have raised a dog like him—such an incredible animal. The rest of the dogs in the team plugged away at that trail like troopers. I was proud of them all.

Those last few miles into Koyuk seemed the longest. As the strip of shoreline grew larger through the blowing, swirling snow, all I could think of was getting out of that wind and feeding the dogs a good, warm meal. I still wasn't hungry myself, but the symptoms were there. I was turning rummy and crabby, moaning to myself, wondering if we were ever going to leave this ice and storm.

Our approach was steady enough, and when I could see the buildings in Koyuk, I knew my battle with the storm had been won. My goal had been reached. I'd worry about the rest of the trail to Nome later.

A handful of people had come way out on the ice to watch. I thought most of them were kids. Only later did I find out that Vera was out there. She was the one who had been jumping up and down on the trail as I passed.

Vera is a special lady. My first race I'd stayed with her, and after a good but short sleep and a warm meal, she had led me by snowmachine to the start of the staked trail. We ended up sitting under the stars talking for more than half an hour before I finally hit the trail.

When I drew up to the crowd, the photographers were out in full force and people were asking me questions left and right. All I wanted to do was park my dogs; then maybe I'd be able to talk. I hiked the dogs up the bank toward town. I had to ask some kids which house was Vera's. I should have remembered, having been there before, but everything was tending to fuzz around the edges. The dogs had had enough of "geeing" and "hawing," so I asked someone to hold the sled while I picked up the leaders' lines and directed the team toward her house. They bunched up along the way, but soon I had them set out in Vera's yard, encircled by a fair-sized crowd.

Right then Vera caught up with me and gave me a big, crushing hug. She was so excited, she was going about a hundred miles an hour. She tried to tell me all at once where to tie the dogs and how her snowmachine had broken and why she hadn't been able to bring me a cup of hot coffee while I was still out on the ice and how much cooking she'd done.

"You're ahead, Libby, better keep going," she told me. "Don't stop for anything. You're going to get there and going to be first!"

The reporters and photographers crowded in while I cut the meat for the dogs, but I asked the first question.

"Who's left Shaktoolik?"

"Cooper, Halverson, Swenson," came the reply.

"Doggone those guys," I said. "When did they leave?"

"Around eleven this morning."

That meant they were behind by at least two hours and as many miles as I'd traveled the previous evening. And the storm was still howling.

"Well," I said, cracking a half frozen smile, "nice person that I am, I hope they have just as miserable a trip as I had."

We'd pulled into Koyuk at a quarter past five in the afternoon. That meant we'd spent about twenty-four hours on the trail from Shaktoolik. Subtracting the twelve hours we'd rested, we'd gone about sixty miles in twelve hours of running time—not too bad, considering we'd had to scratch our way inch by inch.

While digging around in my sled for dog food, I answered reporters' questions about my trip across the bay. I told them about how cold and miserable I'd been, that going out into that storm had been a stupid thing to do. But now I was across and somewhat giddy with success. I exchanged banter with the media people, feeling relaxed and carefree. I told them that after the race I might go to Hawaii. "Good idea," they agreed. Those who followed the race with camera and notebook knew their share of the cold, too.

In quick time all the dogs were eating and resting comfortably on their little piles of straw. The wind wasn't blasting quite so hard in the village, so they could have their bedding. I gathered my half a ton of frozen gear to be dried in the house. I had a bag of wet dog boots to dry, too; I wanted to make sure I had enough for the icy trail ahead.

Vera helped me tote some gear up to her house, talking all the while. She told me she wasn't going to let me leave until all my things were dried. "I know what that's like myself," she said, "and I don't want you out on that trail with damp clothes. It's no good for you."

Soon the area around Vera's stove was a hanging sculpture of my gear. Even my sleeping bag was hanging to dry. The warmth in the house almost bowled me over. Racks of cinnamon rolls sent their odor out from the kitchen, and pots full of goodness-knows-what simmered on the stove. The aromas were intoxicating. Sitting

Vera

*E*very year Vera Napayonek opens her house in Koyuk to the women mushers. She wants them to know that she will always be waiting for them with hospitality and encouragement.

"I enjoy treating the ladies here," she said. "I am an Eskimo lady and they're white ladies and they beat me, run the Iditarod. White ladies can do it. When they come in, I tell them 'I'm full-blooded Eskimo, you beat me, run that Iditarod Trail. If I had a gold medal, I would give it to you.'

"I am real proud of them. One thing I always tell them, no matter what: 'Just try to keep going, even if you don't win, even if you only make first top twenty, even if you don't make first top twenty, you reach the end of the line over there. You set out to reach that thing, you keep going, even if it gets hard. When I know you reach the end of the line, I'm a real proud person.'

"I want all the women—even if they don't win, even if they don't beat the men—I want all the women to reach the end of the line. I'm not much for words, but what I'm trying to say come out from down here, from my heart, with love."

down in a chair was such a luxury, almost too much so. I knew I couldn't stay there for long. I had asked several people to tell me when Cooper and Halverson came, and despite the comfort of Vera's home and a creeping feeling of confidence, I kept wandering over to the window to look for them across the ice. Between trips I slipped off to the bathroom.

At least according to my image in the mirror, I was still all in one piece. No frostbite. I soaked my hands for a few minutes in the warm water Vera had given me and stood with my eyes closed, enjoying the sensation. I pulled a few chunks of ice from my hair and worked out what was left of my braid, then washed my face.

When I emerged from the bathroom, feeling like a regular human being again, Vera herded me over to the table. She had rounded up a small gang to have dinner with us. Art Taylor, the ham operator, was there and, to my surprise, Varona Thompson, whom I'd raced with before, and Rob Stapleton, a photographer who was following the race. Sitting at that table with Vera buzzing around like a bee, I couldn't believe the food being piled in front of me. Vera had outdone herself, and I was thinking that even before she pulled a golden roasted turkey from the oven. Talk about hospitality on the trail!

I made a pretty good showing. I managed to sample everything and still have room for two cinnamon rolls. Then Vera ushered me into an extra bedroom. I planned an hour's nap, leaving her orders to wake me if other teams rolled in. I needn't have worried about oversleeping. Lying down and stretching out my back felt great, but now that I was alone, in that comfortable bed, my mind began racing and wouldn't let me sleep. If I played my cards right, and didn't make any mistakes, it was quite likely that I'd be the first one on Front Street in a day or two. Everything looked so good, my heart was nearly pounding out of my chest as I thought about it. Then the worries began to flow. Two hundred miles of trail lay between me and the finish line. There was plenty of room for mistakes—my mistakes. I didn't doubt the dogs even a little. They seemed to get better the more miles we traveled. They'd had a nice long rest out on the ice the night before, and I figured on a good, five-hour blow for them here in Koyuk, as long as no other teams came along.

The only casualty crossing the bay was a slight case of frostbite on Sister's flanks. It was my first experience with this problem in several years of running in some mighty cold weather. While feeding the dogs, I had noticed a slight reddening of the thin flap of skin on the top front of her hind legs. It shouldn't have surprised me: she'd had pups fairly late in the season, and huskies always blow their coats after having pups. Her winter fur hadn't grown back completely yet. I felt bad for not noticing it as we went across, but it was a mild case and didn't seem to faze Sister at all.

Cold had jinxed Sister once before, when she had delivered another late-season litter several years back. It was a particularly cold, nasty night, with thirty-mile-an-hour winds, so I had gone out to make sure the expectant mother was comfortable and out of the wind in her dog house. To my horror I found a frozen white-and-liver puppy. When I picked it up, it made a noise, a slow-motion, frozen moan. I was shocked; I hadn't expected it to be alive, not in this cold wind. I tucked the pup under my shirt, against my skin, and then moved Sister into a tin shed used for hanging fish. I spread dry grass over the gravel in a corner. It wasn't much warmer, but at least she'd be out of the wind. With Sister situated, I took the frozen pup into the cabin and worked with it for the better part of an hour. Finally it came around, and I set it on a board over a basin of warm water on the wood stove. Now it needed food, so I took it back out to its mother. She had dug a hole in the corner. I pushed the grass back into it and left the pup.

Half an hour later the grass was everywhere but in the nest, and the pup was half frozen again. Clearly, Sister just didn't know how to handle pups in winter. There was nothing to do but bring her into the cabin. I had to tie her to a table leg so that she wouldn't eat Danger the cat between deliveries. That night she gave birth to seven more pups, including Whitey and Stripe.

I glanced at my watch for the twentieth time. When the hour was up, I felt relief. Nome was waiting. I tried to stand, staggered, and then, after my hour of wakefulness, a wave of true fatigue passed over me. I sat back down on the edge of the bed, trying to adjust to gravity from a vertical point of view. After a few minutes I tried again, and the attempt to stand went smoother. I made it into the main room and faded into the nearest chair. Vera gave me coffee but I only held the cup, sitting there staring off into space for several moments before I got around to tasting it. As much as I could have used the caffeine, my body rebelled against its dehydrating effects and I could finish only half the cup. Then I took a cup of my cold medicine, this time mostly for the aspirin in it. I needed a little grease on my wheels to move again.

Darkness had fallen, but still no one had seen any sign of headlights out on the bay ice. I began to feel a different sort of concern for those drivers out there. Instead of worrying whether they were going to catch me, I found myself worrying whether they were lost on the ice. They had to be fairly close to Koyuk; they were probably struggling around trying to find their way. It couldn't have been much fun in the dark.

Someone knocked at the door and a vaguely familiar face entered the room. This was Debbie Altermatt's husband, Randy, who was teaching in Koyuk. I'd never met him, but I remembered seeing his picture at Debbie's house when we were training there before the race. A little sheepishly he handed me a small package, a present Debbie had insisted on: two peanut butter and banana sandwiches. When I was staying with her, she had discovered that the sandwiches were a vice we had in common and thought it would be a good surprise for me. It was.

Sandwiches in hand, I started preparing to move out. I had one more favor to ask of Vera, a refill for my little bottle of seal oil. She looked at me, surprised.

"What you want seal oil for?"

"For me, for the trail, so that I can keep warm."

"Libby, you always have seal oil?"

Then I gave her some moose jerky and a container of *akutug*, another word for *kamamik*, Eskimo ice cream, which I wanted her to have.

"Libby, you always eat *akutug*? Who made this? You made this? Boy, dried moose meat, seal oil, *akutug* . . . I thought blondies never eat that. I know, I got daughter-in-law, she's blonde, and she won't eat seal oil. Next time you come around, I feed you Eskimo."

Somebody in the house mentioned that a group of reindeer herders had traveled the previous day between Koyuk and the next checkpoint, Elim. They might have left some sort of tracks to follow despite the blowing snow. Supposedly, the trail was well-marked the whole way.

When I went outside, the cold slammed into me, shaking my poor body into consciousness. I repacked the sled and checked each dog and put on a few dog boots. The dogs looked up at me with interest. They understood the routine and knew we'd be on our way soon.

I had a protector for Sister's frostbitten flanks that would keep the wind from doing any further damage and maybe make her a little more comfortable. It was a homemade contraption: a neck loop connected with webbing that came up between the front legs, another strap between the back legs and up over the tail, two side strings tied over the back and looped through the tail strap, all to hold the covering material against the dog's sides. The outfit went over the harness.

It was shortly after ten at night when we left after about a five-hour stop. Still no headlamps showed out on the ice. After the tough crossing we'd just negotiated, this traveling seemed a breeze. I was rested and well-fed and all smiles. My gear was dry and cozy, and I was finally getting the feel of the new sled. The load felt light, the trail was packed and hard, a tail wind gave us a boost. The dogs moved out easily.

202

They must have known how close we were to Nome. Judging speed isn't easy at night, but I could tell we were flying.

The first few miles followed along the edge of the bay and then the trail turned up to portage over land. On the portage I could see the reindeer herders' snowmachine tracks, and the trail was marked quite well. My headlight was a must; there wasn't even the faintest glimmer of light from the moon or stars to illuminate the way. I couldn't even tell what type of country I was traveling through. All I could feel were a few little rolling hills, and I had the idea we passed trees scattered here and there.

I never looked back at the disappearing lights of the village, afraid to lose the sensation of speed if the lights didn't fade into the distance quickly enough. About an hour from Koyuk I was skidding sideways on the icy trail when one of my foot boards came loose. I looked down to discover that the bolt fastening it to the sled had snapped. This was more an inconvenience than a problem, but I couldn't put any pressure on that runner and had to ride with both feet on the other runner most of the time. That made steering the sled more difficult.

While stopped I could see the dogs standing in pairs along the narrow beam of the headlamp, the wind roughing up the fur on their backs. Snack time. I walked up to Dugan and Axle in the lead and gave them their fish first. When they had all eaten, I walked the line again, petting and encouraging each one. Tails wagged, and Tip and Whitey shook, kind of an "aw, shucks" response to the petting. Axle was feeling reserved; he sat down and lifted his nose to the stars. Minnow and Bugs rolled around on their backs in the snow. I was marveling at their playfulness when a sharp bark startled me. It was Inca. She dug at the snow with her front paws. "Let's go," she said. "Let's go."

Off into the complete darkness we flew, the wind pushing us from behind. The dogs paddled effortlessly up the hills. I tried to pedal on the upgrades to help them, but they pulled me up so quickly I was more a hindrance than anything.

The loose foot board made steering the inclines and drops tricky. The little two-pronged brake on the sled was difficult to get used to, too. This was the first time it was necessary—I certainly hadn't needed a brake crossing Norton Sound.

The toboggan sled had a brake bar the width of the sled, and I hadn't had to hunt to find it. This sled's brake board was only about four inches wide, and I was having a hard time hitting it. The new sled had a different feel, too, but the change was nice. The sled was light and, despite the broken runner, easy to maneuver, and the handlebar was slightly lower, a better level for me.

That night I had no problem staying awake. The speed of our travel exhilarated me, and so did the knowledge that we were first.

March 19, 1985

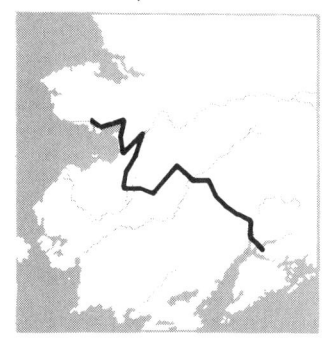

Koyuk to White Mountain: 94 miles

Clear, high 16° and low 6°, with northerly winds of 10 knots gusting to 20.

The dogs maintain a good pace, preserving Riddles's five-hour lead, but a mistake could cost her the race. She is tired, and the long trail through the hills demands all her strength.

Sometime after one in the morning we came out of the hills and the trail flattened again. I guessed we had dropped back onto the ice. Along that part of the trail the markers were farther apart. My concentration on the trail intensified. In the total darkness I couldn't pick out any landmarks to aim for if we went off the trail. And if we got off, I might waste precious time waiting for daylight to find the trail, or we might hit bad ice or even open water. Whichever way I looked at it, losing the trail seemed like a bad idea.

For a while everything went well enough. I could follow the snowmachine trail between the markers, but that grew increasingly difficult. The markers led us out onto a hard, icy surface, where no snowmachine would leave a track. I couldn't pick out much of a trail at all.

Then, with my anxiety increasing all the time, I couldn't see the next marker anywhere. I ground my teeth. But the dogs, if they noticed any lack of trail sign, didn't show it; they kept right on going straight in their happy Iditarod shuffle.

Something in the headlamp beam caught my eye. I'd been scrutinizing the terrain ahead for even the faintest trace of a machine track. We were on glare ice, which didn't offer much hope for seeing the corrugated tracks a snowmachine leaves on snow. What I did see was a scratch on the ice running parallel to our own path. My hopes jumped. It could have been just a small crack in the surface of the ice, but maybe it had been made by one of the reindeer herders' machines, probably from the underside of a ski. I determined to stick to that scratch like glue.

At home we trained on the bay ice quite a bit, and when we weren't on an actual trail, the leaders tended to follow cracks in the ice. This particular scratch was difficult to see, so I had to keep directing them to keep it in my sight. By now Dugan was so attuned to the lead commands, it took just a quiet word now and again, which he followed without missing a step. If he'd wanted to be difficult, he could have made the situation miserable. Stopping and setting the hook while I straightened him out would have been all but impossible on the glare ice. But Dugan made steering almost as easy as driving a car. I wondered how much of my thoughts and feelings were picked up by the dogs. It seemed the more intense our situation, the more solid our unity as a team. During training at home the dogs played their little games and tricks on me. There they knew we were just running around in circles. Somehow they knew the difference between that and the race.

Dugan moved left or right, the degree of his turn varying according to the intensity of my verbal command. A barely whispered "gee, gee, gee" turned us just a few feet to the right. A hard, sharp "GEE!" and he made a forty-five-degree turn. This made excellent practice for Axle, who was a good follower and learned from his partner. The way Axle had improved during the race amazed me. He was not the brightest sled dog, but he performed his duties. And he was one of the few guileless huskies I'd ever known. There wasn't a sneaky bone in his body . . . well, maybe he had one little sneaky bone. He knew he wasn't supposed to harass Danger the cat, but one day, not long after Danger had ambushed him while he was asleep, grabbing him around the neck and taking a bite out of his ear, he succumbed to temptation. But first he paused and held a point, just like a bird dog—except that he couldn't straighten his tail—and only then did he spring for the cat. Luckily for Danger, I called him off.

The darkness made it imposssible even to tell in which direction the land lay. I tried stopping the team for a moment, turned off the headlamp

Athletes in Training

One early racer, who had trained his team in the treeless area around Nome, went to Anchorage with a lead dog who had never seen a tree. Each time she encountered one, she stopped and shied away. The frustrated driver dropped the dog at the first checkpoint.

Today, trainers look for terrain and snow conditions similar to those of the race: flat river running, hills and thick forest, open tundra, and if possible, sea ice. This not only accustoms the dogs to the range of conditions along the Iditarod Trail, it also prevents boredom.

Many drivers begin conditioning their dogs as early as August, hitching the teams to wheeled carts. When snow flies, the real training can begin. Most aim to put one thousand to two thousand miles on the team by the first Saturday in March, when the Iditarod starts, but some work for more.

Some drivers train on a time schedule. Joe May, the winner in 1980, slowly conditioned his dogs until they could cover a hundred miles in twenty-four hours. Others make daily runs of specific mileages, usually thirty to fifty, varying the amount to keep the dogs from getting bored, and giving them an occasional day off. In anticipation of a close race, some drivers condition the dogs for sudden bursts of speed. Most drivers keep records of each dog's mileage in training.

As winter sets in, trainers bring the dogs to a peak of conditioning. Then, a few

weeks before the race, they take the dogs on shorter runs, enough to keep their muscles toned and their interest up, but not so much that they will be tired at the start of the race. The dogs will quickly return to top condition along the trail, and if they are strong, they will be able to maintain a good pace through the race.

and waited for my eyes to adjust to the darkness, hoping to make out a hill or ridge, but it was useless. I still couldn't see any trail markers, either. "Anxious" was not the word for it anymore; "sick" was more like it. Losing the trail here could cost me the race. All I could do was keep following that little scratch in the ice. I kept my eyes riveted to it.

We'd gone nearly five miles without markers, I guessed, when my eyes caught something that made my spirits soar. Such a small thing, but so incredible to behold: a skinny little stick with a length of surveyor's tape flapping from it. Relief. That scratch we'd been following could have been almost anything, a little side track to goodness-knows-where, but I'd placed my bet that sooner or later the track would take me back to the staked trail and I had won my wager.

The markers were few and far between in this area, so I still had to pay close attention to remain on the trail. When we drove back onto snow, I could see faint machine tracks to follow between the markers. We'd run nearly two hours since the last snack. Time to take a break. I dug out some lamb, which the dogs scarfed down greedily. They needed a lot of good food to keep their weight up when they were working this hard. I took a good stretch, too, to loosen up from the tension of the last hour. For all my tons of clothing, I could still move about freely. Vera had patched the ruff of my pullover in Koyuk. The fur had been damp for too long, and in the storm a piece where frost from my breath collected had ripped.

For my own snack, I took a quick drink from my Thermos of juice. I wanted more, but we had at least fifteen or twenty more miles to Elim and I wanted to save enough for one more blast. A couple of handfuls of trail mix and a few pieces of moose jerky made the rest of my meal. Then I sat on the sled with the light off, enjoying the darkness and the silence. A part of me wanted life to be like this always: just me and my dogs, alone in this vast, silent country, our goals always sure, living out of the sled day after day. This was the most seductive feature of the

Iditarod, the reason I would come back time and time again, despite all the suffering that went along with it: this intimacy I had with those fine animals . . . and with the magnificent land of Alaska. I had moved to this state when I was sixteen—and wanted to go so badly that I had arranged to finish my last two years of high school in six months—because I wanted an adventure. I had found it.

I decided I'd better move before I started getting all misty about the race coming to an end too soon. Odd, that while I was in such a big hurry to reach Nome, I was going to be sorry when it was all over.

The miles passed quickly under us in the darkness. Soon I made out the faint outline of the empty houses at Moses Point up on the bank. I'd been there once in the summer when the fish-processing plant was operating and the bay wasn't frozen. I could hardly believe it was the same place. People had been bustling all over and waves lapped all up and down the beach. Now it looked like a ghost town. If there was one spooky spot on the whole trail, it was here.

We passed the town in the eerie silence. Suddenly ahead on the trail, a light burst into view. It seemed too bright for a machine headlight. We were still moving at a good clip, but oddly the light didn't seem to be any closer. If anything it looked like it was going in reverse. No doubt it was an optical illusion; lights had played tricks on me before.

My curiosity about the light kept growing. The dogs didn't act like anything odd was happening, or even give chase. After a while we appeared to be gaining on the strange light. Soon it blinded me to where I could barely see the dogs. It was a machine after all. I almost expected to see a lantern sitting on the seat.

The driver was waiting for me. People in Elim knew I would be coming along, and this guy had come out as a spotter to see how far from town I was. I didn't try to tell him how bizarre his light had looked. I still couldn't decipher the tricks my eyes had played on me. We talked for a couple of minutes and I drank the rest of my juice. Then he turned his machine around and was hitting nearly sixty within the first mile. The noise faded into the distance with just the faintest red glow from the taillight. Then silence.

We continued down the trail at considerably less than sixty miles an hour. A few miles farther and more light games awaited me. A yellow light flashed at me from the bank, a guide to make sure we didn't miss the trail, but I could have sworn the darn thing followed me for at least two miles down the bay. The thought entered my head that they'd put the light on a long, sliding rail just to mess with my mind. I was happy to be well past Moses Point.

The trail took a turn up into some hills to connect with a road that led into Elim. A forest of stately spruce trees thickened on either side of us. I took deep breaths, inhaling the evergreen air. This was a different world from the wind-whipped country we'd come through. The smell of the trees was fresh and clean. The sun would be coming up soon, and everything in the world seemed good. We started descending and then the trail dumped us back onto the sea ice. We were close to the village by this time. The team must have heard dogs barking in town because all of a sudden their ears perked up and they took off at a lope, all excited about what lay ahead. That was exciting, to have a team frisky enough to run a mile or two this late in the race.

The sky was still mostly dark when I pulled into Elim before six in the morning. We'd made the forty-eight miles from Koyuk in about seven and a half hours, averaging seven miles an hour, including the rest stops. A handful of people met me at the edge of town. Fritz and Bessie Saccheus, who wanted me to stay at their house for my short rest in Elim, had headed out the trail to meet me, but somehow we'd missed each other. They were friends of Joe's and he always stayed with them when he went through Elim.

I couldn't see any sense in resting for any length of time with the finish line so close and a mandatory four-hour layover ahead at White Mountain, just another forty-six miles. I planned on two hours, max: long enough to put a good meal into my hounds and fix the broken foot board on the sled.

By the time I'd situated the dogs, Fritz and Bessie appeared. They wanted to help, but there was little for them to do until I finished tending the dogs. Then I could come in for some breakfast.

I cooked a quick meal for the team with lots of water in it. Even though this was a short stop, I had shipped straw here so that the dogs would get the most benefit out of their rest. I took off the dog boots and then turned to Sister's protector. The fabric was damp and I had no spare. The temperature wasn't nearly as cold as it had been, but the wind could start blowing again at any time. She had to have some kind of covering on that little frostbitten spot.

This close to the end of the race, I didn't know if I'd have the time to keep drying the protector, and that thought led me toward a tough decision. For Sister's own good she would have to stay in Elim. I couldn't in good conscience run her when I knew it might cause her discomfort. She was fit to run the distance otherwise. She wasn't a bit tired, and she really should have finished the race after having come so far. She was nine years old. She should have finished her final run on the Iditarod.

The checker, Marlin Paul, Sr., kept reassuring me as I deliberated most of this out loud. He would look after Sister personally and keep her at his house. Later I heard she even came indoors to watch the finish on television. Even though she wasn't going to be at the finish line with us, in my mind she would still be part of the winning team . . . winning? We had many miles to go.

Fritz and Bessie finally talked me indoors for breakfast, and a righteous one it was: big sourdough pancakes, eggs, and bacon. They knew what was good fuel for this kind of weather. They put a bowl of hot bacon grease on the table and I slathered some over my hotcakes. Working hard in the cold, I needed high-octane food.

I learned that Cooper and Halverson had pulled into Koyuk around midnight, almost two hours after I had left. They were now back out on the trail and they were coming. They were as concerned about me as I was about them.

My five-hour lead gave me a cushion, but if their teams were as rested as mine, they could push hard and cut their rest stops short. I didn't think they could catch me, but I didn't want to stand around and give them the chance. Somewhere behind those two, old Iron Man Swenson was following. He was known for his fast dashes along the coast to Nome. I would have to look over my shoulder every once in a while.

Thawed and filled, I was again deeply grateful for the lavish hospitality along the trail. These people didn't have to bring racers into their homes at all hours of the day and night. Race rules required us to carry our own food and mostly take care of ourselves, but Bush hospitality is a tradition and comes out full force during the Iditarod. The big meal and the warmth tried to put me to sleep. For a few minutes I sagged in my chair, staring without seeing. Rising out of the chair was the hard part, but I forced myself up and into a few good stretches. That started the blood flowing again. Outside the cold air perked me even more.

The dogs looked at me from their perches where they were strung out around the house on top of a snowdrift. Reluctantly I dug out a chain for Sister and watched sadly as Marlin Paul, Sr., led her away.

It was one of those superb arctic mornings. The air was fresh, almost vibrant, the slanting rays of the sun covered the snowy landscape in pastels. It was a morning I would have liked to show to anyone who wondered why I lived in the North.

The first few miles were easy going, flat-tracking on bay ice. Soon, though, we'd be turning up onto land to tackle a hill the mushers had come to call Little McKinley, so I tried to limber up on the runners for the workout soon to come.

I spotted a cabin the trail was leading us toward. We would start uphill from there. As soon as we pulled up the bank off the ice, I stopped for a minute to shift leaders. Dugan was doing fine, but I kept thinking he needed a break after leading nearly every step of the way. I tried Axle and Brownie, whom Joe had used a little in lead. I hadn't put him out front for the whole race, or even in training, and that was just as well; he didn't last long on the job. Brownie was probably too accustomed to running in the team. He bungled my verbal commands and wouldn't keep the line taut and generally made a mess of leadership.

Brownie did well enough with Axle to take us to the top, anyway. The climb gave me a hefty workout, making me run behind the sled all the way up. Once we reached the top, I took a breather. The dogs didn't need one, but I sure did. We'd just had a stop and a whitefish snack at the bottom, and it was mostly downhill from there. So as soon as I had caught my breath, we took off again.

I had moved "Duke" into lead with Axle and put Brownie back in the team where he belonged. I kept wishing I could put Minnow in lead instead of swing, but she was still in season and I didn't want her distracting the boys. Dugan and Axle had taken us most of the way to Nome and didn't seem unhappy about it at all. I just wanted to keep it that way and try to give them a break every once in a while.

The day was turning bright enough for sunglasses. Wispy clouds passed high in the sky. A hard, fast trail led us downhill toward Golovin. Wind had blown all the loose snow away and the sun had baked a glaze over the surface. My plastic runners were almost too slick on this surface and I had to brake nearly all the way down with the sled skidding sideways on the icy trail. About halfway, one of the P-Tex runners tore loose, the rough ride proving too much for the glued plastic. Fortunately, that material was laid over some thicker runner plastic, so I wasn't down to bare wood.

Despite the hard surface, the trail down was surprisingly rough and bumpy and I couldn't relax for a second until we had returned to sea level. The sun warmed the air as it broke from behind the moving clouds. Soon we'd be in

Golovin and the dogs would have a chance to rest and cool off for a while. A mile to two from the checkpoint I began talking to my dogs. "Hey gang! Checkpoint ahead. Oh boy." I'm not sure if it was my words or if they heard and smelled the village themselves, but they broke into an easy lope and held it all the way into town. By now the routine was so familiar they looked forward to the excitement of the villages, especially to checking out the local canine population.

With my team charging into a checkpoint after a thousand-mile run, I couldn't have been prouder. I was smiling from ear to ear, inside and out, at the idea of having a dog team that had come this far but went roaring into checkpoints like they were just out for an afternoon jaunt. I pulled into Golovin about noon and stopped where a good crowd had gathered. Then the team nearly had all its expectations for excitement fulfilled. A little black "rat dog" wandered through the forest of human legs, so small even my cat Danger could have whipped it. Stewpot set eyes on it. He started whining and barking and pulling the whole team in that direction so that he could munch on the little fellow. I started yelling, "Get that dog!" Someone reached down just in time and saved it from becoming big Stewpot's lunch.

We had a moment of confusion about where I should go in the village. My main concern was to park somewhere where I'd be pointed toward the outgoing trail. I was such a trail zombie, I had to ask the checker for directions several times before I figured it out.

Tending the dogs took only a few minutes, then I was talked into going inside for at least a cup of coffee. Once indoors, I was persuaded to have a tuna sandwich. As I nibbled dreamily at the sandwich, the little black "rat" peered warily at me from inside a man's coat. Information on the teams behind me was spotty. I didn't want to risk letting anyone catch me, so I had to keep moving. Cooper and Halverson had left Koyuk. As it turned out, they reached Elim about the time I passed through Golovin, which gave me a lead of about thirty miles and almost five hours. Even if I'd known, I wouldn't have trusted it, because the information at that point was so unreliable.

A fellow I thought I recognized was standing near the dogs when I went out. He had visited us in Teller, but he had to refresh my memory on his name, Ralph Willoya. At least I recognized his face. He gave me some encouraging words as I prepared to leave, about how well I was doing and how great the dogs looked. He was a big, steady, quiet, older guy, and he hung around until I pulled the hook and headed out across the ice of the lagoon.

We'd stopped for barely forty minutes. I was anxious to make White Mountain to begin that mandatory rest stop. The sun was out in full force by this time and it had burned away all the high clouds of morning. I let the dogs amble along at a slower pace. They had just eaten a full meal, and the sun made it a little too warm for them. It was okay. We weren't in a big hurry, but we did have to keep moving.

An airplane took off from Golovin and passed low over us a few miles out of town. The dogs were used to being buzzed and barely looked up at the intruder. Flat-tracking across the bay reminded me of our spring training back home: long, leisurely sunlit days and turquoise skies. These long flat stretches made me feel we were moving ever so slowly. Gradually the village faded into the landscape behind us. The sun beat onto my face, making me sleepy. I dozed for a minute or two at a time, standing on the back of the sled.

In time we reached the far end of the bay and the trail turned onto the Nudyutok River which led to the village of White Mountain. We didn't have much farther to go, just a few miles. I noticed ears perking up along the team and then they broke into a lope. They always knew before I did. They were eager to check out another village. Maybe they'd even have a chance at another rat dog. We rounded the next bend in the river and the village of White Mountain lay against a hillside, beckoning. It was three in the afternoon. We had four hours of rest in front of

All's Fair . . .

*D*rivers need to keep an eye on the competition. Many carry AM radios and tune in to KSKO in McGrath and KNOM in Nome, both of which carry race reports, but because the information on standings is often out of date by the time it is broadcast, drivers may turn to other strategems.

As they draw near to Nome, drivers appoint friends to watch other teams to make sure no one slips out of a checkpoint unnoticed and gains an hour's edge. Others sew tiny clocks into their hats so that they will hear the alarm to wake up without alerting competitors who are sleeping in the same room.

Drivers even seek to mislead each other. In 1980 Joe May reached Unalakleet first; his nearest competition was still on the Yukon River. He told a radio interviewer that both he and his dogs were ready to quit, that he didn't know whether he could keep going. His words were broadcast, and it is probable that the drivers behind him heard his confession of weariness. May and his dogs kept going, however, and won the race.

Disinformation is a common strategy of experienced mushers, and rookies consider it a compliment when they are taken seriously enough to require being misled. Veterans expect it but cannot afford to discount what they hear.

In the 1987 race one driver fed false information to a competitor, hoping to make her push her dogs too hard and wear them down. Not wishing to take the chance that the team he said was right behind would overtake her, Susan

Butcher cut short her rest stop. But her dogs had the stamina to keep up the pace, and the deception failed.

us, and then just seventy-seven miles to Nome.

Donna Gentry emerged from the crowd that had gathered and began straightening out the team. I called out, "Is that Long John Gentry up there with my lead dogs?"

I was so proud of my team, the way they had come loping into town, I just had to ask.

"Ever think you'd see dogs come into White Mountain looking this good?" It was an idle question, really; I knew the answer.

I wasn't prepared for the rest of the reception I received. The local people had turned out in full force to watch us roll in, along with a battery of news people. Then I spotted Joe, my brother Mike, my sponsor Steve Jones, Duke Bertke, and Nancy and Jack Studer. It didn't seem right for me to see them there. I had thought so much about seeing everyone in Nome that being with my friends and Joe in White Mountain was almost cheating. I wasn't ready to see them yet, not with seventy-seven miles still to go. But they were part of this effort, too, and they were happy for me and feeling a little pride themselves at how I was doing and their part in it.

Some racers have friends follow them from checkpoint to checkpoint on the race. Although there aren't any rules against it, I've never thought it was fair. Only the people with the big bucks can afford it, and even if your friends don't actually help you do the chores, they can help by giving information on how the trail is, how the checkpoints are set up, and more. For a trail-weary musher, even knowing where to take the dogs in a village eases some strain. Besides, I enjoy being independent out there, doing it myself.

One year I went to White Mountain to watch Joe, and after that I knew I'd never again follow him to all the checkpoints. When I saw him so tired, fumbling around, it was natural to want to pitch in and help him with chores, as I would have at home. It was sheer torture, standing by without being able to help. I had wanted someone to tie my hands behind my back. Now Joe needed his hands tied.

Everybody wanted pictures. As soon as I had

215

the dogs situated on a little hill toward the end of town, I obliged them. They took a few shots with me and a small group of Eskimo women, all of us with our parkas on. I'd worn mine even though it wasn't all that cold. When you're a little run down, you chill easier, so I wore it just in case. After a few photographs I peeled it off and put on my lighter jacket to do the chores. People around the sled made the tasks a little more difficult. All the talk sidetracked me.

I tossed everything out of the sled and slit open the bags of dog food. As I stood there looking at this mess, Joe came over, now that the crowd was thinning, to give me a quick hug and a kiss. It must have lasted all of one second, but those photographers were on the ball and caught us in the act. Should have known better.

Soon the charcoal roared and the dog food bubbled in the cooker. While it cooked, I went through all my gear, laying aside anything that could be sent home to lighten my load. I had to shoo some kids away so that the dogs could rest better. The veterinarian came by to look at the team and make sure they were fit enough for the last leg into Nome. Jim Leech, the head trail veterinarian, said he thought all the dogs looked very good. I *knew* they were in good shape.

We'd been invited to James and Jenny Oksuktoruk's house across town. As soon as I had fed the dogs, we caught a ride up there. Jenny showed me to an empty bed in a small room. I fell asleep instantly and just as quickly Joe was shaking me awake again. An hour had passed. I had forty mintues left until my enforced four-hour stop ended and I could leave. No other teams had reached White Mountain yet. From the reports I'd heard, I still had several hours on Cooper and Halverson, and I think I might have been going a little faster than they were, too. We'd covered the distance from Koyuk to Elim more than an hour faster than they had. But there was no use taking chances.

The one-hour snooze left me incredibly groggy. I probably would have been better off to have skipped it. I felt sick and cold and stiff all over. This had become the norm after my cat-naps: hit the pillow feeling good, if a little tired, but wake up feeling like a sled had run me over. In my stupor I had to sit in a kitchen chair for a few minutes to let the world come into focus. Once I was on my feet everything came a little easier; automatic reflexes took over.

Again I'd known the hospitality of strangers on the trail and I thanked the Oksuktoruks. They'd even taken in Joe and Mike and fed them. Very nice people.

The dogs looked up when I arrived, but they weren't going to stand up until I gave the word. They were trail-hardened veterans now, and they weren't going to waste a bit of energy. Putting boots on a few feet took about ten minutes. and then all I had to do was pack the sled. While I worked, Joe kept telling me, "Just a short way to Nome, now. Piece of cake." I wished it were true. What bothered me was the long, tough trail at night through the Topkok Hills. I was in a hurry, but I wasn't going to rush. No one was in sight yet, so I had at least four hours' head start. I gave the dogs a minute to stretch and shake out the effects of their own naps. Then I hooked the tuglines to their harnesses and we were ready for the last dash, seventy-seven miles through the Topkok Hills, the Safety checkpoint, and then to Front Street—the end of the trail.

Joe stepped away. "See you in Nome," he said.

I whistled up the dogs and we took the outbound trail. At just after seven in the evening it was still fairly warm, fifteen or twenty degrees above zero. I wore my pullover for the cold later in the night. Most of the sky was clear with just a sweep of high clouds in the west. That promised cooler temperatures before morning.

The evening was beautiful and again a twinge of wistfulness crept into my mind at the thought that this race soon would be over. I might race again, but it would never be the same as this one. This was special. I had new experiences and new friends I'd never forget.

My attention turned to the trail and the dogs. All the tuglines were tight, no sign of annoyance showed in the stance of their ears or in their gait. They all looked so good and trotted so

217

smartly down the trail. Dugan and Axle were leading. In swing with Inca was Penny, my sweet little invisible dog.

Stewpot began to lively up as we moved into evening. He was always happier running at night. Joe contended it was because he was part wolf, something I doubted, but the instincts were there.

We'd gone about ten miles when I heard a snowmachine a long way back. Some reporters had said they'd be coming along in a little while. I turned around to see how far behind the machine was—the country was fairly flat and I could see for several miles—and just as I turned, I saw the sled behind the machine tumble and pitch its rider into the snow. The driver never saw the flip and kept going. I stopped and tried to signal the driver to look behind him, but he didn't catch my meaning. When he came even with me I told him he'd lost a rider. He looked back surprised. Then he turned and zoomed away for his lost passenger. It looked comical from my vantage point, but if I'd been the one dumped, I probably wouldn't have thought it was so funny. If I ever had to ride the sled behind one of those things, I'd have a rope tied to the driver so I could give him a good yank if things got too wild.

They drew even again, this time with the crew intact. Soon they disappeared ahead and the evening fell quiet again. And what an outstanding evening it was. This was beautiful country of unblemished snowy hills dotted here and there with stunted spruce. The sunset had just begun coloring the sweeping clouds. At the peak of one hill I was even inspired to pull out my camera for a quick shot.

The fire in the sky cooled after a time, and the land and sky turned deepening shades of blue. Light remained for a long time after the sun went down. We followed the bank of a river where a few inches of powder covered the trail. The traveling was easy.

We reached the first of the Topkok Hills at just about dark. I snacked the dogs and reluctantly dug out my headlamp. I had waited as long as possible to put it on because it was a bit restrictive: the wires around me and the headband to hold it, and the battery pack made extra weight to carry. Nothing much, but even the little things can be irritating after a while.

After dark, when we drove into the hills, the fun began. A breeze picked up, particularly on the hilltops. We had to do quite a bit of sidehilling traversing these slopes, and my sled kept sliding off the trail on the downhill side. The wind out of the north helped push me off the trail. I constantly had to muscle the sled uphill on the icy slopes.

Going up the hills turned out to be somewhat easier than going down, for a change. At least going up, the sled would stay in the trail and the pulling was easy enough for the dogs with the light load and icy surface. Once we neared the tops, I had to pull the sled constantly toward the uphill side, standing with both feet on one runner, always fighting the sled to keep it in the trail and straight rather than sliding sideways down the hill. Going downhill was frantic, braking and pulling the sled against the wind at the same time. My arms and shoulders began to feel a little sore. The sliding made tough going for the dogs, too. Every once in a while, the sled slipping downhill would jerk the dogs along with it. The trail had to take one last good shot at us before we were through, it seemed.

Once, going down a hill, I lost the trail. I parked on a steep slope and walked around in search of the faint traces of blown-over trail. I found the problem: I had gone straight where we should have taken a sharp turn. And if I hadn't stopped the team where I did, we would have had to return uphill for quite a ways to rejoin the trail—that is, if I could have found the markers from farther away. I hardly dared to blink for fear of losing the trail again.

The bare round hills went on and on; we cruised precipitously down one and struggled up the next. They all seemed the same in the dark. My patience again was stretching in the strenuous workout those hills gave me. At least they couldn't last forever.

At the bottom of one hill we stumbled upon an A-frame shelter cabin next to a little creek of frozen overflow. The trail seemed to stop at the cabin but I knew that couldn't be. I walked around a bit and found we were supposed to go straight on through, across the overflow and into bushes. Walking around for a minute felt good. It stretched me out after the tight muscling on the sled.

As long as we were stopped, I figured the dogs might as well have a bit of lamb. They looked up expectantly at the sound of the plastic bag being pulled from the sled. Before we hit the trail again, I tried to pick up one of the Nome radio stations on my Walkman. I wanted to hear how the others behind me were progressing, but nothing came through except static.

I closed up the sled bag and we kicked into gear with a short scramble over the ice in the creek, pulled up through the bushes and then found the staked trail that took us up and down more hills. At the top of one I caught the Nome signal on the radio and learned that Cooper and Halverson had pulled into White Moutain almost an hour after I'd left. They had to wait four hours, too, so I still had five hours on them. I'd have to encounter some major disaster for them to catch me with that kind of lead, but I never discounted that possibility. The way my luck can go, I wouldn't quit worrying until we were in Nome.

More hills passed under the runners. Then, finally, we reached the last summit of the Topkok Hills. I could make out the vague leveling of land below us. With some measure of relief I descended that last slope. This stretch of trail had a reputation for weather nearly as bad as Shaktoolik, and over the years more than one of the top racers hadn't made it across those hills. Some actually had to scratch when their dogs quit or the weather became overwhelming, their races ended almost within sight of Nome.

We started down the long decline to sea level. About halfway down I saw some lights, and when I caught up, I found the snowmachine crew stopped for coffee. The driver said he'd probably detour to Solomon for gas and warned me not to follow them there. Solomon is a small village about thirty miles east of Nome, but it's not a checkpoint on the race. No problem, I thought. I'd just follow the staked trail, piece of cake. Then they took off, a red taillight disappearing into the black night.

Once we reached the beach, the trail led us back into the blasts of the north wind. I knew this same wind was tearing at the teams still crossing the ice on Norton Sound.

We headed due west, parallel to the shore, and those gusts of wind took us from the side, tossing my little sled off the trail. At first the wind was little more than a nuisance, just making more work to keep the sled on the trail. The fact that the trail had a slight downhill cant away from the wind didn't help much.

A particularly strong gust tumbled the sled over and I went crashing into the snow. Where I'd been so happy with the dogs' strength and willingness to keep going, now they worked against me. The team showed no intention of honoring my "Whoa!" command. While I hung on for all I was worth, cussing away at a high decibel level, they dragged me face down through the snow. It seemed like several minutes before I could work the snowhook loose and set it. When they finally stopped and I righted the sled, they looked back at me as if to ask, "Hey, what's holding up progress here?" The rest of the night was going to be very long indeed.

The snow was normal for the coast, scoured and packed by the wind into the density of concrete. For the dogs, that hardpack made it just as easy to pull the sled on its side with me dragging along as it was to pull it upright on the runners. At least the hard snow made it easier for me to hang on and skid along, better than plowing through loose powder. Easy or not, by the third or fourth time the wind tumbled me over, I was growing a little annoyed with dogs who didn't have the courtesy to stop for their boss when she was sliding along on her face.

To compound the problem, all the markers

221

were on the downhill side of the trail and I had the worst battle trying to keep from mowing them down with the sled. I tried commanding Dugan to the seaward side of the markers, and he'd do that for a while, but he was a stubborn little guy and figured part of his duty as lead dog was to follow the trail, not some ditch. So he'd take us back uphill. We'd come up on a marker and I'd have to jerk the sled uphill away from the stake, hoping to clear it before we slid back down. Despite my best efforts we wiped out a few as we passed.

We did have our moments of relief. Once, when we passed close to a cabin, the dogs slowed to take a long look. I knew it had to be Tommy Johnson's place and I'd heard a good story about it.

A few years earlier we'd lent some of our dogs to Ray Lang for the All-Alaska Sweepstakes Race. When he ran into a hellacious storm right in this area, he'd used this cabin for shelter and taken the dogs right in with him. The next year Joe was on this last stretch of the Iditarod, and the dogs were trotting along at their regular pace when all of a sudden they broke into a lope and dragged him up to this cabin, hoping to be let in again. Some of those dogs were in my team, and although they did give the cabin a good once-over, they seemed more intent on the westbound trail. Maybe they knew that direction led to their nice, warm dog barn, which was a better haven than this trail cabin.

Past the cabin we fought through more of the same terrain, dodging markers, tipping over, dragging, sliding. Skidding down one slope, I noticed Stewpot grabbing for something. He missed and looked back at it, and as we passed, out of the corner of my eye I saw a fat, blond, furry rodent rolling end over end across the snow. The animal must have been a lemming, the first I'd ever seen. Stewpot kept looking back at it. He'd missed the little rat dog, and now he'd missed a lemming, but he wasn't going to let another snack escape. For the next hour or so, every lemming-sized hunk of snow that blew his way he grabbed for, just in case.

March 20, 1985

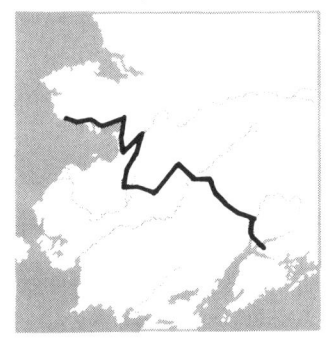

White Mountain to Nome: 77 miles

Mostly sunny, high 18° and low 5°, with northerly winds of 7 knots gusting to 13.

Riddles takes a wrong turn not once but twice, losing time. She is still ahead, however, and as the dogs run the last miles into Nome, the reality of victory hits home.

The next checkpoint, Safety Roadhouse, was just twenty-two miles from Nome. We'd been traveling along the beach for quite some time, so I knew we had to be pulling in there soon. Then I spotted a faint light up the trail. That would be the checkpoint. It would take a long time to get there—it always does—but at least it was something to shoot for.

Following the trail, I could have sworn we were moving up a hill, even though memory told me it was mostly flat around Safety. On the slope I had to dig the brake into the snow every once in a while to keep the sled going straight. Ever so slowly the light crept closer, and I began to make out the shapes of houses. Peculiar, I thought. This doesn't look anything like Safety. Where the heck was I? Cooper and Halverson were grinding after me, and here I didn't even know where I was.

The source of the light turned out to be a streetlamp of sorts, a floodlight mounted on a pole. Even though it was after one in the morning, lights showed in the windows of one house. I gave Dugan a "gee" command to turn him toward it. The dogs thought all this was curious; surely this wasn't a checkpoint. For one thing, no one had come out to greet them. They all stood watching to see what I'd do next. I tromped over to the house, glancing back at the team to make sure they weren't going to make a break for it. All heads were turned toward me, watching, but indicating no apparent plans for dashing on to Nome without me. I walked up the steps and tapped on the door.

In a moment the door opened and I squinted into the bright glare of a Coleman lantern. An older Eskimo man peered out, probably a little surprised to be greeting company at this hour. I was more tired and out of it than I had realized. Without ever saying who I was or what I was doing there—probably it was obvious—I blurted out, "Where am I? Is this Safety?"

"No," he said. "This is Solomon."

Solomon! A little village on the way to Nome but several miles away from the trail. Lost miles, and lost time. I wasn't the first one to make this mistake. Many racers have missed the trail in this area and gone through the village. Rick Mackey did it the year he won the Iditarod.

I groaned. It couldn't be. There had been no Y in the trail. I'd followed markers all the way. How could I have screwed up like this? The night was black enough, I supposed. Those guys behind probably still couldn't catch me, but the extra miles had taken away some of the cushion we enjoyed.

"Can I get you a cup of coffee?" the man asked.

I asked for water instead and gulped it down, then panicked. "How do I find Safety from here?"

He smiled. "Don't worry. Those guys won't catch you. Just follow the markers. They go right to Safety."

I turned the team around and headed for the first stake. I hoped it wouldn't take too long to reach Safety. It seemed the wind had changed, but I didn't pay much attention. I was too busy kicking myself for having gotten onto the wrong trail. A few miles out of Solomon, I began concentrating on the trail and saw brake marks from a sled. That seemed odd. But no, just a coincidence that someone had been dog teaming around there earlier in the day, using a sled the same size as mine, and a two-pronged brake, just like mine . . . Then it hit me. Everything came together: the change of wind, the sled tracks, the brake marks.

"Oh, you *dummy!* Those are *your* brake marks, and you are heading back toward White Mountain."

I shuddered to the point of physical pain,

imagining what it would be like to run into Cooper and Halverson and maybe Swenson at the bottom of Topkok, gaily running in the wrong direction. I was really messing it up. But then, this was Iditarod. Just when you thought you had it made, *wham!* It threw you a curve . . . or you threw yourself one.

I turned the dogs around, giving Dugan a "come gee," which he seemed willing enough to do. If he could have talked, he probably would have given me that command long before. He had to know by the scent of the trail that we were going the wrong way. A few of the dogs turned around and gave me funny looks:

"Does the boss know what she's doing?"

"Seems a bit touched tonight."

"We'll have to humor her a little."

I fretted and muttered under my breath all the way back to the floodlight where we'd parked just a half an hour earlier. Again I stopped the dogs by the light. The lights were out now in the house where I'd talked to the old man. My headlight batteries were losing their juice and the lamp was fading. I fished around for my spare headlight. I found it, for all the good it would do: the batteries were frozen and the lamp was useless. I was going to have to make do. Taking a deep breath, I started walking around, scoping the area, looking for the right trail, the one heading west. I shined the dim light toward the trail I'd just covered twice, then tried to find a reflector in line with them where that trail would go if it went straight through these old buildings. I walked around, peering around corners, until Eureka! There it was. Faint and far away a marker, the *right* marker. At my call Dugan and Axle swung the team around toward me. For once the snowhook held.

"Hey guys. Look what I found. The right trail."

They'd probably known all along which way to go, but like good dogs all over the world, they let me think I was the smart one.

Now I had a trail to follow, a checkpoint ahead, and the sound of pads hitting the snow. The night was still a challenge, though—plenty of miles left—and as tired as I was, I could still

225

make mistakes. With my batteries going out, finding the markers was difficult, and the wind blowing the trail half away didn't make it any easier. I had to pay attention. But drowsiness was creeping over me, my eyes wouldn't stay open. The wind pushed me down the trail past trail markers as if in a dream. I ran out of trail several times, and each time I vowed not to go more than a short distance. But the leaders seemed to find the way better than I could. It took us nearly an hour to reach Safety checkpoint. It was mostly thanks to Dugan and Axle that we got there. Every time I woke up from one of my trances, I was amazed to see we were still on the trail. When we finally saw the lights of the new Safety Roadhouse, it was an accomplishment to celebrate.

Safety wasn't what you'd call a lively place at this time of year, but the warm yellow lights made me think I was going to visit a long-lost friend. When I finally set my hook outside the roadhouse, it was four-thirty in the morning. The wind was still pushing at my back.

The checker, Jim Cole, a Nomeite and Iditarod veteran, came out with his clipboard for me to sign the sheet. Then he found my dog food in the pile of bags. A few reporters, mostly familiar faces by this time, watched as I slit open the sack and divided up slabs of lamb for my eager team. Moving around off the sled got my blood circulating again, and I began waking up. It took a few minutes to shake off the daze.

Nome was just a short jaunt away, but I wanted to give the dogs a good rest. The trip from White Mountain through the Topkok Hills had been a long, tough haul for them. But worse was the mental wear and tear on me for having taken the wrong trail and gotten turned around. So I decided on a two-hour stop at Safety, as much for me as for the mutts. As I left them and walked up to the lodge, they were already circling and digging, looking for comfortable spots with their backs to the wind. A few were already down and licking their paws clean.

The lodge, a new structure built to replace the old roadhouse, which had burned down, was dimly lit. That suited me just fine: bright lights and white walls would probably have killed me right then. A handful of somewhat bedraggled people milled around; a few others were parked at the bar. Many of them were reporters who had followed the entire race. No wonder they looked a little weatherbeaten. And after eighteen days and more than a thousand miles on the trail, I fit right in.

First things first. All my frozen gear needed to be thawed and dried by the stove. Then I joined the folks at the bar for a bowl of hot soup and a glass of juice. Everyone had questions. The atmosphere was relaxed, though, and they gave me room to take it easy and rest for a while. I was in a great mood, despite being tired. I'd planned the layover to rest the dogs, but I kidded the reporters, telling them I was waiting because I didn't want to roust everyone in Nome out of bed to watch me finish.

"I'll stay in Safety a bit," I said, "and arrive in Nome at a civilized hour."

Reuben, the fellow serving up the soup, asked if I needed hot water or coffee for my Thermos. Right. Forgot about that. I went out to fetch the Thermos. The air felt refreshing after the warmth of the lodge. As I walked over to my sled, I saw a curious sight. Dugan and Axle had curled up on the seat of one of the snowmachines parked near by. Those lead dogs were no fools. Why waste a nice, soft cushion? One of Axle's blue eyes followed me as I walked back to the lodge, the other hidden as he lay with his tail curled over his nose. Nothing else moved in his whole body, just that eye, making sure I wasn't going to do anything without him.

I accepted seconds on the soup and talked about the trail and the storm with Speedy, a hard-core mushing fan. Every year when he has leave from the British army, he hightails it over to Alaska to do volunteer work for the Iditarod. He also helps out on the Yukon Quest, the long-distance race between Fairbanks and Whitehorse in the Yukon Territory. He listened wide-eyed as I told him my adventures.

The heat in the room began to overcome me,

making just keeping my eyes open difficult. I finished the soup and took a big stretch. If Joe could have seen me and known what I was thinking, he would have had a fit. Safety was not the place for a nap. When the leaders go through, they check in, throw everything out of the sled they don't absolutely need, check out, and beat it for Nome, usually with challengers right on their sled runners. No, Safety wasn't the place to stop.

But the room was warm, and there were cots set up along a wall, and I had that five-hour lead out of White Mountain. The guys behind me would have to have atomic dogs to catch me. So I did what came naturally. In the last checkpoint before Nome, just twenty-two miles from the finish, I walked over to one of those cots, stretched out on top of someone's sleeping bag, and tried to take a nap.

I never knew the real meaning of "tired" until I had run the Iditarod. Sleep is one of life's luxuries, not to be taken for granted. I had asked to be awakened in half an hour, but as I never did fall asleep, I rousted myself off that bunk. Maybe this time it was easier because I knew it was the last time before Nome.

For some reason, I hadn't sent any new headlamp batteries to Safety. We only had an hour or so until daylight, but an hour was plenty of time for us to lose the trail again if I couldn't see the markers in the pale beam of a weak headlamp. No one in the roadhouse had the right type of batteries; the old ones had to do.

Outside, in the cold morning darkness, I made a quick rummage through the sled, tossing out anything I could do without to lighten the load. Jim Cole said he'd make sure someone hauled this extra gear into Nome for me. I made one last check of the mandatory gear. I didn't want to lose the race on a disqualification because I was missing a snowshoe. I had it all.

Dugan and Axle climbed down from the snowmachine seat when I called them, stretching and yawning. The rest rose to their feet.

"Last haul," I told them. "Let's go to Nome."

They were eager to go. All I had to do was

point them in the right direction. They looked so fit I felt I could have turned them around and gone back to Anchorage. Minnow wriggled around on her back, scratching herself in the snow, then rose and sneezed a couple of times.

"Watch out! Rabid dog!"

I teased her and gave her a few petting thumps on the side. She wagged her crooked tail furiously. Inca stretched out her front legs, yawned, then play-barked at me, clicking her teeth together. She looked up at me with eyes that seemed to say, "I'll do anything for you, boss."

Axle and Dugan stood at the front, all business, looking back at me as I worked my way up the line. I kneeled in the snow in front and gave them little scratches behind the ears and told them what good dogs they were. When I'd finished, they both shook their fur, Axle undulating from nose to tail, as if slightly embarrassed from the attention.

They watched for me to pull the hook, and once it was up we were on our way. The team moved slowly at first. I'd fed them heavily at Safety. But by the time the sun began lighting the sky over the sea ice, we were moving along smartly. The headlamp had faded into dimness, and twice I had to stop to search out a marker. It wasn't all that tough, though, and the sunrise held the promise of a beautiful day. Cape Nome, a huge bluff that had given the city its name, was a few miles up the trail. I'd been warned the trail would be rough around the cape, but it didn't meet expectations. We weaved around massive blocks of ice crushed against each other by pressure from the sea; the sled slammed into a couple of them on the tight turns, but this rougher stretch lasted only a mile or two.

Past the cape, the squat cabins at deserted summer camps collected snowdrifts along the shore. I relished the silence and those last few miles alone on the trail. Words of an Emmylou Harris song popped into my head.

I was born to run,
to get ahead of the rest
and all that I wanted

229

*was to be the best,
just to feel free
and be someone.
I was born to be fast,
I was born to run.*

In a few places the trail sloped toward the beach just enough to throw my sled off the track. I had to keep wrestling it to the uphill side. Perfect weather blessed us—sunny but not too warm for the dogs. Many people profess a hatred for winter and snow, something I don't understand when I see one of these dazzlingly clear mornings. Some could call this country a barren wasteland, but I knew better. It has a rare beauty, and I thrive on it. Those of us who live here appreciate its beauty, knowing also its capacity for savagery.

The snarl of snowmachines off in the distance broke into my reverie. Ten or fifteen minutes later I saw them, a handful of photographers waiting near a steep bank we had to traverse. They made their shots while I concentrated on guiding the sled down the bank. Then they all roared off, zooming up the trail.

I dug around in the sled looking for my Walkman. It was coming time to snack the dogs so I stopped, set the hook, and gave every dog a hunk of whitefish. They seemed anxious, as if they knew how close to Nome we were. And maybe they did. Dogs have great memories for places they've been before. Just for kicks I decided to tune in the radio to hear what they were saying about me. But as it turned out, listening to the reports was strangely disquieting. It hadn't really hit me that I was going to win this race. Victory had seemed more a figment of imagination than a definite possibility until hearing someone else talk about it, on the radio, turned the figment of imagination into a hard reality, breaking through the wall of casual pessimism that had kept me conveniently sane through all that had happened so far.

In the place of that pessimism was a thickening numbness. It must have been a survival mechanism to help me cope with the overload of emotion. With the worst of the trail behind

A Happy Fan

When Libby Riddles had arrived in Koyuk, Vera Napayonek had felt confident that she would win. But it was not until the television cameras picked up Riddles coming into Nome that the reality of victory hit.

"I sit down and cry right there," said Napayonek, pointing to a chair. "I sit down there, all the tissue right there, going crazy, just cheering. I was so happy for her. First woman to ever win the Iditarod race. I wish I was there to hug her. 'Libby, Libby, Libby,' I cried."

me and the finish line so near, it suddenly felt like it had been too easy to reach this point, too easy to be nearing this Everest of a goal I'd set for myself. I had been prepared mentally to struggle for years if that had been necessary, but here it was, only fifteen miles away. I tried to force the thoughts back. I couldn't think about it too much. But that's all that was on the radio. The DJ dedicated a song to all of us out on the trail. The song was sung by Hobo Jim, an Alaska picker from the Kenai Peninsula and an end-of-the-trail fixture. I'd heard it a million times, but now, listening with only one ear, so to speak, I suddenly started paying attention and heard the last verse as if for the first time:

I just pulled out of Safety,
I'm on the trail all alone
I'm doing fine and picking up time
And running into Nome.
There's no sled tracks in front of me
And no one on my tail.
I did, I did, I did the Iditarod Trail.

That did it. Those words had been written just for me, and I have to say, this tough dog driver lost it. There were tears running down all over my face. Everything had hit center all at once. Such a feeling to be on the edge of my dream. It just felt so good it hurt.

I had to turn the radio off for a while to regain myself. When I did, more motor noises came through, the thwop-thwop-thwop of a helicopter. Soon the machine was hovering in front of us whipping the snow into our faces. A cameraman leaned out an open door, filming the team as we moved down the trail. The miniature snowstorm they kicked up was less than entertaining, but it wasn't the first time we'd had snow in our faces. So we gritted our teeth and squinted our eyes and drove on into the ministorm, taking it as part of the job. They made their footage and then thwopped off toward Nome, leaving natural weather in their wake.

The closer our approach to Nome, the more machines we encountered.

People waved and hollered and clapped for me and the dogs as we passed. I smiled and waved back. These people gave me the courage to try the radio again. It sounded like Nome was going wild. Being from Teller, which is a mere seventy miles away from Nome and thus practically a suburb, at least by Alaska standards, I figured on a warm welcome, but it sounded more than warm. The radio announcers kept saying this was the first team from the northwest part of the state to win the race. Now the racers from this area—Joe, and Herbie Nayokpuk and Roger Nordlum and Jerry Austin and Isaac Okleasik and many more—are all tough, and yet here I was, the first from the area to win. The thought was boggling.

The people from Teller and Brevig were going to be pretty happy. They'd always been proud of the dogs from their villages, and many of them had at least some part in getting my team into the race this year. Not the least of their help was monetary. The Teller Entertainment Committee, whose main business was the bingo games in town, had paid my $1,049 entrance fee, and despite the difficulty of raising money in a place where most people don't have much ready cash, they had given me a check for another $2,000 to help me with my expenses for the race.

As we neared Howard Farley's camp, just four miles from Nome, I wondered whether the dogs would remember that we'd worked there the previous summer. It had been Howard's job, but when he had decided to do some commercial fishing in Norton Sound, I had spelled him. Twice a day, seven days a week, I drove twelve dogs down the sandy beach to meet the bus. We would run back alongside the road with the bus while all the tourists snapped pictures. It had been good training for the young dogs, good conditioning for the older animals, and good practice for me, harnessing and unharnessing the dogs quickly so that I could go answer questions from the people on the tour. For my last run I had left the yearlings at Howard's camp and hitched up my Iditarod team, the same dogs I was driving now; they gave me quite a spin down the beach, and even the bus driver noticed the extra power.

Now we were up on the tundra on the north side of the road, away from the beach. As we passed Howard's camp, my team barely looked at his dogs. Here I'd been worried they might cross over for a visit, but all they did was give a quick look and chug along down the trail. The buildings of Nome were in sight now and I saw more action along the trail all the time. The team sensed the excitement as we passed by the Fort Davis Roadhouse and they broke into a lope. Not bad for a bunch of dogs who had just come twelve hundred miles. The sudden burst of speed gave me a thrill. What heart these dogs had, after so many days on the trail. Oh, the things I was going to do for them when this was all done! A box of dog biscuits and a steak for each one, mountains of fresh straw to lie on, days of leisure to soak up the sun.

I couldn't foretell the approaching chaos and that was probably good. I had never once thought about what would happen afterward. My hopes had taken me only as far as the wooden arch over Front Street. All I'd ever really hoped for was to earn the respect of my fellow competitors and to let these dogs Joe and I had raised from pups prove they were as good as any team around.

If anyone had told me that I was on the verge of becoming a national representative for my sport and an Alaska heroine, my poor little brain would have short-circuited. I had never thought much about being the first woman to win the race. I thought of myself as just a sled dog racer, not a woman sled dog racer. But there was no denying that if my winning encouraged other women not to underestimate themselves, then I was happy to have helped. It's just that I considered it accidental.

What fills me with pride was that I'd proven myself to be a real Alaskan, even though I hadn't been born here. For someone who'd grown up as a tumbleweed, always moving, this was a great personal accomplishment: to feel I belonged among those people whom I admired so thoroughly.

But all of this, and much more, came later. For

233

the time being, I pedaled behind the dogs innocently enough. As long as there was trail in front of us, there was business to attend to. A photo crew stopped me to strap a video camera onto my sled. Their nervous hustling was amusing. After all, the nearest team was more than twenty-five miles away.

We moved off again onto a confusing trail that crossed from one side of the road to the other.

In the crowd I recognized Dave and Sue from Teller. I stopped for a minute to talk with them while I tried to figure out whether we were on the right side of the road. The other side looked more likely, so they gave us a hand crossing. I appreciated their nonchalance. It was as if they were just helping me with a tangle on a training trail, and that attitude had a calming effect.

We dropped down onto the sea ice again for a short way and then I was off the back of the sled, running by the sea wall up the ramp that opened onto Front Street.

When I reached the top and saw all the people who were flanking the street, smiling and waving and shouting, my heart started pounding in my chest and the jumble of emotions turned me almost numb. I smiled.

The dogs never broke their pace through all of this, although Axle did look from side to side a bit, and Dusty, who hates crowds, pulled back on his neckline in protest. Sister should have been here with us, that was my only regret, but as I learned later, she was watching on television.

The last few hundred yards were like driving into the eye of a hurricane. The crowd fell in behind me, following, and all around along the street they shouted and cheered.

I caught sight of the wooden arch at the finish line and made out Joe and Mike up there, waiting. The dogs looked so fresh coming down the street, doing a high-stepping trot. I was more proud of them than I could say.

The team disappeared into a crowd behind the finish line and then my sled stopped. The race was over. Joe reached me first, gave just a quick squeeze, then was swept into the crowd before I could give him a good hug. Mike wormed in with a ten-gallon smile, and I could hear the Teller crowd going wild right beside me. Even before Mayor Leo Rasmussen officially welcomed me to Nome, the microphones were waving in my face.

"How does it feel, Libby?"

I could never explain in words, but I will hold the feeling all my life and no one can ever take it away.

"What I feel is, if I died right now, it'd be *okay.*"

Epilogue

Duane Halverson crossed the finish line two and a half hours after Libby Riddles, followed by John Cooper, Rick Swenson, Rick Mackey, Vern Halter, Guy Blankenship, Herbert Nayokpuk, Sonny Lindner, Lavon Barve, Tim Moerlein, Emmitt Peters, Tim Osmar, Jerry Austin, Terry Adkins, Roger Nordlum, Glen Findlay, John Barron, Raymie Redington, Burt Bomhoff, and twenty others. Joe Redington, Sr., had scratched at Shaktoolik; Chuck Schaeffer dropped out at Shageluk; Victor Katongan pulled out at McGrath.

Ralph and Helmi Conaster of Eagle Island won the Iditarod Trail Committee's award for the checkpoint of the year, as thanks for the food, comfort, and encouragement they had offered the weary mushers.

Dugan and Axle took the golden harness award for the top lead dogs.

Terry Adkins was officially recognized for his sportsmanship, which consisted in part of having caught and stopped Libby Riddles's runaway team on the first day of the race. After he reached Nome, Riddles thanked him with a double Yukon Jack in the Bering Sea Saloon.

Sister watched the finish on television while recuperating from her frostbite. Although the 1985 race was to have been her last Iditarod, the next year she was recalled from retirement and, at the venerable age of ten, led Joe Garnie's team into second place, winning the 1986 Iditarod golden harness award.

Dugan was dropped from the 1986 Iditarod at Elim because of illness but ran Minnesota's Beargrease race in 1986 and 1987. Axle was also dropped from Garnie's team in 1986, at Ophir. The two brothers are Riddles's most dependable leaders.

Inca, Riddles's favorite dog, was bred to Dugan and produced one pup, which died of parvo; she has had three female puppies by Binga.

237

Bugs, ever the bad boy of the dog yard, has become a playboy. Because he taunts his male teammates, Riddles keeps him surrounded by female dogs.

Despite the instructions on his shipping papers, Stripe was flown to Anchorage instead of Nome, and two weeks passed before he rejoined his teammates in Teller. In 1986, wearing his booties, he finished the Iditarod as one of Garnie's best dogs.

Minnow and Tip, the largest of Riddles's dogs, continue to race.

Penny was bred to Axle and produced four pups. Garnie's other racers—Brownie, Socks, Whitey, Dusty, and Stewpot—are all still on the trail.

Libby Riddles received the humanitarian award, given by the race veterinarians to the driver who took best care of the dogs during the competition. She also won the 1985 Pro Sportswoman of the Year award, given by the Women's Sports Foundation, and was written up in *Sports Illustrated* and *Vogue*. She has not yet been to Hawaii.

About the Authors

Libby Riddles was born in Madison, Wisconsin. In 1972 she moved to Alaska and lived in a cabin near Nelchina. Once she became involved in sled dog racing, she worked summer jobs—with the Bureau of Land Management, at a fish-processing plant, for a warehouse—and sewed fur clothing to support herself and her dogs during winter training and racing. She now lives outside Nome, in a cabin she built in 1987, and continues to breed and train sled dogs at her Blazing Kennels.

Before Tim Jones began approaching life as a hobby, he was an editor for the *Chicago Tribune, Wall Street Journal, Anchorage Daily News, Nome Nugget,* and other newspapers. Now he seeks to make a living from the pursuits he would enjoy on weekends if he held a traditional workweek job. In summers he captains a tour boat in Prince William Sound, sharing with visitors the beauties of one small part of Alaska. In winters he lives in his cabin near Talkeetna, within sight of Mount McKinley, and writes. His first book about the Iditarod, *The Last Great Race,* was published in 1982. He is now at work on a novel.